IRELAND'S
SECRET WAR

Marc Mc Menamin is an author, documentary maker and teacher originally from Ballyshannon, Co. Donegal. He holds an MA in History and a PGDE in Education from the National University of Ireland, Galway, and works as a teacher in Oaklands Community College, Edenderry, Co. Offaly, where he teaches English, History and Politics and Society.

He has produced a number of award-winning radio documentaries for RTÉ Radio 1's *Documentary on One*, including *Richard Hayes, Nazi Codebreaker*, which was a finalist in the Best Radio Documentary Category at the 2018 New York Festivals. His 2013 radio documentary *Peter Daly – Good Cop/Bad Cop?* was shortlisted for numerous prizes including the 2014 Prix Europa and Prix Italia awards, while his 2015 radio documentary *Seamus Darby and the Goal that Made Champions* was shortlisted for Sports Documentary of the Year at the 2016 Celtic Media Awards. Marc also occasionally works as a reporter for RTÉ Radio 1's *The History Show*, and has worked as a researcher and assistant producer on a number of documentaries, most notably Virgin Media Television's *Sinn Féin: Who Are They?*

Based in Dublin, Marc is an avid fan of cycling, Donegal GAA and the Republic of Ireland soccer team, and tries to get home to Ballyshannon as often as possible. *Ireland's Secret War* is his second book, following *Codebreaker* in 2018.

DAN BRYAN, G2 AND THE

IRELAND'S

LOST TAPES THAT REVEAL THE HUNT

SECRET WAR

FOR IRELAND'S NAZI SPIES

MARC Mc MENAMIN

GILL BOOKS

Gill Books
Hume Avenue
Park West
Dublin 12
www.gillbooks.ie

Gill Books is an imprint of M.H. Gill and Co.

978 07171 9288 5

Designed by O'K Graphic Design, Dublin
Print origination by Bartek Janczak
Edited by Jane Rogers
Proofread by Tess Tattersall
Indexed by Eileen O'Neill

Printed by CPI Group (UK) Ltd, Croydon, CR0 4YY
This book is typeset in 11 on 16pt, Minion Pro.

A CIP catalogue record for this book is available from the
British Library.

5 4 3 2 1

MIX
Paper from
responsible sources
FSC® C171272

FOREWORD

The first 30 years of 20th-century Irish history have been scrutinised much more carefully than the years leading up to and during World War II, and Ireland's role in that conflagration has been misunderstood and undervalued, both during the war and since. Ireland's neutral position, its quiet tilt toward the Allies, surely contributed to the country's transition from Free State to Republic. However, Irish neutrality was not without its critics. Both pro-German factions and those convinced that the policy helped the Allies criticised the country's stance. Although Irish neutrality was benevolent to the Allies, anti-Irish sentiment was widespread in the US as well as in Britain, and even today many Americans believe that Ireland's neutrality was a cover for its covert Nazi sympathies.

The first people to write about Ireland in World War II were journalists such as Sean O'Callaghan and Enno Stephan, who exposed the German spy Helmut Clissmann. By the time I came to the topic, many of the participants were willing to talk about their experiences, and quite a bit of, but not all, documentation was accessible. One cannot overemphasise the value of first-hand oral accounts and other primary sources, and the papers of those who play a role in historic events should be housed in reputable archives so that those who evaluate the past can have adequate materials to lead them to intelligent judgments.

Marc Mc Menamin has rigorously examined documents that earlier journalists and historians either did not have access to or overlooked. For instance, he has scrutinised interviews with Douglas Gageby, of the *Irish Times*, as well as the testimony of Commandant James Power, the man in charge of the Athlone internment camp. In his previous book, *Codebreaker,* Mc Menamin expanded our knowledge of activities of the German colony in Ireland prior to and during World War II. *Codebreaker* is the definitive biography of Dr Richard Hayes, who broke the Abwehr code that the failed spy Hermann Görtz brought to Ireland.

One of the men who implemented the Irish position in World War II was Col. Dan Bryan, a genial, intellectual man whose life and writings reflected the highest standards of government service. Mc Menamin has made ample use of Bryan's papers, as well as of the interviews that I conducted with him and others many years ago. Mc Menamin now provides us with an excellent description of Bryan's early life and stresses the importance of the goals expressed in his treatise 'Fundamental Factors Affecting Irish Defence Policy'. Mc Menamin believes that sometimes one person is labelled a hero while someone else, a real hero, is overlooked. His examination of Bryan leads him to conclude that the man has been as undervalued as Ireland's policy of neutrality; that he was heroic in his conduct of his duties, and that he deserves greater respect and renown.

Mc Menamin represents a new generation of historians, anxious to go beyond previously accepted stories. He has written an important book, which you are about to read. If his conclusions generate controversy and further investigation into Ireland's role in World War II, he will have done a great service to the historical profession as well as to the general reader.

Carolle J. Carter
Professor *Emerita*
Menlo College
Atherton, California

ACKNOWLEDGEMENTS

This book would not have been possible without the help of many people; I will do my best to enumerate them here. First and foremost, a huge debt of gratitude is owed to Sarah Liddy, Teresa Daly and all at Gill Books for agreeing to publish this book and for recognising the value of this story from the outset. Thanks also to my editor, Rachel Thompson, and copyeditor, Jane Rogers, for their diligent work with the manuscript. A huge thanks also goes to Laura King for her help with the wonderful photo section.

My thanks to Professor Carolle Carter for all her help, advice and generous access to her personal archive. This book stands on the shoulders of her pioneering work at a time when access to archives was restricted so I'm very much indebted to her, as I'm sure are the many historians of this period of Irish history. I'd also like to acknowledge Prof. Carter's husband, Jesse Kitchens, who ferried Madeleine and myself around northern California during our visit. He is one of life's great gentlemen.

The assistance of the staff at the National Library of Ireland, National Archives Bishop Street and the British National Archives at Kew has been indispensable; without their help not one word of this book would have been possible. A special mention is reserved for Dr Sandra Collins of the National Library of Ireland, who hosted me there to give lectures on my work. Her enthusiasm for this subject and that of the life of her predecessor, Dr Richard Hayes, has not gone unnoticed and is greatly appreciated. Similarly, a huge debt of gratitude is owed to Faery Hayes, Sheila O' Sullivan, Brian Costello and Brian D. Martin, as well as to Michael C. Murphy (ex-J2), whose help in terms of sources and insights has been second-to-none.

I would like to thank the staff and students of Oaklands Community College Edenderry, County Offaly, where I have worked for the last number of years. I am extremely privileged to work alongside such talented colleagues and with such inspirational students, whose enthusiasm for history makes my job a joy every single day. I am particularly indebted to Principal Brian Kehoe and Deputy Principals Richard Murphy and Mairead O'Shea, who make our school such a stimulating and vibrant community of learners, and who have all been so supportive of my writing career outside of the classroom. Since my first book, *Codebreaker*, was published in 2018, our former principal Gerry Connolly sadly passed away after a long illness. Gerry was a huge mentor for me as both a teacher and as an adult. I will be forever grateful for his encouragement, his guidance and his faith in me, and for giving me my first real start in education. He is missed, and thought of often in Oaklands by myself and many others.

A massive thanks is owed to the team at RTÉ's *Documentary on One*, who helped me secure the tapes in California that were used as primary sources for the writing of this book, and their ongoing support of me as a documentary maker. In particular I'd like to pay tribute to series producer Liam O'Brien, who is an amazing storyteller and whom I admire greatly. I have been honoured to count him as a friend and mentor over the last few years and I'm deeply grateful for all his help and advice. Thanks also goes to Lorcan Clancy and Myles Dungan at RTÉ's *The History Show* for their shared enthusiasm for bringing history to life.

My friends have been a huge source of fun in my life, which, as any writer will tell you, is crucial. Sometimes time away from the manuscript is as important as daily attention to it, and I'd like to thank my friends for providing that escape that is so vital to the creative process. I'd like to particularly mention Triona O'Neill for all her encouragement, as well as Johnny Keenaghan, Brian Mullaney, Daire O'Neill, Daniel Mc Garrigle, Simon Mc Garrigle, Paul Gerard Duncan, Shane Harron, David Langtry, Michael Dore, Conor Sweetman, Terry O'Doherty, Chris and Joe Mc Gurrin and Paul Cleary. Also to my friends Richard Fitzgerald, Aaron Ó'Maonaigh, Brian Drummond and Mary Elaine Tynan, whose advice on various matters relating to this book is much appreciated.

A special thanks goes to my mother, Florence; father, Patrick; and brother, Jason; as well as to Anna O'Carroll and the wider Mc Menamin family. Your support and encouragement have made the writing of this book possible. I doubt a word of it would have been written without your support and I feel so fortunate to have such a wonderful family who inspire me every day. Thanks also to my aunt Margaret Golden, for her company, warmth and mutual love of history; as well as to my cousins Jonathan and Catherine Golden, for being such wonderful role models growing up. Another huge thanks to the Murphy family, especially to Raymond and Étain, who have been so supportive and kind to me throughout the duration of this project and indeed since I first met them. Your advice and encouragement are so appreciated, and I am forever grateful.

Finally, to my dearest Madeleine, to whom this book is dedicated. Thank you for being the wonderful person that you are and for being such an inspirational, kind and loving partner. This book, as indeed most things, would not have been possible without you. All my love always.

CONTENTS

PROLOGUE: AN OLD BOX OF TAPES   XV

I   The Storm Clouds Gather   1

II   Forging Alliances   21

III   The Art of Diplomacy   42

IV   Upping the Ante   62

V   The Parachutist   82

VI   Neutrality Under Pressure   102

VII   Our Friends and Allies?   123

VIII   Prisoners of War   145

IX   Endgame   165

X   Unsung Heroes   185

EPILOGUE: A JOURNEY WEST   205

BIBLIOGRAPHY   209

Viris fortibus non opus est moenibus.
(To brave men, walls are unnecessary.)
AGESILAUS THE GREAT, KING OF SPARTA (C.375 BC)

PROLOGUE: AN OLD BOX OF TAPES

This story is a sequel of sorts to my 2018 book *Codebreaker: The Untold Story of Richard Hayes, the Dublin Librarian who Helped Turn the Tide of World War II*. I felt very strongly when writing that book that it was important to tell Dr Hayes's story, which had been sadly neglected in the historical record of World War II in Ireland. Hayes had done amazing deeds for the country and was instrumental in breaking a number of German codes during the war. While he was celebrated in the intelligence communities for his achievements in cryptography, he was less esteemed in Ireland, where he is probably better known as an academic and librarian. His *Manuscript Sources for the History of Irish Civilisation* is still consulted widely by historians and researchers alike.

The book was largely built on the 2017 radio documentary *Richard Hayes: Nazi Codebreaker*, broadcast on RTÉ Radio 1's multi-award-winning *Documentary on One* slot. The press coverage that followed the book's publication led to numerous offers of TV projects and film scripts inspired by Hayes's story. Naturally this piqued my curiosity as to whether there might be film footage or audio tapes of Hayes and Dan Bryan (whose name came up repeatedly during my research on Hayes – indeed, in truth you can't separate one man from the other), perhaps in a private collection that had hitherto lain undiscovered. While there is some material in RTÉ's television and radio archives of both men, in which they mostly talked about other topics – Hayes on Islamic art and Bryan on the War of Independence – material on World War II was thin on the ground. This got me thinking about a book I had consulted while writing *Codebreaker*. *The Shamrock and the Swastika*, a ground-breaking study of German espionage in neutral Ireland during the Emergency, was written by Professor Carolle J. Carter of San José State University in northern California, who carried out the research for it between 1970 and 1973. The book had its genesis in Prof. Carter's master's thesis, which she carried out under the supervision of Professor Charles B. Burdick, one of the foremost authorities on World War II and the author of 10 books on the subject, as well as numerous scholarly articles and book chapters. He is still regarded as a pioneering historian on the history of the German High Command throughout the war.

After much research online I discovered that there was a large archive at San José State University, named, in the professor's memory, the Burdick Military History Project. I was aware that Prof. Carter's book had been mainly written using personal interviews she had carried out with Dan Bryan and Dr Hayes during the early seventies while on a research trip to Dublin. Was it possible that Carter's audio tapes, recorded so many years before, still existed? I decided to contact San José State University directly. After navigating my way around the college switchboard, I was advised to put my request in writing to Dr Jonathan Roth, who today presides over the Burdick collection. Within 24 hours I received a reply from Dr Roth putting me in contact with the university archivist, Carli Lowe. Carli offered to look through the Burdick collection for material relating to Ireland and found that the archive included primary sources consulted by Professor Burdick in his research, as well as research notes and personal correspondence.

While nothing immediately seemed to pop up in the library catalogue of the collection in relation to Ireland during World War II, Carli suggested that I speak directly with Prof. Carter. I immediately emailed her to introduce myself and inquire if she still had copies of the tapes that she had used in her research for *The Shamrock and the Swastika*. The email I received the next day opened a Pandora's box that eventually became the basis of this book. I suggested to Prof. Carter that we should organise a Zoom call to talk through things further and so that I could explain my rationale for wanting to obtain the tapes she had recorded so many years before. During the course of our initial Zoom call, I discovered that the tapes in Prof. Carter's possession were utterly priceless. They were in effect the untold history of World War II in Ireland told from the point of view of the main protagonists. A precious resource that existed nowhere else in the world.

Prof. Carter had carried out the interviews on vintage audio cassette tapes using old-style field equipment, over multiple visits to Ireland between 1969 and

1971. Naturally, I was worried that these tapes might not have stood the test of time. After all, they had been in storage in the professor's attic for the best part of 50 years. Over the course of one of our many Zoom calls Prof. Carter told me she would catalogue the material in her attic, a 'fun thing to do to alleviate the boredom of lockdown'. At the time California was suffering badly from the Covid-19 pandemic, with record daily cases and deaths, despite the best efforts of Governor Gavin Newsom to halt the course of the virus. Prof. Carter and her husband were adhering to California's 'shelter in place' order, so the chance to catalogue the tapes was a welcome distraction from all the bad news.

After a week I received an email from her telling me that the tapes were in a very healthy state and that she had catalogued and labelled all the material on them. She had also gone through her notes and research and had a wealth of information from the period that she felt would be of use to me. I read the list Prof. Carter had compiled with utter fascination and sheer excitement that I would be able to hear the voices of those from the war in Ireland tell their own stories.

The earliest tapes date from August 1969 and were recorded in the Republic of Ireland as Derry was about to explode into the violence that became known as the Battle of the Bogside. The first tapes consisted of interviews with Helmut Clissmann, a prominent Dublin businessman, originally from Germany, who had been involved with the Abwehr, the intelligence service of the German Wehrmacht during World War II. Another interview recorded in 1969 was carried out in Enniscorthy, County Wexford, with Stephen Hayes, one of three wartime Chiefs of Staff of the IRA. This tape is a unique audio recording of an IRA Chief of Staff from the 1940s. Also included in the 1969 batch of interviews was a tape of the testimony of Commandant James Power of Athlone, a member of the Irish intelligence services dealing with Nazi prisoners interned in Athlone during the war. One of the most interesting tapes from these 1969 recordings was a tape of IRA leader James O'Donovan (also known as Jim and Seamus), who helped establish the initial links between the IRA and Nazi Germany just before the outbreak of the war in 1939. O'Donovan travelled several times to Berlin and his oral testimony of the period is fascinating.

Prof. Carter returned to Ireland the following summer to carry out interviews with retired members of the Irish intelligence services, including

Richard Hayes, as well as with the writer Francis Stuart, who himself had been embroiled in espionage with Nazi Germany during this period. By far the most important tapes were a series of seven interviews with Colonel Dan Bryan, the head of Irish Military Intelligence for the bulk of the duration of the war. Bryan was a towering figure in the history of the Emergency and is perhaps one of Ireland's least-known heroes. He masterminded Irish intelligence services throughout the war and was regarded by those who knew him with whom I have spoken, and by historians of the period, as a man of honour. The Bryan interviews, which were mainly carried out during Prof. Carter's last visit to Ireland in 1971, were perhaps the most important of all the tapes since they were the oral testimony of the man who knew most about Ireland's secret war against Nazi Germany.

It occurred to me that these tapes were so important that it was crucial that they be preserved and that, once the details in the tapes were properly logged to tell the story of their contents, some sort of project should be put in place for this purpose. Prof. Carter agreed and gave me her permission and her blessing to use the tapes in whatever way I saw fit. Thus the idea of this book, and an accompanying radio series with RTÉ, was born. If the content of the tapes was as significant as I thought, it was important that the public should get to hear them and read more about them. A huge bee in my bonnet is the fact that the history of World War II in Ireland is often undersold or misrepresented in the history curriculum taught in schools. The curriculum is the foundation stone on which a lot of the Irish understanding of the war is built and sadly at present it is mostly a tale of glimmer men, rationing and little else. Irish history is often taught through a nationalist lens, so it is hardly surprising that this basic version of the war in Ireland is uppermost in the public consciousness. Finally, I felt that these tapes, if presented in the right way, could, alongside some of the already great scholarly work out there on the period, begin to change the conversation in Ireland about the war. But one big problem remained. How do you get a big box of audio tapes from California to Donegal in the middle of the biggest global pandemic in a hundred years?

There was only one person who could help me resolve this quandary: Liam O'Brien, the series producer of RTÉ Radio 1's multi-award-winning

Documentary on One series. Nobody gets the worth of a story more than Liam, and nobody understands better how to tell it. Since Liam took over the *Documentary on One* strand in 2006 it grew from a little-known programme to one of the most successful radio documentary units in the world, winning over 250 international awards and becoming the envy of public service broadcasters throughout the world. So I called Liam and we had a long conversation about the box of tapes in California and how to get them to Ireland. We both agreed that transporting the tapes themselves was out of the question; the risk of damaging them was too great. Liam agreed with me that we should use the tapes to form the basis of a radio documentary series, along the lines of such recent RTÉ programmes as 2020's *The Nobody Zone* and 2021's *Gunplot*, with this book to accompany it. The best course of action, we felt, was to get the tapes converted into digital audio files that could be sent over the internet to Ireland, where we could listen to the content and restore the audio if need be. Liam promised the finances to do this and was an enthusiastic backer of the project from the outset.

Then began the process of trawling the internet to find a suitable place to digitise the tapes. Making digital copies of anything that was recorded as far back as the 1970s is a laborious process. The audio has to be played in real time while the files are copied into a computer program. Given there are almost 35 hours of audio in the tapes, this would be no mean feat.

After searching numerous audio shops in southern California that could do the conversion process, I was able to narrow the possibilities down to three or four businesses in the San Francisco Bay area. Of course, Covid ruled out many of the businesses as they were severely curtailed by the pandemic, which at this stage was affecting the United States worse than any other country in the world. I had almost given up hope when I decided to get in contact with Sean Sexton at the Digital Roots Studio in Oakland, California. Sean couldn't have been any more helpful and we arranged to have the tapes picked up at Prof. Carter's house and then transferred to digital files before being dropped back. By the time all this had been arranged it was much safer in terms of Covid in California, so the professor insisted that she and her husband would bring the tapes to Oakland themselves – they were dying to get out of the house after having spent so long in lockdown, and it would also be a great opportunity to go for a drive in their new electric car. Sure enough, the tapes and transcripts were dropped off and three weeks later I received an email from Sean to say that he had digitised all the audio and would send it over to me later that night. In the meantime, I was in Donegal, having returned home for the Christmas break from my job as a teacher, and I had planned on spending two weeks at home. I ended up staying for two months. As soon as Covid cases began to improve in California they began to spiral out of control in Ireland; schools here were closed, and it would be April before all students returned to their classrooms.

Sean began to send the audio files over on a Saturday afternoon. Given the sheer volume of audio, it took quite a bit of time to download the files. It was going to take at least an hour, so I decided to have a beer to congratulate myself on all the hard work getting the files as far as my computer in the first place. As I sat with a sense of anticipation, I couldn't help being struck by the marvels of technology. Only a few years ago such a feat would have been impossible and these tapes would likely have never seen the light of day, at least not in Ireland. As I mulled over how things had changed, a ping from my laptop let me know the downloads were complete and that it was now, after all the effort, time to listen to them.

I opened the first recording. It came from an interview with Dan Bryan in 1971, long before I was born. Expecting to hear some sort of fearsome five-star general, I was struck by Bryan's speaking voice. This gallant man, who had singlehandedly helped thwart the Nazi's plans for Ireland, sounded more like a rural GP than a military man, with his soft-spoken intonation and a hint of a rural Kilkenny accent. I couldn't help marvel at the sound of his voice and it reminded me very much of a line from the 2014 film *The Imitation Game* about another unsung hero of World War II, the famous codebreaker Alan Turing: 'Sometimes it is the people no one imagines anything of who do the things that no one can imagine.' That is certainly true of Dan Bryan and Richard Hayes.

It was also incredible to hear the voices of Helmut Clissmann, Stephen Hayes and Jim O'Donovan telling their own stories of the war. I was struck in particular by Hayes and O'Donovan, who, even though they disagreed with each other within the IRA, both felt that they were continuing the pure republicanism of the 1916 leaders. Hayes sounded like a typical rural Wexford man, while O'Donovan's Roscommon accent hadn't been in any way diminished by years spent living in Dublin and elsewhere. In his own way, Clissmann also takes the listener by surprise, sounding more like a businessman – which he was at that stage – than a former intelligence agent for the Abwehr. His interviews, like those of the others, were thoughtful and reflective and very much true to his own version of events. It is only by taking all these tapes together, alongside the body of secondary source literature that exists out there, that one can begin to paint the bigger picture and to sketch the story of Ireland during the war through the eyes of those who lived it.

With the tapes finally in Ireland, work began in earnest to try to develop a radio series with them, which I hope will see the light of day sometime soon. I also began to draft what would eventually become this book. From the outset I was determined that the book would tell the story as much as possible in the first person, so there are many quotations from the various protagonists. Naturally, there will be gaps in any narrative and what is contained in the tapes isn't by any means a definitive account of the period. Therefore, I have filled in some of the gaps using testimony taken from files released by the Irish Department of Foreign Affairs as well as Foreign Office and MI5 and MI6 files from the British National Archive at Kew. I have also consulted Dan Bryan's papers and a portion of an incomplete memoir dictated to the historian Eunan O'Halpin, which were all deposited in Bryan's alma mater, University College Dublin. To flesh out the story further, I have drawn on a rich body of second-ary sources on various aspects of this period written by Professor O'Halpin, Dr Mark Hull of Kansas, journalist Enno Stephan, who was the first person to write about German espionage in Ireland during WWII, and of course Prof. Carolle Carter herself. I have also consulted works by historian T. Ryle Dwyer, perhaps the best-known authority on much of the history of the war years in Ireland. In doing so I have been able to sketch a broad narrative of the war in Ireland, inserting the first-person testimony of those interviewed in the tapes at appropriate intervals. I have augmented all this with the extensive archival research I have carried out over the last number of years.

This book does not purport to be the definitive history of the war in Ireland. It is intended to illuminate this period for the casual reader of Irish history and to illustrate that there are many facets of it, such as World War II era, that have been neglected in terms of commemoration and acknowledgement over the years. The story presented here isn't entirely chronological, as various events over the period intersected and overlapped, and to follow a strictly chronological approach would not do justice to the bigger picture; neither would it, in my opinion, be as entertaining. The narrative unfolds in an episodic manner, dealing with the major issues and themes of the war: the origins of G2; republican intrigue; Allied attitudes towards Ireland; Nazi spies; and so forth. What I hope will set this work apart from others is that I have consciously tried to make it about the individuals involved and to allow them, as much as possible, to drive the narrative from their own perspectives. It can often be said that personalities loom large in the telling of Irish history. For example, the World War II period is often read as the triumph of de Valera – but the reality is much more nuanced, and de Valera was often at odds with Bryan and others in the intelligence services. This history hopes to document the period using oral testimony in a bottom-up fashion and bring previously unheard voices to the fore.

As I write, Ireland is coming to the end of the greatest national emergency since the days of World War II. Covid-19 has wreaked untold havoc, the likes of which have not been seen on this island in a century. What has been notable has been the sacrifice of those nameless faces in the medical profession who have put their lives on the line for the common good. This book is a tribute to that same spirit, a spirit that characterised the lives of Dan Bryan, Richard Hayes and many others during the course of World War II, people whose selfless interventions and quiet patriotism did a great service to this country during one of its darkest hours. What follows is the story of Bryan, G2 and the hunt for Ireland's Nazi spies and how we as a country are still learning to reckon with the legacy of World War II. In order to tell that story, it is necessary to go back to the beginning. Back to the most unlikely of places, back to rural Kilkenny at the turn of the century. As Ireland approaches its centenary as a nation, I hope that someday I will be able to pass a statue of Dan Bryan and Richard Hayes in Dublin or, indeed, Kilkenny or Limerick. But perhaps most of all, I hope that having read this book many others will also share in that aspiration.

I

THE STORM CLOUDS GATHER

I regard certain events during World War II as the high point of my career.

COLONEL DAN BRYAN, FORMER DIRECTOR OF IRISH
MILITARY INTELLIGENCE, DUBLIN, 16 FEBRUARY 1984

Perhaps all tales of heroism begin in the most unlikely places. This story is no different. And, while this tale is multifaceted, first and foremost it's the story of how one man, Dan Bryan, the son of a small middle-class farmer from County Kilkenny, masterminded the most sophisticated security operation in the history of the Irish state. A clandestine operation that helped thwart a Nazi invasion of Ireland during World War II, the story of which has remained hidden in plain sight for over 80 years. It's also the story of republican/Nazi intrigue and the competing narratives of patriotism that characterised the early years of de Valera's Ireland. In truth, the fate of independent Ireland rested on the shoulders of Bryan, a most unconventional army officer who resisted the narrow definitions of republicanism espoused by some of his peers in the National Army and who truly saw the gravity of the looming threat of Hitler's Brownshirts and Mussolini's Black Brigades as the dark clouds of fascism began to gather over Europe in the 1930s. Bryan was undoubtedly one of Ireland's greatest unsung heroes, and his origins in rural Ireland were far from the corridors of power in Irish Military Intelligence in Dublin, where he oversaw Irish state security for over a decade.

Dan Bryan was born in a small rural townland near Gowran, County

Kilkenny on 9 May 1900. He lived the early part of his life on the family farm with his widowed grandmother Bridget and his parents, John and Margaret Mary (née Lanagan), of Maddoxstown, County Kilkenny. Dan, the eldest child, was followed by eight brothers and five sisters. The family farm of 500 acres, inherited by Dan's father from his own father (whom Dan was named after), gave the family financial security. Young Dan had a happy childhood, working with his brothers and sisters on the farm. By the time Dan was a young boy his parents were able to employ three farm hands and a domestic servant.

John Bryan was a firm believer in the power of education and put considerable financial resources into the schooling of his children; he had to let go of two of the farm hands to put four of the children through school. As the eldest, Dan held a certain level of responsibility and had to help with the family's financial situation. With his father's encouragement, he went to University College Dublin to study medicine (though he had initially wanted to study law). When he left Kilkenny and made his way to Dublin, he was taking his first steps into an Ireland that had changed utterly since the turn of the century.

The Dublin of this period was a hotbed of republican activity and the city had been convulsed by the fallout from the 1916 Rising, the scars of which were still visible. Many of the landmarks on O'Connell Street lay in ruins and the General Post Office, the site of Pearse's reading of the Proclamation, was a burnt-out shell – it wouldn't open to the public again until 1929.

Dan initially roomed at various boarding houses on the South Circular Road and on the Rathmines Road in south County Dublin. He loved life in the city, but Kilkenny was always close to his heart and he returned home once a month to visit his parents. He settled easily into life as a student at UCD, but it wasn't long before he became aware of the many separatist organisations that had emerged in the city in the wake of the Rising. Dublin was hot with nationalist fervour, manifest in cultural and political institutions such as the Gaelic League, the Irish Republican Brotherhood (IRB) and the GAA. A separate, unique Irish identity was espoused in most walks of life and it was no surprise that Dan became hugely influenced by the spirit of the time, despite his wealthy land-owning family background.

The British occupation of Ireland left scars that ran deep throughout the Irish countryside, with old resentments harking back to the penal times and beyond, and Kilkenny was no exception. Following the executions of the 1916 leaders, anti-British sentiment was rife. Such a changing of the tide culminated in May 1917 when former Easter Rising participant W.T. Cosgrave, who would become a colleague of Bryan's in later years, won a by-election in the county.

After two years as a medical student Bryan joined the Irish Volunteers as a seventeen-year-old in November 1917 and served in C and G companies of the 4th Battalion of the Dublin Brigade. He almost immediately became involved in raids, armed patrols and observation work and carved out a reputation as a formidable and dedicated Volunteer. Owing to the erratic British response to the public outcry in the wake of the 1916 executions, the Dublin Brigade was allowed to blossom. Indeed, in the months up to when Dan Bryan joined, most of the remaining leaders from the Rising had been released from Frongoch internment camp in Wales and many had reintegrated into the Volunteers. The Dublin Brigade grew into a considerable force, which benefited from new enlistees who had travelled to Dublin from the countryside in search of work or for education. This influx of Volunteers was timely as the group planned to actively resist conscription during the latter part of World War I. In April 1918 the Dublin Brigade helped organise a general strike against conscription and organised attacks on British food exports, which they redistributed to the city's poor. Dan Bryan had experienced a political awakening that would go on to define the rest of his life.

As the political situation deteriorated, the Dublin Volunteers campaigned for Sinn Féin in the general election of December 1918. They also stewarded their rallies and were embroiled in riots involving families who had relatives in the British Army. The political landscape of Ireland changed utterly when Sinn Féin won the election and formed Ireland's own parliament, Dáil Éireann. On 19 January 1919, the Dáil met for the first time, in Dublin's Mansion House, and declared Irish independence. The first military blow for independence was struck on the same day in Tipperary when Volunteers, led by Seamus Robinson, with Dan Breen among them, shot dead two Royal Irish Constabulary (RIC) constables at Soloheadbeg as they transported gelignite to a nearby quarry. Both RIC men were Catholics, one a native Irish speaker.

All Volunteers across the country took an oath of allegiance to Dáil Éireann and soon began to refer to themselves as the Irish Republican Army (IRA). The bloodiest day of the new conflict with the British occurred on 21 November 1920, when IRA Director of Intelligence Michael Collins orchestrated the assassination of the Dublin Castle G Division detectives known as the Cairo Gang. The IRA had eliminated a crucial cog in the British intelligence network in Dublin. The British responded on the same day – Bloody Sunday – with an indiscriminate attack on civilians at a Dublin and Tipperary football match at Croke Park and the assassination of Volunteers Dick McKee, Peadar Clancy and civilian Conor Clune. Bryan, who by this stage had shown huge aptitude for carrying out observation work, played his own role that day as a scout on Baggot Street Bridge during the attack on the Cairo Gang. In January 1921 Bryan was appointed assistant battalion intelligence officer in the IRA, working in his new role with fellow Volunteers Seán Dowling, Seán MacCurtain and F.X. Coghlan. It was in intelligence that Bryan was to excel. During the entire period of the War of Independence and the Civil War he didn't, to popular knowledge, even fire a weapon.

The War of Independence ended with the truce of 11 July 1920. Bryan supported the Treaty and the new Irish Free State. In June 1922, he joined the new National Army as an officer on the general staff and quickly made a name for himself. He began working in army intelligence during the Civil War that was to follow, commanding a group of agents who were widely feared in Dublin for their wide-scale arrests of anti-Treaty republicans. Bryan often worked on his own late into the night and regularly held meetings with various agents and informers. He was a teetotaller (and remained one all his life) and didn't smoke, and because of this he very often cut a solitary figure in the army. On 4 September 1923 he was promoted to the rank of captain and in February 1924 formally moved into the intelligence branch of the nascent Irish Defence Forces, a move that would help steady the ship when the army faced the biggest challenge of its brief existence with the Irish Army Mutiny in March 1924. The dispute was caused by a proposed reduction in numbers following the Civil War, and by rank-and-file dissatisfaction with the lack of territorial gains after the delineation of the border between the Free State and the new political entity of Northern Ireland. Indeed, Bryan's skills would come to the fore in this dispute, solidifying his growing reputation as a future leader in the Defence Forces.

During the 1920s Military Intelligence became a formidable force in gathering information on subversives and those seen as enemies of the state. It crushed the remnants of the republican movement who refused to recognise the Free State, rendering them almost impotent. Its jurisdiction covered foreign affairs as well as internal security matters. Its role in internal security brought it into contact with republicans as well as the Free State's secret civil police force, the Criminal Investigations Department (CID). Based at Oriel House on Dublin's Hawkins Street, the CID had a reputation for torture and murder. While there is no suggestion that such methods were sanctioned by the government of the day, they did prove effective in establishing the rule of law in the state. The CID was disbanded after the Civil War, and in late 1925 responsibility for political surveillance was transferred to the new police force, An Garda Síochána. This process included the transfer to the Gardaí of over 30,000 political files, informers and agents held by Military Intelligence.

Following the scaling down of army intelligence Bryan was transferred to the Defence Plans division of the army, and in 1927 he attended the five-year review conference of the Treaty defence arrangements as well as the Imperial Conference in London. By 1931 Intelligence had been colloquially rebranded G2, an American designation used as part of the continental staff system to refer to army intelligence, security and information branches around the world. The continental staff system used in structuring military staff functions was based on one originally employed by the French Army in the nineteenth century. Each staff position in a headquarters or unit is assigned a letter prefix corresponding to its function and one or more numbers specifying a role.

The Irish system consisted of four divisions. G1 handled personnel, G2 intelligence, G3 operations and G4 logistics. All were overseen by the Chief of Staff and the Assistant Chief of Staff. Policy was directed by the

Department of External Affairs, later to become known as Foreign Affairs, over which the minister of the day had authority. In addition to this there were four regional commands located in the western, eastern and southern areas of the country and in the Curragh. The net cast by the intelligence apparatus in Ireland was extensive and it could rely on the support of C3 (the Garda Security Section), the Garda Aliens Section, Garda Special Branch, the Naval Service and the Coastal Service, as well as the departments of Immigration, Posts and Telegraphs, and Justice.

Bryan became acting director of G2 in 1931 and fitted in well into the new system. He knew the importance of maintaining relationships with various sections of the community and he maintained informal contacts within the republican and labour movements. During this time Dan found great personal happiness when he fell in love with Eleanor Mary Barton-Fraser, known as Ellen, of Ballsbridge, and they married in 1930. The couple lived at 9 Heytesbury Lane, Ballsbridge, and Ellen was a great support to Dan throughout his career in the army.

Bryan's cool and calm demeanour was to serve him well in his role as Acting Director of Intelligence. These attributes were ones that were badly needed as the 1930s, one of the most tumultuous decades in the history of the state. After over a decade in power the ruling Cumann na nGaedheal party, led by W.T. Cosgrave, lost eight seats – and its majority – in the 1932 general election. It had fought the election on its record of having provided 10 years of stable government, but public patience had worn thin following the 1929 Wall Street Crash and the global economic depression that followed. Buoyed by a manifesto promising protectionist policies, industrial development, self-sufficiency and improvements in housing and social security benefits, Fianna Fáil won 72 seats, an increase of 15 from the 1926 election.

Fianna Fáil was still five seats short of an overall majority, but it still looked like the only party capable of forming a government. Discussions got under way immediately after the election and Thomas J. O'Connell's Labour Party agreed to support Fianna Fáil. The party could now form a minority government. The changing of the guard was to prove the first major challenge to Bryan and his colleagues in G2. It was clear that Civil War divisions still ran deep in Irish society and there was huge trepidation that the army would resist the peaceful transfer of power to de Valera's party, although, as Bryan recalled in the first batch of the interviews recorded by Prof. Carter, this was merely conjecture:

I've mentioned this question of doubt when Fianna Fáil took over and briefly there was an atmosphere that when they took over that the army might resist them and stage a *coup d'état*. This view of certain elements in Fianna Fáil is certainly confirmed by the story that Fianna Fáil TDs came to Leinster House to take their seats on the occasion quietly armed with revolvers. Briefly, I would say that there was never any serious suggestion of a *coup d'état*. There was all kinds of wild talk and speculation but nothing else that I know of. It is well to say here too that this atmosphere soon broke down into a position of personal good relations and the creation of those good relations may have been due to considerable extent to the personality of the Minister of Defence, Mr Frank Aiken, although his personality and policies in other respects have been subjected to the most drastic criticism.

In June 1933 Bryan graduated from the infantry officer's course, during which he showed his independent streak; for his thesis he wrote a document that initially drew the ire of his superiors but would later go on to redefine Irish security policy. This was timely. In the same year in Germany Adolf Hitler's Nazi Party (officially the National Socialist German Workers' Party, NSDAP) took power for the first time. Closer to home, General Eoin O'Duffy's quasi-fascist Blueshirts were posing their own problems for de Valera's government. G2 was tasked with surveillance of the group, which had arisen out of the Army Comrades Association and other elements in the army. O'Duffy would prove to be a vehement critic of de Valera, which indirectly gave G2 a new lease of life.

After a three-year sojourn in the Chief of Staff's Office Bryan returned to intelligence work in 1935 and was soon promoted to the rank of Deputy Director under Colonel Liam Archer, eight years senior to Bryan. Archer and Bryan differed in many ways, but they both wanted to keep Ireland neutral during the war. A native of Phibsboro, Archer had joined the Irish

Volunteers in May 1915 and was attached to F Company of the 1st Battalion of the Dublin Brigade, under the command of Piaras Béaslaí. Archer also fought in the Easter Rising in 1916 and with the engineering section of the IRA during the War of Independence. Promoted to commandant, he took up a position as a postal worker to help Michael Collins in the intelligence section of the IRA. He joined the National Army in 1922 and was given command of the Signals Corps, a unit that specialised in communications and information systems essential to army operations. Archer was appointed Director of Intelligence in 1932 and alongside Dan Bryan was instrumental in G2's reorganisation.

It soon became apparent to both men that war in Europe was looming for the second time in the twentieth century. Bryan became obsessed with studying foreign press reports and security briefings and was convinced that any major European conflict could have dire consequences for Ireland. He was acutely aware of both how vulnerable Ireland was to the threat of foreign invasion, and how subversive elements such as the IRA could be manipulated by Nazi Germany and fascist Italy. Both Bryan and Archer were very aware that G2 had a unique and important role in protecting the state. The problem was that prior to the 1930s Ireland faced mainly internal security threats from republicans and other subversive elements. Never had the state been so vulnerable to outside threats. Archer and Bryan approached the Chief of Staff, Lieutenant General Michael Brennan, to communicate their concerns. In a memo to Brennan, Bryan outlined the gravity of the situation and his fears that the dangers to the state weren't being taken seriously by the government: 'The International Situation gives cause for great unease. I fear this unease is not felt outside this department.'

The Chief of Staff forwarded the memo to the government, along with his own memo strongly agreeing with Bryan's and Archer's analysis. The warning was met with deep concern by the Taoiseach, de Valera, who immediately set in motion plans to set up a Cabinet Committee on National Defence.

Archer advocated immediate rearmament in line with what G2 had observed in other European nations. In the meantime, Bryan wrote a document entitled *Fundamental Factors Affecting Irish Defence Policy*. The document took a three-pronged approach. Its primary objective was to consider the military consequences for Ireland of a war in Western Europe or in the Atlantic with Britain as one of the main belligerents. The second objective of the document was to consider what military courses of action, if any, were open to Ireland in such a war. The third considered what the results would be if any of the methods outlined in the plan were adopted. Bryan described in very clear terms Ireland's fundamental defence flaws, as well as the wealth of forces needed in the event of a major war on the continent, and he stated his belief that Ireland was sleepwalking into a disaster of epic proportions if its present course wasn't altered: 'The Saorstat people are further not prepared in practice to provide sufficient forces to guarantee even relative freedom from outside interference.'

He also set out the options of neutrality, default or non-recognition, co-operation or resistance for consideration by the government, weighing up the likely success of each option in very clear and stark terms. For Bryan, Ireland's geographical position was of fundamental importance. It was an asset in terms of its strategic location but also a huge problem given the country's total lack of defensive measures, trained manpower and limited economic resources. Such flaws were, in his opinion, down to an abysmal lack of knowledge by civil servants and government ministers of defensive measures necessary to protect the state, which further compounded the already grave situation. Bryan recommended neutrality as the best option for Ireland and advocated that the country pursue defensive measures and security procedures modelled on those used by Britain during World War I. The document was circulated among government ministers and debated widely in the corridors of power. Indeed, Bryan's *Fundamental Factors* was the only major policy document outlining the Irish defence situation that was compiled in the years leading up to the outbreak of the war in 1939.

Even though Bryan's memo was widely distributed among government minsters, it was ultimately set aside. It wasn't until after the invasion of Czechoslovakia and the Rhineland that de Valera and his Cabinet were spurred into action. It was as if they had awoken from slumber to find the house already on fire. The government now faced the unenviable task of trying to equip for defensive purposes an army that they had neglected and run down for a decade. Such neglect had left neutrality the only viable option for the country. Indeed, Ireland's feeble state from a defensive point of view drew derisory comments from many quarters. The infamous William Joyce, known as Lord Haw-Haw, and famous for his wartime broadcasts from Germany, lamented: 'The Irish army wouldn't beat the Tinkers out of Galway.'

Undeterred, Bryan set about utilising the more positive aspects of Ireland's strategic situation to its advantage. Deep water ports and, crucially, the Treaty Ports (Cobh and Berehaven in Cork and Lough Swilly in Donegal) were sufficient for Ireland to develop security arrangements, and preparations were put in place by de Valera and the Cabinet. De Valera's acquisition of the Treaty Ports was to prove a huge asset in the months and years ahead. Perhaps most crucially, and unpalatably for many in government and military circles, was Bryan's belief that if any security operation was to be successful, Ireland had to reassess its relationship with the old enemy.

It was soon clear that the Treaty Ports were to be essential for Ireland to be recognised as a separate neutral entity from Britain in the event of a European war. Even during World War I, US authorities had selected Berehaven as a base from which troops en route to France could receive protection; so Ireland's coast was already well established in the international public consciousness. Bryan's assessment of Ireland's security status was extensive. He noted that Lough Swilly, the Shannon Estuary and Galway and Killary harbours could provide safe anchorage for entire fleets of ships of either Allied or Axis forces. He felt that these could be protected from U-boat or Allied submarine attacks as well as aerial bombardment, if certain measures were put in place – the inlets were wide enough to provide natural protection.

Bryan also noted the fact that up to 75 per cent of sea communication passed through the English and St George's Channels as part of the North Atlantic trade route to the major European ports. The Irish Sea acted as a natural barrier, allowing the creation of a flank that was vulnerable to submarine attack. This would be of huge concern to the British. It was also something that Bryan had long mulled over. Throughout his life Bryan had a deep and passionate love of military history. His knowledge was to stand him in good stead in the preparation of *Fundamental Factors*. The vulner-ability of an Irish Sea flank could have led to a silent economic blockade of Britain, one which Bryan knew as a student of history could have dis-astrous consequences. Similar situations had occurred during Napoleon's reign; and during the American Civil War President Abraham Lincoln pro-claimed a blockade of 3,500 miles of the Atlantic and Gulf coastline to stifle Confederate trade routes. A similar approach could not be countenanced if Ireland was to remain neutral in the war.

In reality, co-operation with the British was the only viable option. Indeed, by 1937 it was all but agreed on by both countries. Anglo-Irish defence co-operation had been inevitable since the Treaty Ports were reluc-tantly returned in 1938. The British believed that the ports would be available to them in the event of a war and that it was better to return them and work together in a spirit of co-operation rather than try to retain them and have to defend them against a hostile Irish population. Indeed, the British believed that it would take an entire army division as well as anti-aircraft guns to defend the ports against the Irish Army. Their thinking was that while not having the ports was detrimental, the cost of retaining them was even more so.

Irish Army resources were scant and they were poorly prepared for the war to come. The Irish Air Corps was particularly ill equipped. In the weeks leading up to Hitler's invasion of Poland in September 1939, the only fighter aircraft available to the Defence Forces were four Gloucester Gladiators. These were British-built biplanes used by the Royal Air Force (RAF) that had been exported to Ireland during the late 1930s. Although they soon became obsolete, Gloucesters acquitted themselves fairly well in dog-fights against the more superior Axis planes such as Junkers or Stukka dive bombers. They were used in almost all theatres of the war and flown by the RAF in France, Norway, Greece and Malta. Four planes, however, were simply not enough to defend the whole island of Ireland.

Ireland's weakness in the air was matched by an equally pathetic numer-ical strength in terms of personnel. By the outbreak of the war in 1939 the entire mobilised Defence Forces consisted of 19,136 men: 7,600 reg-ulars; 4,300 A and B reservists; and 7,236 volunteers. The Irish Army was neither trained nor equipped for any sort of war. Ireland was in many ways extremely vulnerable, a sitting duck for any invading force.

But the mainstream body politic was both deluded and naive. Many members of the government and opposition, and the civil service, had been members of the Old IRA and had fought in the 1916 Rising, the War of Independence or the Civil War. With the exception of military men such as W.T. Cosgrave and Richard Mulcahy, many in officialdom still clung to a romantic notion of guerrilla warfare as a means of defending the country. This idea couldn't have been further from reality. The murderous ferocity of Hitler's Panzer divisions had been unleashed on many unsuspecting nations, and such highly mechanised warfare would have completely overwhelmed the Irish defences. While the Irish spirit of resistance was certainly not dormant, it wasn't a match for the advances in technology and military expertise that the Germans, and indeed the British, could call on. Bryan was also aware that the Germans hadn't respected the neutrality of countries such as Belgium, Greece and Persia during World War I. Ireland was also the only European state without compulsory military service, something that Bryan felt would amplify the miniscule manpower that Ireland could muster in the event of an invasion. A policy of neutrality, with a degree of co-operation with the Allies, was the only feasible option for Ireland to take at the outbreak of war. Such co-operation would have to be kept secret, and a policy of overt neutrality would have to be shown towards Axis powers.

Bryan's writings spurred the government into action and plans were put in place to provide an adequate defence response. Using World War I as a basis for planning, censorship of the press and of general communications was put into place. In 1936 a ministerial committee on national defence was established. It consisted of an amalgamation of key figures from the departments of Defence, Justice and Local Government. The committee was tasked with co-ordinating all governmental activities that affected national defence. Such joined-up thinking would be crucial in terms of strategic planning.

In the early days of the war G2 was led by Liam Archer, while Dan Bryan worked essentially as his deputy. Over the course of the Emergency many men passed through the ranks of G2, including Lieutenant Colonels Childers and de Buitléar, Captains Henry and Leonard, Commandant Quinn and

Lieutenant Rúaidhrí de Valera. Second Lieutenant Douglas Gageby played a hugely significant role as an intelligence staff officer. Gageby, originally from Belfast, went on to become editor of the *Irish Times* from 1963 to 1974 and again from 1977 to 1986. He held the position of Junior Officer in G2's headquarters, which was in a building known as the Red House (also the codename for G2) on Parkgate Street. During Gageby's time there were roughly 50 or 60 intelligence officers working out of the Red House. Gageby's role, since he was fluent in German, was mainly gathering and translating German documents. Language fluency was an essential trait in intelligence work and it was a skill that Colonel Éamon de Buitléar shared with Gageby. He was fluent in Irish, French and, most crucially, German.

When Liam Archer was promoted to Deputy Chief of Staff in 1941, Dan Bryan became Director of G2. Bryan was able to put his own men into crucial roles and restructure the organisation as the war progressed. His personal staff consisted of Major Joseph Guilfoyle and Professor Joe Healy. Healy had been seconded from his role as Professor of Spanish at University College Cork to work as a linguist for G2. Born in Cobh in 1905, Healy spoke Spanish, Portuguese, French, German, Italian and Irish.

Bryan was known as an astute leader, and he made sure to draw on the informal contacts he had kept from his old IRA days. These, he felt, would be crucial for the upcoming intelligence operations during the war. One of the most influential figures drafted into G2 during this period was Florence 'Florrie' O'Donoghue. Born in Rathmore, County Kerry in 1895, O'Donoghue had been involved in intelligence work during the War of Independence and had built up a considerable body of contacts. During the Civil War he had remained neutral, eventually setting up a faction in the south known as the Neutral IRA, which he claimed numbered up to 20,000 volunteers at one time. A network such as this was a huge asset and O'Donoghue was sought out by Bryan, who gave him a senior role in G2. During his tenure O'Donoghue recruited many ex-IRA men into the National Army.

During Bryan's tenure G2 was reconfigured into seven sections. An administration section dealt with gazette and war establishment as well as map requisitions. The information section, which dealt with combat

intelligence books and requisitions, was led by a Captain Kelly, who worked
directly under Bryan. It also had at its disposal three sergeants, one corporal
and one private. G2's external security section dealt with postal censorship,
one of the most important sections of the intelligence service. Three com-
mandants, five lieutenants and two captains were assigned to this section.
The naval service had a permanent presence in the security section of G2.
Internal security within G2 was dealt with by one commandant, one lieutenant and two NCOs. One of the most important subsections within G2
was the reconfigured coastal and air defence security division. The resto-
ration of this area of defence was crucial to maintaining neutrality during
the Emergency. Another crucial subsection within G2 was the publicity
department, which dealt primarily with press censorship, press liaison,
photography and film censorship. Aerial photographs were of particular
interest. Domestic and foreign press were monitored, and press cuttings
were meticulously filed. The final section was signals security, presided
over by Commandant Sean Nelligan and Captain John Patrick O'Sullivan.
Nelligan's brother David had worked as Michael Collins's spy in Dublin
Castle during the War of Independence and had later gone on to serve as
the first Director of Intelligence for the Irish Army.

O'Sullivan was born on 7 November 1889 on Valentia Island, County
Kerry. As a young man he gained a scholarship to King's College, Bromfield,
England, going on to study at the British School of Telegraphy. He joined
the crew of the SS *Campania* shortly afterwards, and served as a wireless
operator and telegraphist on a number of ships. O'Sullivan joined the
Signals Corps of the newly created army in 1922, at the request of Michael
Collins. By 1933 O'Sullivan had become the first commissioned officer of
the Signals Corps of the Irish Army. He transferred to GHQ to work full
time in G2, where he became a valuable asset to Bryan during the war years.
O'Sullivan even set up a listening station in his own home in St Lawrence's
Road in Chapelizod to monitor radio signals for subversive activity. As well
as Nelligan and O'Sullivan the section also had at their disposal a team of
three female typists. Signals security was to prove a hugely important section
in G2 during the war, handling sensitive intelligence matter in relation to
post-invasion France, aircraft flights over Ireland as well as the monitoring of

convoy communications. In addition to this, the Signals unit also recorded ship numbers and various communiqués along the Irish coast.

G2 was well structured, but it was always short of staff. However, it was able to mount a very successful pre-war surveillance operation which gathered information on subversive elements in Irish society. It was particularly concerned with the movements of German and Italian aliens and liaised with Garda Special Branch when monitoring these individuals. Most of the men involved in G2 were ''22 men', or veterans of the independence campaign. This brought its own unique problems but it did enable those in charge in intelligence to use a wide variety of contacts to carry out surveillance work. For instance, the pre-war Director of G2, Liam Archer, kept files on any suspicious individuals or organisations and meticulously monitored any perceived threats to the state, both domestic and foreign. In fact, the greatest potential danger to Ireland lay within its own borders; many of the disgruntled ''22 men' in the IRA were prepared to use any means necessary to launch a renewed offensive against the British state. Any liaison with German or Italian intelligence would be the biggest threat to the state and to Bryan and his colleagues in G2. It was necessary for G2 to bolster its ranks to protect the Irish state from the greatest security threat it would face since its creation – a potential Axis/IRA partnership.

Mindful of this threat and in order to further supplement its ranks, G2 drew upon the Local Defence Force (LDF). Originally formed in 1939, and first known as the Local Security Force (LSF), it was to act as an army reserve during the war. On 22 June 1940 the organisation was split into two distinct entities, one attached to the regular army and the other to An Garda Síochána. The LDF was organised nationwide based on the district and division system used by the Gardaí. It was trained by the army and a member of the Gardaí was assigned a supervisory role over each local unit, usually under the title District Administrative Officer, to oversee the daily administration of the force. In rural areas the LDF was organised into rifle platoons. In urban settings, where resources allowed, it became more specialised. Urban units were able to deploy engineers and signals specialists, something not possible in smaller areas. By March 1941 the LDF had 88,000 reserves in its ranks. Units were armed with Springfield 0.300 rifles which were originally sourced from the British War Office, but ammunition for the rifles was often in short supply. Eventually recruits were issued with miniature rifles as well as small numbers of handguns and grenades. A lack of resources also extended to fatigues suitable for Irish weather. But by 1942 most of these issues had been resolved. The army's First Division, which was primarily responsible for the defence of the south coast of Ireland, was placed under the stewardship of Commandant Michael Joe Costello, who served as O/C of Southern Command from 1940. Costello was highly regarded for his background as the army's Director of Intelligence 1924–6 and from his days in the Old IRA. Costello did an exceptional job in the southern region with scant resources.

Bryan and Archer decided to extend their intelligence-gathering capabilities to the LDF and established an intelligence section within the reserve unit. The group became known as the Supplemental Intelligence Section (SIS) and was mainly attached to LDF units in the southern region of the country. Crucially, SIS members were known only by code numbers and were given very specific intelligence-gathering tasks and clear instructions on how to report their findings. Often their primary function was maintaining coastal look-out positions to keep an eye on any potential invading forces. Bryan put Florrie O'Donoghue in charge of the SIS in the southern region and while recruits received no pay, their postal and telephone costs were reimbursed every month. The SIS command structure was modelled the pre-1921 IRA Battalion areas. O'Donoghue swelled the ranks of the SIS by appealing to ex-IRA men and stoking their memories of the guerrilla war against the British. If there was an invasion, the SIS would be called on to use the same approach, and O'Donoghue even trained new recruits in guerrilla tactics. The organisation was active mainly in Waterford, south Leinster and Munster and was never extended to the rest of Ireland; Bryan felt that any invasion would take place in the south of the country. Bryan and Archer had cast the net wide and had put themselves and G2 as an intelligence organisation in a prime position to detect any penetration into the state by foreign subversive organisations.

Despite a lack of resources in certain areas, the army put considerable work into establishing the Coast Watching Service, set up in 1939 to guard against a seaborne invasion of Ireland by Axis powers – or, indeed, by Allied powers in a pre-emptive strike. More than 80 sites around the coast from north Louth to Donegal were selected and look-out posts were positioned at strategic locations at these sites, from which teams of men carried out watch duties over the sea. A network of 83 look-out posts (LOPs) were built around the coast of Ireland and manned by members of the LDF. The coast watchers were responsible for identifying and reporting on shipping and aircraft movements and also on any communications between ship and shore. LOPs were manned 24 hours a day by pairs of men working 8- or 12-hour shifts. One man operated the telephone inside the LOP while the other patrolled outside. The men had to report every activity observed at sea or in the air in the vicinity of their LOP. Each LOP was assigned a unique identifying number starting with LOP 1 in County Louth and continuing in a clockwise direction around the coast, finishing with LOP 82 at Malin Head in Inishowen, County Donegal. Speaking in an interview with Prof. Carter, Bryan felt that the Coast Watching Service was of huge importance to Ireland's strategic defences:

> One of the things that we did in Ireland before the war was to set up – that is we were ready to put into action – a coast watching service. The Coast Watching Service was really intended to deal with the submarine problem; we thought in World War I the submarines off the Irish coast were quite close to Ireland, we'd have a lot of problems with submarines in the near coast and that kind of thing. The Coast Watching Service was really intended to deal with the submarine problem and the war at sea, but under new conditions of the submarine war, the submarines were driven far out in the Atlantic and the submarine war was fought far out in the Atlantic.

It was very prescient of Bryan to establish the Coast Watching Service; even though submarines wouldn't be an issue for Ireland in this conflict, the war in the air was a very palpable threat. The service was to prove a very useful asset in this regard, according to Bryan:

What the Coast Watching Service became useful for was something that we hadn't anticipated and that was that we had the Luftwaffe flying over Ireland and this was a portion of the Intelligence Service. The thing we all liked to boast about is that once we got working, no aircraft flew into the country over the coast but they were observed, and you see when the aircraft came in, it was reported. Then the people, there were four stations around the country receiving reports, knew it was flying in a certain direction and they then warned the other. They rang other places, had they seen the aircraft and that. I should say, the only permanent centres were the ones around the coast, but every military post and Garda station was under orders. They did it very effectively for some years – to report any aeroplane they saw flying over the country day or night.

In addition to the various intelligence-gathering methods deployed by G2, the organisation had opened a secret dialogue with MI5, the British security service. German, Japanese and Italian diplomatic missions as well as the German expatriate community in Dublin were causing grave concern among government figures, prompting Secretary of the Department of External Affairs Joseph Walshe to make contact with the British Dominions Office with a view to co-operation between the two states on counter-espionage.

Born in Killenaule, County Tipperary in 1886, Walshe was to have a storied career in the Irish diplomatic service and is regarded today as the father of the Irish Foreign Service. During the course of the war Walshe maintained diplomatic relations with high-level British officials as well as with the United States and Germany. Despite Irish neutrality being official policy, Walshe advised that Britain be provided with intelligence reports from G2, as well as other forms of assistance. Walshe knew that Ireland was under threat of invasion from Britain and from Germany and in military terms Ireland lacked any sort of credible military capacity to repel any potential invader. He was acutely aware that throughout the war Ireland would have to rely on the soft power of its diplomatic service to protect its neutrality. It was through Walshe's initial intervention that Bryan and Archer were able to establish an informal intelligence co-operative arrangement with MI5.

This informal alliance unofficially became known as the Dublin link.

Originally established in 1909, the Security Service, also known as MI5, is the UK's domestic counter-intelligence and security agency, and is part of its intelligence machinery alongside the Secret Intelligence Service, Government Communications Headquarters, and Defence Intelligence. MI5 was originally small in terms of personnel, but by the time hostilities broke out between Britain and Germany in 1939 it had grown to become a formidable intelligence agency.

As a result of Walshe's initial intervention, Archer and Bryan travelled to London in October 1938 to meet with MI5 Director of Counter-Espionage Guy Liddell. Liddell had been a security officer in the intelligence service since 1919 and by 1939 had risen to the role of Director of Counter-Intelligence. The result of the meeting was an agreement to co-operate on intelligence matters and the establishment of an Irish Desk within MI5, which was to be headed by Liddell's brother Cecil.

The Liddell brothers had a deep understanding of Irish affairs and had visited the country regularly. They had family ties to Warrenpoint, County Down and were very much aware of the unique political sensitivities between Britain and Ireland. They were both frequent visitors to Dublin's Lambay Island, which was owned during the war years by their cousin, Lord Revelstoke. Until arriving at MI5, Cecil had virtually no intelligence experience, having worked mainly in the advertising industry. He was brought in with the specific task of dealing with Irish affairs, a sensitive role, and Guy firmly believed that he could have no better asset in this role than his brother. Cecil initially worked in the Irish section on his own, but in May 1940 he was assigned a second staff member, John Stephenson. Stephenson had a background in law and, like the Liddell brothers, had family links to Ireland. His father, Sir Guy Stephenson, was the Assistant Director of Public Prosecutions in charge of the prosecution of Sir Roger Casement in the wake of the Easter Rising.

Although the relationship between G2 and MI5 would be tested at various stages during the war, it would be the single most valuable partnership in the maintenance of Irish neutrality through the entire conflict. The Liddell brothers were to establish crucial friendships with Archer, Dan Bryan and

Joseph Guilfoyle of G2. While Bryan and Archer were able to maintain this clandestine security alliance, both men were deeply aware that their willingness to co-operate with the old enemy would not have been a popular decision with many of their colleagues. Many of the senior officers in the Defence Forces were veterans of the campaign of independence, some of whom maintained a marked dislike of the British. Indeed, in certain sections of the army there was a false assumption that the Germans were to be trusted more than the British, and even that Adolf Hitler's Nazi regime could help the Irish state reclaim the lost territory of Northern Ireland. It was therefore essential that G2's intelligence co-operation with MI5 was kept top secret and that only a few key people were allowed within the inner circle. The Dublin link was very much dependent on the political relationship between the two countries throughout the war. De Valera gave some latitude in terms of the strictness of neutrality by declaring the caveat that while Ireland would be neutral it would not allow itself to be used as a base from which to attack Britain. This in turn gave political justification for the Dublin link to work successfully. In the years ahead the relationship would be tested to the extreme.

Dan Bryan, the young lad from Gowran, had come a long way since he first arrived in Dublin as a medical student. He was now the head of the Irish Intelligence Service and facing into the most devastating conflict ever to confront humankind. Ireland had never before been so vulnerable. As Bryan was beginning to learn, however, Irish ties with Nazi Germany ran very deep. Contact between the Nazi apparatus and the republican movement with a view to co-operation had begun in earnest many years before Bryan walked the corridors of power in the Red House. The future of independent Ireland was at stake and Bryan would need every skill at his disposal to prevail.

II

FORGING ALLIANCES

Oh, here's to Adolph Hitler,
Who made the Britons squeal,
Sure before the fight is ended
They will dance an Irish reel.

WAR NEWS, 21 NOVEMBER 1940

Hiberno-German relations stretch back over the centuries. From the Ballinderry Sword, with its German inscription, thought to date back to the ninth century, to the first performance of Handel's *Messiah* in the new Music Hall on Fishamble Street in 1742, to the German Palatines of the eighteenth century and the cabaret performances of Agnes Bernelle in the 1920s, there have always been strong cultural ties between Ireland and Germany. Before World War I Ireland had a small German population, mainly working in the hotel business or in skilled trades such as victuallers, hairdressers and grocers. Irish independence in 1922 would see a marked change in the numbers and skill sets of Germans arriving into Ireland, when the pendulum swung sharply towards academia.

Perhaps the most defining moment in Irish–German relations in the early twentieth century was the role of Siemens-Schuckert in the Ardnacrusha hydroelectric scheme. After independence it was hoped that the new Irish state would be able to stand on its own two feet and rely on its own natural resources. When Irish engineer Thomas McLaughlin joined Siemens in Berlin in 1922 he soon raised the idea of harnessing the power of the River Shannon to provide electrification to the country. Out of this exchange the Shannon Scheme was born and soon became the world's first national electricity system. German involvement in the scheme was a huge selling point and ultimately saw the scheme adopted by the Cumann na nGaedheal government. The project was a resounding success and provided a template for other electrification projects around the world. The German imprint on the scheme was clear in the design process and the skill of the workmanship. It also provided for a steady influx of skilled German workmen, many of whom married Irish women and stayed on to live in Ireland after the project's completion.

Ireland's links with Germany weren't confined to engineering; strong cultural ties soon developed in the arts and sciences as well as in industry. This was mainly driven by a lack of expertise in some areas in the fledgling Free State. As a result, major roles in state bodies such as the Turf Development Board and Forestry were filled by German nationals. The arts also boasted German nationals in some leading roles. For example, Colonel Fritz Brase was appointed head of the Irish Army School of Music. Brase emigrated to Ireland in 1923 at the invitation of General Richard Mulcahy and soon grew to great prominence in Irish social circles. An accomplished band leader, he soon became a frequent performer with the army band at Dublin's Theatre Royal. Other Germans who held prominent positions in the arts were Friedrich Herkner, Professor of Sculpture at the National College of Arts, and Dr Adolf Mahr, director of the National Museum. Under Mahr's stewardship of the museum, Germans with an interest in folklore and Celtic mythology were encouraged to visit Ireland for extended periods of study. These cultural exchanges brought many Germans into contact with Irish nationalists and those with republican sympathies for the first time. These contacts were built upon in the years ahead as the political situation began to deteriorate on the continent.

In the years following the Wall Street Crash of 1929, alongside the political instability of the Weimar Republic, Adolf Hitler had grown from a political outsider to a reasonable alternative to the establishment. This was achieved through relentless propaganda aimed at a public who had grown weary of successive government failures to restore economic and social stability. The electoral strength of NSDAP grew in successive elections; the Nazi Party grew from 2.6 per cent of the vote in 1928 to 18 per cent in the 1930 election. Hitler himself won 36.8 per cent of the vote in the 1932 presidential election, in which he ran against the incumbent, President Hindenburg. Although Hindenburg was returned, his position was significantly weakened by the increase in the Nazi vote. Through various political intrigues with conservatives such as Franz von Papen, Hitler was able to secure the Chancellor's office in 1933, despite not having a majority in the Reichstag. On the death of Hindenburg in 1934, Hitler established himself as dictator. Now he sought to extend his influence to other European countries, including Ireland, where there were subversive elements with which Nazi Germany had common cause. Plans were immediately put in place to reach out to republican elements through the German expatriate community in Dublin and other parts of the country.

The advent of National Socialism as the dominant political order in Germany had a dramatic impact on German activities in Ireland. The Nazi Party was able to organise overseas affiliated political organisations, the largest of which was the Auslands ('foreign') Organisation (AO) of the NSDAP, which was headquartered in Berlin. The AO was subdivided into national groupings, known as Landesgruppen, based in different countries. The Dublin branch of the AO was formed in 1934 and its membership primarily consisted of members of the German intelligentsia who were involved in the arts. Adolf Mahr, director of the National Museum, became leader of the AO in Dublin. The Dublin membership never numbered more than 30 but it had enough clout that Mahr was able to influence the German–Irish Trade Agreement of 1935. Despite being delayed until 1939, the deal was a huge boost for the agriculture sector:

> Arrangements have been made for the export to Germany in 1939 of cattle, eggs, meat products, and herrings in prescribed proportions. The German government are free to purchase other Irish products, including butter and horses, in such quantities as they may require from time to time. The new Agreement provides that as from the 1st January next agricultural products will be purchased by Germany in the open market here, thus obviating the necessity for special price arrangements between the governments and eliminating any risk of loss to the Irish government.

Not only did the AO extend its influence to trade agreements, it also kept abreast of any domestic political developments and regularly transmitted intelligence to senior figures in the Nazi High Command. The Dublin branch of the AO was given to frequent and ostentatious displays of national pride, often held in prominent restaurants and hotels; and on occasion it organised large gatherings in the Kilmaccurragh Park Hotel in County Wicklow. Such public displays of nationalism brought the group to the attention of Dan Bryan and G2, who set up round-the-clock surveillance of many of the members of the AO.

The group wasn't the only fascist organisation that G2 had begun monitoring. Italian fascists had also established a political group in Dublin, the Fascio di Dublino Michele D'Angelo, which was connected to the Italian Fascist Overseas Organisation, essentially an Italian version of the AO, and which met frequently at an Italian café in the city centre. The group was led by Trinity College Professor of Italian Count Eduardo Tomacelli. Count Tomacelli purchased a property at 35 Eglinton Road in Donnybrook after having arrived in Dublin from Naples in 1935 to take up his teaching post. He was immediately put under surveillance by G2 and the Garda Special Branch. Bryan was able to utilise two G2 plants in Trinity codenamed 'Rome' and 'Paris' to report regularly on Tomacelli. The close relationship between the Count and the German Legation was noted, with Bryan remarking that the Germans were working 'hand in glove with the [Italian] Legation'. The pro-fascist activities of Tomacelli and his colleagues proved to be a huge source of distress to the Italian community in Dublin who had fled in exile from the Mussolini regime.

It was through academia that some of the most potent connections with Germany were inadvertently established, mainly through a foreign exchange organisation that sought to strengthen and promote cultural links with the country. It is perhaps because these links were established through universities and were cultural in nature that they managed to slip through the net and were not subject to the same scrutiny by G2 as the AO and the Italian Fascist organisation. The Deutsche Akademischer Austauschdienst (German Academic Exchange Service) sought to provide a platform for cultural and linguistic exchanges of German students and academics. Many of the students who came to Ireland as part of the programme were studying Celtic studies and folklore.

The group was led by a native of Aachen, the spa city near Germany's borders with Belgium and the Netherlands. Born on 5 November 1911, Helmut Clissmann, the second son of a banker and schoolteacher, first came to Ireland in 1933 as a student and exchange lecturer in Trinity College Dublin, where he soon became the representative of the German students at the university. Clissmann always strenuously denied that his initial intentions in Ireland were anything more than cultural in nature. When asked by Prof. Carter in the tapes whether he had been asked to do anything else, such as 'keep his eyes open' or 'liaise with the German Legation', Clissmann replied 'No'. He was then asked by Carter to account for rumours to the contrary, and he said only that, 'Some people must have come to some wrong conclusion.' Indeed, there is no evidence that Clissmann's business in Ireland at this point was anything other than academic and cultural in nature.

Alongside his academic life Clissmann developed contacts within the republican movement in Ireland through his cultural endeavours and family acquaintances. Before 1933, on a private visit to Dublin, he had become acquainted with the editors of *An Phoblacht*, Frank Ryan and Peadar O'Donnell, both prominent figures on the left of the IRA.

Clissmann soon blended into life on campus as an exchange student and later worked on a doctoral thesis entitled 'The Wild Geese in Germany' on his return to university in Frankfurt. These studies may well have bolstered his burgeoning interest in Irish nationalism, and Clissmann was shortly to become personally acquainted with some of the major figures of the War of Independence and their family members. These would include Seán MacBride, son of Maud Gonne MacBride and Major John MacBride, who had been executed for his role in the Easter Rising. Major MacBride was a venerated figure and the family carried that aura with them. Perhaps the most important figure with whom Clissmann was to become associated with during this period was War of Independence veteran Tom Barry, who would go on to form links with other students in the exchange programme.

While in Ireland, Clissmann was appointed by the German Academic Exchange Service to extend exchanges of student lectures, authors, musicians, etc. In addition to this role, the Goethe Institute in Munich also appointed him as a teacher of German and he held classes for several years in Mount Street. His activities in pre-war Dublin appear to be entirely cultural, for example arranging for the choir from his native Aachen to perform in Dublin. Clissmann's links with Ireland were further strengthened by his marriage to Elizabeth 'Budge' Mulcahy.

A native of County Sligo, Budge was born on 5 August 1913, the eldest of four daughters of Denis and Mary (née Murray) Mulcahy, both teachers at Sligo Technical College. The Mulcahys were known in Sligo as a fiercely republican family and Denis was interned for a time in Newbridge camp during the War of Independence for refusing to take the Oath of Allegiance to the British Crown. While he was interned, Mary ran Sligo Technical College. From an early age Budge was involved in the republican move-ment and during the Civil War, aged only nine, she acted as a courier for anti-Treaty IRA men on the run. After attending school at Sligo's Ursuline Convent, she studied Irish and French at University College Galway, gradu-ating in 1933. She spent a year studying abroad at the Sorbonne in Paris and married Helmut Clissmann in 1938. Clissmann's best man at the wedding in the Unitarian Church, St Stephen's Green, was a friend from his native Aachen who had also come to Ireland through the exchange programme. Joseph 'Jupp' Hoven originally travelled to Ireland to study folklore and in the course of his stay paid several visits to various parts of the country, including Northern Ireland.

Following Hitler's rise to power in January 1933, all students leaving the Fatherland to study abroad were obliged to join the Nazi Party as a prerequisite for obtaining travel papers and funding. Clissmann became a card-carrying member of the Nazi Party. This wasn't uncommon at the time, as Budge Clissmann recalled: 'You couldn't get an exchange student place unless you were a member of the party. So he [Helmut] just joined but that does not mean that you were a member with any enthusiasm.'

Clissmann's marriage to Budge Mulcahy meant that he got to know many people in the republican movement. In addition to Barry and MacBride he soon became acquainted with Maurice 'Moss' Twomey, Seán Russell and Jim O'Donovan. These contacts were notable – all of these men, apart from

O'Donovan, would hold the position of IRA Chief of Staff: Twomey from 1926 to 1936; MacBride briefly in 1936; Tom Barry from 1936 to 1937; and Seán Russell from 1938 to 1939. O'Donovan, an ESB manager, later acted as the IRA's liaison officer with Nazi Germany from 1938 to 1941.

Clissmann himself left Ireland on 11 September 1939 on board the mail boat the *Cambria* in a general recall of German citizens following the outbreak of the war. He was called up for active service in July 1940, and his knowledge of Ireland was soon to be used for political and military missions to Ireland. Despite Clissmann and Hoven's acquaintances with the republican movement, it was through Barry that first contact between the IRA and Nazi Germany would be made.

Tom Barry, arguably one of the most recognised names of the Irish War of Independence, was a respected guerrilla fighter who is synonymous with the Kilmichael Ambush on 28 November 1920 and numerous other engagements with British forces. Born on 1 July 1897 in Killorglin, County Kerry, Barry had an unusual start in life for a guerrilla fighter – his father, Tom Senior, was a member of the RIC. Barry is the earliest known intermediary between the fledgling Nazi state and the IRA. In his native county, however, Barry was and remains a folk hero.

Cork was the most active county in Ireland during the Anglo-Irish War and as a result it was also the bloodiest. The Kilmichael Ambush was the largest ambush during the conflict, carried out a week to the day after Bloody Sunday. Sixteen members of the Auxiliary Division of the RIC (ADRIC) were killed by Barry's flying column. Three IRA men, Pat Deasy, Michael McCarthy and Jim Sullivan, were also killed in what Barry described in later years as a 'false surrender' of some of the Auxiliaries. The Kilmichael Ambush was militarily a great success and a propaganda coup for the IRA. It also won Barry the admiration and respect of many of his fellow countrymen, as the harassment of the local population in West Cork by the Auxiliaries and the Black and Tans was well documented. He became a republican icon in Cork in the aftermath of the war, opting to take a different path from that of one-time colleagues such as Dan Bryan. Bryan would later note that perhaps Kilmichael was the peak of Barry's revolutionary career and that his subsequent dealings with Nazi Germany were something he would prefer to be forgotten:

I got that story and I pursued it and it's never become public. The IRA man was a man called Tom Barry. If you went to Cork almost anyone would tell you where to find Barry. His wife Mrs Tom Barry is President of the Irish Red Cross. Now ... she lives in Cork but they have offices in Dublin. I knew somebody that was an OC [Officer Commanding in the IRA] down there who told me this and he left me under the impression that this was correct. Hoven had met Barry and gone to Germany. He travelled from Belfast down to Cork to meet him. Barry has written his memoirs since his War of Independence days but he has never mentioned this particular episode in it. He was one of the principal guerrilla fighters in the war against the British but he hasn't achieved anything since. Barry has never mentioned that publicly. There are certain things in relation to him where I'm beginning to wonder how well founded they are. I would say he would talk about it if asked. He was a bit erratic and unpredictable.

For Barry, like many who shared his republican outlook, the war with the old enemy was very much ongoing as long there remained a British presence in Ireland. He was prepared to utilise any opportunity possible to further the republican cause. For Barry and his generation the idea of a military alliance with Nazi Germany perhaps wasn't such a shocking proposition. Such was the visceral hatred of the British among certain elements in republicanism that an alliance with Hitler was not an unreasonable step to take. On numerous occasions in Irish history militant nationalists had taken advantage of British military and political crisis overseas to launch rebellions. Perhaps the only notable exception was the Indian Rebellion of 1857. Indeed, the Easter Rising, coming at the height of World War I, can be seen as the ultimate expression of this idea. Ironically, Barry was at the time of the Rising serving as a corporal in the British Army and stationed in Mesopotamia in the Ottoman Empire. Dropping his rank in protest at British suppression of the rebel forces in Dublin, he returned to Ireland in 1919.

It is hardly surprising that the old adage of England's difficulty being Ireland's opportunity was repackaged and repurposed by republicans to advocate for an alliance with Nazi Germany on the basis that they were at war with the British.

The earliest IRA contacts with Nazi Germany are believed to have been initiated by Barry in 1937 when he travelled to Berlin alongside Hoven. By now Barry was Chief of Staff of the IRA, a role he was to hold until 1938. In his capacity as Chief of Staff he was tasked with investigating the capacity for co-operation between the Germans and the IRA. Barry saw this in terms of support for a guerrilla war and a sabotage campaign against England. The Germans showed some interest in this proposal but attached to it very specific terms. In return for a promise by the IRA to limit its targets to British military installations in Northern Ireland, Germany would provide assistance in various forms. Barry brought these proposals to the IRA General Army Convention in 1938, but the tide was turning against him within the republican movement and much of the power now resided in the IRA's more militant wing, led by Seán Russell. By April Barry had been ousted and Russell had taken over, largely due to the popularity of an alternative IRA plan, later to become known as the S-Plan. Barry returned to his role as a docker with the Port of Cork. A reluctant supporter of the Provisional IRA in his later years, albeit a critic of pub bombings, he died in 1980 and is buried in St Finbarr's Cemetery in Cork City.

As Hitler's grip grew on all facets of German life and the Nazi Party grew in strength and dominance, the opposite was the case with the IRA. The old guard was rapidly becoming an irrelevance in the new political era led by the fascists in Europe. The movement had been reduced to a disgruntled rump in the years following the Civil War, and since the defection of Éamon de Valera to mainstream politics when Fianna Fáil was founded in 1926, there had been a dearth of leadership in Sinn Féin. What was left behind was a disparate group of extremists with a rainbow of political hues, ranging from traditional Catholic ideologues in the vein of Patrick Pearse to a left-leaning faction inspired more by Lenin's Russia than by Rome. In many ways the movement was in disarray. This was encapsulated in the formation of the Republican Congress, a dissenting voice within republicanism led by Frank Ryan, Peadar O'Donnell and George Gilmore. The group lit the spark for a significant rift within the IRA which was to have a major impact on the group's outlook. The restructuring of the IRA would lead to a metamorphosis from a rag-tag group of poorly organised gunmen to a more streamlined modern outfit with a clear set of goals and objectives that would find common cause with Nazi Germany, a country with which it shared a distaste for all things British. In order to transform the organisation, it was essential to unite all groups within the IRA to a common cause. Prof. Carter's tapes reveal Dan Bryan's view:

> Mr de Valera helped to lead them into a Civil War in '22 against Collins, Griffith and Cosgrave and ... in '32 he did what Collins, Griffith and Cosgrave did in '22 and ... there's no essential difference between the settlement in '22 and what he did in '32 and ... they're very bitter for that reason. They say, 'that so-and-so encouraged us to fight a Civil War against Griffith and Collins and then he went and did the same himself'. This involves more than the oath and mind you, I hold myself that there's a good lot to their contention. He [de Valera] made a fool of himself in '22 by going into the Civil War. I hold that de Valera's later constitutional successes were built on the foundation made by the people who took over in '22.

In an almost mirror image of G2, many of the main players in the IRA during the 1930s were "22 men", or veterans of the independence struggle. By 1938 many of the main players in the movement had disengaged themselves from active service. Barry had returned to his work in Cork Port; Moss Twomey had retired to open a shop on Upper O'Connell Street; O'Donovan had returned to his role with the ESB. During this period all maintained a tenuous relationship with the IRA. The departure of so many of the main figures led to a power vacuum within the organisation that allowed Seán Russell to come to the fore.

Born on Lower Buckingham Street in Dublin in 1890, Russell was a militarist and a die-hard supporter of armed struggle, who held senior roles in the movement during the War of Independence. He was a veteran of the 1916 Rising, having joined the Irish Volunteers in 1913. During Easter week he was an officer in the 2nd Battalion of the Dublin Brigade with

Thomas McDonagh. In the aftermath of the Rising Russell was interned in Frongoch internment camp in Wales. During the War of Independence, he was appointed to the role of Director of Munitions in 1920, a post that would see him rise to the top of the ranks of IRA GHQ. He took the anti-Treaty side during the Civil War and was imprisoned for a short time after hostilities ended in 1925. On his release he was still wedded to the course of the pursuit of the Irish Republic that theoretically existed, in direct conflict with the Irish Free State to which Bryan and others had given their allegiance. To that end Russell and Gerald Boland were dispatched to Moscow to establish links with Alexei Rykov's Soviet Russia in an effort to garner arms and political support. During this visit Russell became acquainted with the use of ciphers for the purposes of sending coded messages.

The history of ciphers and coded messages in Russia can be traced back over many centuries, and some of the first political cryptography can be dated to the reign of Peter the Great in the early eighteenth century. While initially primitive in nature, Russian ciphers came of age in 1754 in the reign of Peter's daughter, Elizabeth, and by the twentieth century Russian ciphers had gained a special notoriety. They were studied in detail by William Friedman, the US army cryptographer who ran the research division of the army's Signal Intelligence Service in the 1930s, and parts of its follow-on services into the 1950s. In Friedman's view:

> By 1916 Imperial Russian diplomatic cryptography was outstanding, far ahead of anything anybody else had at that time. They involved substitution and additive-based systems with very elaborately concealed indicators. These systems were also described as frequently cumbersome in appearance, [but] adroit and cleverly devised. Following the overthrow of Imperial Russia in 1917, the Bolshevik successors, in an apparent eagerness to reject all vestiges of Tsarism, initially abandoned the complex and relatively secure diplomatic systems. Government bureaus, military headquarters, police, etc., compiled their own codes and ciphers, and, until 1923, employed mostly primitive substitution and single transposition systems.

Coded messages would prove to be a valuable asset to republicanism in its attempt to forge links with Nazi Germany.

On his return from Moscow, Russell reported his findings to Seán Lemass, the notional republic's Minister for Defence. In a twist of fate, de Valera, Boland and Lemass would soon abandon the IRA to enter constitutional politics. Afterwards, Russell was promoted to the role of IRA Quartermaster General in 1927, a position he held until 1936. He immediately set about reorganising the IRA, travelling the length and breadth of Ireland from 1929 to 1931 to rally the demoralised membership. His activities didn't go unnoticed by Military Intelligence and the Garda Special Branch and he was arrested the night before he was due to give the annual Wolfe Tone Commemorative Oration in Bodenstown in 1931. On his release, Russell travelled to the United States in 1932. Sensing a shift in the IRA following the creation of the Republican Congress, Russell sensed an opportunity to rise to the top of the movement and sought to curry influence in republican circles in the United States to help him achieve his ambition.

During his tour of the States, Russell visited many Irish American strongholds, and he met with Clan na Gael leader Joseph McGarrity. A native of Carrickmore in County Tyrone, McGarrity was hugely influential in Irish America and respected by republican activists back in Ireland. Clan na Gael, which could trace its heritage back to the Fenian Brotherhood, was deeply committed to securing an Irish republic. Gaining its support would be crucial for Russell's bid to take the reins of the IRA. Alongside McGarrity, Russell conceived a mass bombing operation to take place on the British mainland. It was hoped that a renewed offensive against the British at a time of political tension with Nazi Germany would create instability and encourage an intent to withdraw from Ireland among the mainstream British body politic.

Buoyed by this new plan, Russell returned to Ireland, but his euphoria was to be short-lived as he was promptly arrested by his colleagues in the IRA under suspicion of misappropriating funds and losing arms from an arms dump. Temporally sidelined by his former colleagues Barry and MacBride, it was not until much later that Russell returned to a more prominent role in the movement. In April 1938, an IRA General Army Convention was called and Russell, with the support of McGarrity and others, was elected to the Army Council. His bombing campaign, for which planning had begun in earnest, was adopted as IRA policy. Soon afterwards, Russell became Chief of Staff of the IRA and recalled his old colleague Jim O'Donovan to help prosecute the bombing campaign against England. Meanwhile in Germany, the Abwehr, the German army's intelligence service, looked on eagerly, sensing an opportunity.

Throughout the period 1921 to 1944 the Abwehr served as the intelligence branch of the German armed forces, the Wehrmacht. Following its defeat in World War I and the Armistice in 1918, Germany had agreed to the terms of the Treaty of Versailles. Ratified in 1920, the agreement sought to enact punitive measures against Germany. In an attempt to assuage French fears of German rearmament, the German military was sharply curtailed. As part of these measures German intelligence-gathering was severely limited; the Abwehr, like the rest of the German army, was restricted to a purely defensive function. But it eventually became involved in offensive planning. In early 1938 Hitler reorganised the Abwehr, incorporating it into the German High Command and reconstituting it into an elite intelligence-gathering agency.

Initially the Abwehr dealt exclusively in human intelligence derived from field agents and intelligence reports. From January 1935 to February 1944 it was led by Admiral Wilhelm Franz Canaris, who was headquartered in Berlin. Canaris reported directly to the German High Command, while intelligence reports were directed to the centralised Oberkommando der Wehrmacht (OKW). Intelligence was then filtered through to various intelligence desks within the German military structure. These included the army, the navy (Kriegsmarine) and the air force (Luftwaffe). Known as a shrewd operator, Canaris was born in January 1887 in Aplerbeck, near Dortmund. He was decorated as a war hero for his role as a submarine captain during World War I. Canaris was initially a supporter of Hitler's policies and was strongly attracted to the Führer's desire to re-arm Germany and rebuild the German Navy. However, his approval of Hitler was to be short-lived. Canaris had been an eyewitness to the killing of civilians in Poland when SS troops in Bedzin set fire to a synagogue, burning 200 Jews to death. This, coupled with Hitler's purge of his enemies in the Night of the Long Knives in 1934, pitted Canaris ideologically against the Führer. Despite his reservations, Canaris was prepared to carry out intelligence work on behalf of the regime. In neutral countries like Ireland the Abwehr disguised its operations by attaching its operatives to German diplomatic missions, particularly legations, which were forerunners to embassies. Under Canaris's tenure the Abwehr grew into a formidable organisation which soon turned its eyes to Ireland in the wake of Russell's rise to the top of the IRA.

In January 1939 Russell and the IRA put into action their bombing campaign, the Sabotage Plan or the S-Plan. The IRA immediately set about attacking civil and economic targets on the British mainland. The campaign was notable for its ruthlessness and the London Underground was attacked on several occasions. Operations were also carried out in Manchester and Birmingham. Northern Ireland was specifically forbidden as a legitimate target. Russell and the IRA claimed its legitimacy as the rightful government of Ireland by publishing in a republican newspaper a statement of 'authority' signed by seven TDs from the Second Dáil of 1921–2. It was believed that this Dáil was the legitimate government of Ireland as it had been the last sitting of the parliament before partition of the island of Ireland under the Government of Ireland Act 1920.

The campaign reached its zenith in mid-January when a written ultimatum was delivered to the British Foreign Secretary, Lord Halifax, giving the British four days to withdraw from Ireland. The message had been written by Jim O'Donovan, whom Russell had persuaded to rejoin the IRA to help train some of the younger recruits. Posters bearing the IRA's declaration were placed on walls of railway stations in both Northern and Southern Ireland as well as in tube stations in London.

Throughout the entire IRA operation Scotland Yard and MI5 had placed the IRA under surveillance. Agents were dispatched to Dublin to seek the arrest of IRA members suspected of orchestrating the bombings. While the British authorities had managed to track down some of the suspects, their arrest warrants weren't honoured by the Irish government, much to the ire of Her Majesty's government. The British authorities instead had to bide their time. They struck gold when they apprehended IRA man Joseph Kelly, who was carrying a copy of the S-Plan. The police also recovered recipes for making bombs as well as republican poetry, coded documents and ciphers. By the time it came to an end, the campaign had been responsible for 300 explosions, 10 deaths and 96 injuries.

The Germans felt it was time to take matters further and in late February 1939 the Abwehr decided to send Oscar C. Pfaus to Ireland to establish contact with Russell and the IRA to see if common cause could be agreed between the IRA and Nazi Germany. Pfaus arrived at Dún Laoghaire on the mail boat the *Cambria* in the guise of a journalist for a German newspaper. He was briefed for his trip by an expert on Irish affairs named Franz Fromme. Fromme became quite adept in the planning of intelligence operations in Ireland. An academic, like many of the German community in Ireland, Fromme had written a book on the Irish independence struggle and had in the course of his time in Ireland acquainted himself with the widows of some of the country's most noted revolutionary figures. He knew Kathleen Clarke, the widow of executed 1916 leader Tom Clarke, and Caitlín Brugha, the wife of War of Independence veteran and inaugural Ceann Comhairle of Dáil Éireann, Cathal Brugha. Because of his experience in Ireland Fromme was deemed suitable to give intelligence briefings on the country to any would-be spies.

Despite Fromme's briefings and background knowledge, Oscar Pfaus arrived in Ireland with no meaningful contacts in the republican movement. After, in error, initially approaching Eoin O'Duffy's Blueshirts, Pfaus was introduced to the IRA through a Mrs E. Martin, a member of the Irish Hospitals Trust. Pfaus's error in contacting the Blueshirts betrayed his lack of knowledge of Irish history and politics, but in contacting the Hospitals Trust he was soon put right. The Irish Hospitals Trust oversaw the draws of the Irish Hospitals' Sweepstake, a lottery established in the Irish Free State in 1930 as a means to finance Irish hospitals. The draws, which aimed to raise funds from the Irish diaspora, took place in Ireland a couple of times a year. The draws were nothing short of spectacular, featuring showgirls, floats and all the trappings of showbusiness. Winners were drawn from every corner of the world, but the primary market was the United States.

The sweepstakes were originally set up by Dublin bookmaker Richard Duggan, Welsh-born Captain Spencer Freeman and Joseph McGrath, once an associate of Michael Collins. Despite the fact that gambling bans were in place in many US states, the sweepstakes proved to be hugely successful in America. In 1932 the prize fund was estimated to be £2.3 million, the equivalent of €151 million in 2020. The profits were used to fund the construction of the Irish health service, but this cloaked a much more sinister reality. The trust had long been infiltrated by the IRA. Overseas tickets were sold illegally and in defiance of gambling bans and returned to private addresses. Tickets were laundered through Old IRA contacts and the republican movement benefited hugely. This, in addition to aid from Joseph McGarrity, who acted as an agent for the scheme in the States, helped to fund the bombing campaign in England.

After making contact with the Hospitals Trust, Pfaus was invited to meet the IRA. He was to go to an office supply store on Upper O'Connell Street on 13 February 1939, where he was picked up by Moss Twomey and taken to Clontarf. There the already very nervous German met with Chief of Staff Seán Russell as well as Director of Munitions and Chemicals and author of the S-Plan, Jim O'Donovan. Despite O'Donovan thinking that Pfaus was something of 'an SS type', the meeting was a success and Pfaus agreed to pass on the IRA's interest in collaborating with the Germans. The IRA would send a contact man to Berlin to discuss matters further and to negotiate for the supply of arms, transmitting equipment and additional funds. O'Donovan himself said he would fulfil this role and travelled to Berlin in mid-1939 using the codename Agent V-Held.

While Pfaus had been successful in making contact with the IRA, he had been under constant surveillance by both G2 and MI5 throughout his visit. G2 had observed him nervously burning documents in his hotel as well as any correspondence he had had while resident in the country. Sensing that he was being watched, Pfaus left Ireland somewhat precipitately and returned to Germany.

In many ways O'Donovan was an ideal agent to make contact with the Abwehr. A veteran of the War of Independence, he had married Monty Barry, the sister of IRA martyr Kevin Barry. He was well educated and had graduated from UCD with a degree in chemistry. While he had declared himself to be retired from the IRA, he had been coaxed back into the organisation by Seán Russell and had been the main driving force behind the S-Plan. He was tasked with training a new generation of IRA volunteers for the subsequent bombing campaign. In many ways O'Donovan found himself thrust into the role as he felt there was a lack of 'talent' within the ranks. Speaking to Prof. Carter, his tape reveals his disdain for what he felt was the poor calibre of IRA recruits:

> I wasn't interested in the first place, because why should I be interested? This was an extraneous job that was sort of forced on me you see. I mean that I very reluctantly engaged in, not that I didn't put my heart and soul into it. I did everything that I could. I did far too much considering that I had no function. I told you that a couple of times already that I was not a member of the IRA and I'm a purely extraneous person or an outside person who is lending a hand, but it turned out to be more than a hand. I found myself doing every damn thing because there was nobody else there. There was never anybody with brains particularly. I mean you could tick them off with the fingers on one hand, the numbers that were any good here.

In total O'Donovan made three trips to Germany, acting under Russell's orders. He set up a courier route for messages via London, and procured a radio transmitter; but the Germans were reluctant to provide arms and ammunition because they considered the bombing campaign provocative. O'Donovan was deeply suspicious of the Germans, whom, he felt, distrusted the IRA. 'Everyone was observing everyone else through keyholes, there was a lot of keyhole looking going on.'

By the time O'Donovan returned from his final visit to Germany major changes had taken place within the IRA. In March 1939 Russell departed for the United States in order to carry out propaganda work on behalf of the IRA and to further the cause against the British, and Adjutant General Stephen Hayes was appointed Chief of Staff. Originally a native of Enniscorthy, Hayes didn't command the same respect as Russell. Prof. Carter's tapes reveal that O'Donovan was incensed at Russell's departure, feeling that his reasons for leaving weren't genuine:

Seán Russell went away needlessly; it was not necessary to go to America to raise money, money was not needed. There was a little bit of money available and the activities of the IRA in the 1930s didn't require much money. It was nonsense for Russell to take a course in sabotage. He knew all about it and didn't need any lessons in it.

O'Donovan also didn't approve of the appointment of Hayes as Chief of Staff; he believed Hayes was a heavy drinker. Despite the misgivings, Hayes had given a pledge to Russell that he would be on his best behaviour in Russell's absence. In reality there was no love lost between the two men. In a recording with Hayes himself he reveals his criticism of Russell's leadership:

He was an idealist, not down to earth, very genuine and very honest. His mind wouldn't be thinking the same lines as Frank [Ryan]. Frank was socialist, really socialist, you know. He wasn't a fascist. As far as economics and that and what the country was going to be like afterwards economically was immaterial to him. All he wanted was Ireland free. There were differences between James Connolly and Patrick Pearse. Connolly was down to earth, Pearse was an idealist. Connolly knew what he was fighting for. Russell, well, he was more like Pearse.

O'Donovan felt that Russell leaving was a blow to the organisation given that German–IRA co-operation was, according to him, solely Russell's idea. Hayes was the natural choice to succeed O'Donovan as he had been on the IRA Army Council in the months leading up to the bombing campaign in England. Born in 1902, he was a veteran of the War of Independence and had been interned by the Free State government during the Civil War. Hayes had a background in republicanism which dated to his childhood when he was a member of Fianna Éireann in Wexford. As well as militant republicanism he was heavily involved in the GAA and won a Leinster football title with Wexford in 1925 as well as serving as county secretary on more than one occasion. Through his role within the GAA Hayes had become a popular figure in Wexford, and his contacts at the port of Rosslare were vital to the importation of arms.

On his appointment as Acting Chief of Staff in April 1939 Hayes set about continuing the offensive against England and regular meetings were held above a shop at 97A Rathgar Road. Unbeknownst to Hayes, the Garda Special Branch had the building under surveillance and the address later became the scene of one of the most notorious incidents of the Emergency when Detective Sergeant Patrick McKeown, from Armagh, and Mayo-born Detective Garda Richard Hyland were both shot during a raid of the address on 16 August 1940. Both men were posthumously awarded the Scott Medal, the highest honour in An Garda Síochána, in August 2021. Despite ongoing planning Hayes's efforts were to prove futile and, despite attracting considerable attention, the S-Plan was not a success. All Hayes succeeded in doing was provoking a severe reaction from the Dublin and London governments, while inadvertently helping to herald the successful passage of the Offences Against the State Act 1939 through the Oireachtas. This Act gave the Gardaí, through its Special Branch and in liaison with G2, wide-ranging powers to deal with the IRA.

Hayes was put under constant surveillance and narrowly escaped arrest on 9 September. However, much of IRA GHQ was apprehended and significant amounts of cash were seized. Hayes himself was forced to live in various safe houses with the constant threat of arrest looming over him. His appointment as Acting Chief of Staff was to prove to be hugely controversial in republican circles, with many, including O'Donovan, believing Hayes to be a government agent. As the intrigue continued in Ireland, matters took a grave turn in Europe. The policy of appeasement of Hitler espoused by British Prime Minister Neville Chamberlain failed utterly. On 1 September 1939 Germany invaded Poland. Nazi propagandists falsely claimed that Poland had been planning, with its allies Great Britain and France, to encircle and attack Germany and that Poles were persecuting ethnic Germans. Two days later Britain declared war on Germany. World War II had begun.

Whether or not he was a government plant, Stephen Hayes had taken over the IRA at a time when its resources had been hugely diminished. Hayes felt that the IRA needed to re-arm and that munitions were badly needed. Through his connections in Wexford, he was able to procure a radio that he used to make contact with Germany to renew acquaintances. During the course of these communications, he requested arms and cash, but he was actually planning a more daring operation, one that he felt would put the IRA front and centre of the ongoing campaign against the British. Hayes had decided to strike the biggest arms cache in the state – the Magazine Fort in Dublin's Phoenix Park. On 23 December the IRA struck and managed to steal over 1,084,000 rounds of ammunition, nearly the entire reserve stock of the Defence Forces. The raid only sought to escalate the government's determination to suppress the IRA rather than to alleviate their arms issues in the long term. Taoiseach Éamon de Valera was determined to deal with the IRA once and for all and render them impotent.

In a series of government raids carried out using intelligence provided by Bryan and G2, over 850,000 rounds of ammunition were recovered and Hayes's radio was seized from Ashgrove House in Rathgar. O'Donovan and other republicans had used it to make various propaganda broadcasts that had unwittingly enabled G2 and the Garda Special Branch to trace the location of the radio set. The Carter tapes reveal Bryan felt that overall, the Phoenix Park raid was a disaster for the IRA:

The fact that most of the ammunition was recaptured must have had a very bad effect on the morale of the IRA. It was due to the fact that although they had made detailed arrangements for the coup on the Magazine Fort, they had no satisfactory arrangements for the effective division and hiding of the ammunition once they got it. It is also an interesting fact that one of the men who had most to do with the organisation of the coup, I'm sure his name was Thomas Doyle, was employed as a junior civil servant in the Department of Defence which is of course located with Army Headquarters in Park Gate.

The effect of the Magazine Fort [raid] was that the army who kept away, the army who kept away from the IRA and, who in general, knew nothing about it until then, began to receive the reports about IRA activities and from then on quite an amount of information came to intelligence from army sources.

Undeterred by the security spotlight cast on the IRA, Hayes sought to make further contacts with the Abwehr. He sensed that the war was initially going in Germany's favour and he was interested in doing a deal with the Nazis should they be successful: 'You see Germany actually looked like winning the war at that stage in the early stages and we were more or less interested in if they were winning the war, what kind of deal we could make with them.'

The Abwehr was more than willing to send a number of spies to Ireland to further bolster the links that had already been established between the IRA and Nazi Germany. However, despite G2 and the Garda Special Branch's initial successes against the IRA and the Abwehr, there were more sinister developments in diplomatic circles in Dublin; whispers of secret radios and illegal transmissions. As Bryan and G2 were to soon learn, the roots of German espionage in Ireland were deep, right to the centre of foreign and domestic diplomatic missions in Ireland. The situation was growing graver by the day, and it was clear the appetite of republicans to collaborate with the Germans was very strong. The fate of independent Ireland was at stake and only Bryan and G2 stood in the way of the Nazis' appalling plans.

III

THE ART OF DIPLOMACY

But it was difficult to withhold one's contempt from a country such as Ireland, whose battle this was and whose chances of freedom and independence in the event of a German victory were nil.

NICHOLAS MONTSERRAT, *THE CRUEL SEA* (1951)

As Bryan, G2 and the Irish government desperately tried to deal with the unfolding situation, an unassuming Irish academic and writer slipped under their radar as he made his way quietly to Berlin to re-establish contact between the IRA and Nazi Germany.

Francis Stuart was unlikely to raise much suspicion from the security forces. Born to Irish Protestant parents in Australia, Stuart was very much part of the establishment. He had been educated in the English public school system, attending Rugby School in Warwickshire as a boarder. His time at Rugby, which instilled in Stuart an intense distaste for the British and the ideals of imperialism, was to shape the course of the rest of his life. He joined the elite of Irish society when he married Iseult Gonne in 1919, and by 1920, he had renounced his Protestant upbringing and converted to Catholicism. Iseult's mother Maud had been married to Major John MacBride, who had been executed for his role in the 1916 Rising. It is perhaps not surprising, given the Gonne family connections, that Stuart became involved in militant Irish republicanism. Through Iseult's half-brother, Seán, Stuart eventually became involved with the republican movement. He took the anti-Treaty side in the Civil War and, like Russell and O'Donovan, rallied behind Éamon de Valera as the upholder of the Republic proclaimed in 1916.

Stuart and Iseult travelled Europe following the death of their first child in infancy but returned to Ireland on the outbreak of the Civil War; Stuart became involved almost immediately, editing leaflets and running messages for de Valera. He also became involved in gun-running and was interned after a botched arms raid. On his release he published his first collection of poetry, *We Have Kept the Faith*. The title is telling, and it comes as no surprise that the collection won him the admiration of the republican movement. Stuart continued working for de Valera in a clandestine capacity until 1926, when de Valera left Sinn Féin to form Fianna Fáil. Stuart now found himself on the political margins. When, as Taoiseach, de Valera sought to suppress and intern IRA members, Stuart and his contemporaries such as O'Donovan and Russell became dissidents without any sort of meaningful political base.

During the mid-1930s Stuart accepted an offer to lecture on Anglo-Irish literature at Berlin University. Although very much enamoured with the role, he returned to Ireland in order to work on his marriage to Iseult, which at this stage was in trouble. By 1939, his marriage had failed and he was suffering from financial problems. He made the decision to take up another academic post in Berlin, seeking permission to travel from the Department of External Affairs under the pretext that he was going to Switzerland for health reasons. His real intention was to attempt to revive the IRA's links with Nazi Germany. The authorities immediately became suspicious and duly informed Dan Bryan and G2, who urged External Affairs to show caution; they believed that Stuart was actually hoping to travel to Germany. Ultimately G2 was unable to prevent his travel documents being issued as the Department of External Affairs was forced to adhere to the policy of neutrality.

In order to secure his passage to Germany, Stuart broached the topic with the German Minister to Ireland, Dr Eduard Hempel. Hempel had first been posted to Ireland in 1937 and, while initially not a member, he had been pressured to join the Nazi Party in 1938. The fact that Hempel was not a member of the party when he was posted to Dublin suited the Irish government, but it was unable to object to him joining the party after being appointed. Hempel had taken up residence in Gortleightragh, a house in the Dublin suburb of Monkstown, and was more than willing to carry out party policy. His official work as Envoy Extraordinary and Minister

Plenipotentiary (rather than ambassador) was carried out at the German Legation at 58 Northumberland Road in the heart of the city. At the Dublin Horse Show in 1938 he had given the Nazi salute in the presence of President of Ireland Dr Douglas Hyde, Taoiseach Éamon de Valera and Tánaiste Seán T. O'Kelly. During his time in Dublin, he was accompanied by his wife Eva and three children, Andreas, Constantin and Liv. Two other children, Berthold and Agnes, were born during their father's time in Dublin.

Stuart travelled to Monkstown to confer on his trip to Berlin with Hempel. The two knew each other through Iseult, a relationship that was to prove advantageous to Stuart's plans. Hempel told the German Embassy in Switzerland that Stuart would be arriving and to provide him with the necessary visas. He also made contact with Berlin to advise them that Stuart would arrive in the city in mid-November 1939 and to treat his arrival with confidentiality; he believed that it could provoke difficulty with the British authorities, whose intelligence service MI5 was monitoring the situation. Hempel felt that Stuart's academic background painted a more responsible image as an Irish nationalist than that of the more militant members of the republican movement. He was also mindful of how delicate Irish neutrality was, and dealing with Stuart provided what he believed was a more moderate approach.

This assumption proved to be naive. As soon as his papers were organised Stuart was approached by Seán MacBride to deliver a message to the Abwehr in Berlin. He also met with Stephen Hayes at the home of Jim O'Donovan before making his way to Switzerland with an exit visa from England and a transit visa through France. After a brief stay in Switzerland Stuart obtained a Swiss visa and entered Germany in January 1940.

Through Hempel various introductions had been made to ease Stuart's entry into society in Berlin. He was provided with papers identifying him as an Irishman lecturing in the city at the request of the German government. In addition to this he was provided with documents that allowed him to travel to and visit places that were restricted to German citizens during the war. Stuart made contact with the Abwehr in February 1940 and relayed a message from the IRA to replace the confiscated transmitter and to send funds to help with the ongoing war against Britain. He also requested that somebody be sent to Ireland to act as a liaison officer between the IRA and the German High Command. After his arrival in Berlin, Stuart was contacted by Helmut Clissmann to see if he would be interested in doing a lecture tour of Germany. Stuart declined the request and instead began writing for William Joyce, the infamous propagandist Lord Haw-Haw.

Stuart remained in Germany throughout the war and broadcast talks for Irland Redaktion, the German propaganda radio service in Ireland. From 1942 to 1944 these broadcasts were transcribed by Irish Military Intelligence and MI5 via the BBC. Stuart's broadcasts were highly nationalistic and promoted greater integration with Europe. The broadcasts have been described as neither anti-Semitic nor anti-Russian, but 'coded references' to international banking conspiracies were said to have been made in some of them. He was interned at the end of the war before travelling to Paris and then to London. Stuart returned to Ireland in 1959 and continued writing prolifically. He denied ever having supported the Nazi regime when asked about it in interviews. In 1996–7 he was elected to the position of Saoi by Aosdána, the Irish Arts Academy, a decision that sparked protests due to his wartime exploits. He eventually retired to Fanore, County Clare and died in February 2000.

The Stuart affair, and in particular his dealings with Eduard Hempel, raised a huge question for Bryan and G2 about how to deal with the various diplomatic circles active in Dublin and abroad and how they could be exploited by the Germans. The extent of the influence of Nazi Germany on Irish affairs went far beyond Irish borders. The Irish community in Germany, despite its small size, provided a perfect platform for the Nazi High Command to plan and mount espionage activities in Ireland. This, of course, raised the suspicions of both G2 and MI5, which had an interest in Irish matters due to the peculiar legal and constitutional situation of Ireland following the adoption of de Valera's Constitution (Bunreacht na hÉireann) in 1937. De Valera had deliberately decided not to fully remove all ties to the Commonwealth in the new Constitution. Because Ireland was not declared fully independent, it remained a British dominion under the remit of the Dominions Office in London. The Statute of Westminster of 1931 had removed nearly all the British parliament's authority to legislate for the dominions, essentially making them tantamount to sovereign nations in their own right. In many ways the Act was a milestone in the development of the dominions as separate states. While it had allowed de Valera to remove the vestiges of monarchy from the Irish Constitution, the failure to declare itself a Republic left Ireland in a peculiar position. While it could declare itself neutral during the war, if citizens of the state were seen to give aid to His Majesty's enemies, they could be charged with treason. This was of course an offence that was punishable by death.

Therefore, while Anglo-German collaboration was a clear and demonstrable act of treason punishable by death, Irish citizens who chose to collaborate with Nazi Germany found themselves in a very peculiar legal grey area. As a result, diplomatic missions at home and abroad that were connected to Ireland were of course of special interest to the British security services. They also provided a considerable headache for Dan Bryan and G2, who were tasked with monitoring both Irish diplomatic missions abroad and foreign diplomatic missions operating in Ireland.

Perhaps one of the most troublesome diplomats in the build-up to the war was a representative not of any foreign country but of Ireland itself – the Irish Minister in Berlin from 1933 to 1939, Charles Bewley. His tenure was not only marked by controversy but also posed a security and public relations problem for the government. It was widely feared that Bewley's presence in Berlin would be an asset to the Abwehr and the wider German intelligence community. These fears were realised, and Bewley became a thorn in the side of the security services.

Charles Henry Bewley was born on 12 July 1888 in Dublin to Henry Theodore and Elizabeth Eveleen Bewley. After receiving his initial education in Park House, Bewley gained a scholarship to New College Oxford. During his time in Oxford, he converted to Catholicism, having been raised as a Quaker. After Oxford he returned to Dublin and was called to the bar in 1914. Following a brief career in law, in 1921 Bewley was posted in an unofficial capacity as a trade representative to Berlin, a posting that began his diplomatic career in earnest. He showed little interest in the posting, complaining that his duties were mundane.

In 1922, he attended the Irish Race Convention in Paris as a delegate from Germany. The Free State government decided to send a delegation that would represent all Irish people, and according to government papers the selection process of delegates was intended to reflect that.

The Cabinet decided to send a delegation to the Irish Race Conference in Paris, and it was decided that this delegation should represent the Irish people, not any particular party. The Cabinet decided to nominate four persons and to ask President de Valera, the leader of the opposition, to nominate four others to go as a joint delegation to Paris. The persons nominated by the Cabinet were: Mr Eoin MacNeill, Mr Michael Hayes, Minister for Education; the Lord Mayor of Dublin; and Mr Diarmuid Coffey. To this delegation was added Mr Douglas Hyde, and a fifth delegate was nominated by President de Valera. The members nominated by President de Valera were: President de Valera himself, Countess Markievicz, Miss Mary MacSwiney, the Lord Mayor of Cork and Mr Harry Boland.

The Irish Race Conventions were a series of stand-alone events held by Irish nationalists with the support of Irish America. They were most often held in the USA, but the 1922 convention was held in Paris in order to assert to the rest of Europe Ireland's emerging status as an independent country. Bewley's attendance at the event should have solidified his status as a trusted Irish diplomat, but controversial anti-Semitic remarks he made in Berlin to Sinn Féin activist Robert Briscoe, who was Jewish, severely damaged his reputation. Despite his remarks, Bewley only received an oral warning and was allowed to remain in his post. Bewley later explained the exchange with Briscoe in an official memo, in which he tried to offer some explanation for the remarks:

On the evening referred to by Mr Briscoe I went to a café in which I had on several previous occasions met Mr Briscoe. He was not there himself. One of the staff asked me whether he was Irish Consul, I said he was not. I was told that he stated that he was Irish Consul. I said that he was not, and added that it was not likely that a Jew of his type would be appointed. (The conversation was in German.) I regret having made the latter remark and have already expressed my regret to Mr Briscoe. At the moment, a German Jew who was sitting near said I had insulted his race, and after a short further conversation I left the café. Altogether four or five persons were present, and I do not think all of them were in a position to hear. However, I frankly acknowledge that the remark was not a proper one to make, and I have expressed my regret to the proprietor of the café, who was present, if I hurt the feelings of any customer.

Bewley later left the diplomatic service of his own accord, returning to Ireland to practise law in 1923. However, the incident was a sign of things to come. Bewley rejoined the Foreign Service in 1929 and was posted as Minister to the Holy See, a role he stayed in until 1933, when, in a controversial move, he was posted to Berlin, a mere couple of months after Hitler had come to power. From Berlin he reported regularly back to Dublin on events in Germany. Initially the reports gave detailed accounts of the development of Nazi policy, but they gradually became more and more focused on Bewley's anti-Semitic views. In one report he seemed to take the view that Jewish people were themselves responsible for any punitive measures taken against them. Matters came to a head in 1938 in the wake of Kristallnacht – the Night of the Broken Glass, the pogrom against Jews carried out by Sturmabteilung (SA) paramilitary forces and sympathetic civilians. Bewley claimed in his report that 'There had been no deliberate cruelty perpetrated against Jews in Germany and that, among other matters, Jews ran the international white slave trade and were a demoralising influence on the communities in which they lived.'

The government in Dublin judged him unfit to carry out his duties in a responsible manner and recalled him to Ireland, but before long he was back in Berlin, travelling to Germany following Britain and France's declaration of war on Germany. Back in Germany, he worked as a freelance journalist and became acquainted with the German Foreign Ministry, for which he compiled a lengthy report on the military value of the IRA to the German war machine. He attempted to put his knowledge of Ireland at the disposal of the German Foreign Ministry and while the Germans felt he was a somewhat useful asset they found him 'timid and lazy'. However, Bewley was successful in developing and maintaining contacts with the Germans throughout the war, which made him a major security problem for the Irish state. Indeed, it was through Bewley that various contacts between Nazi Germany and the IRA were created and developed throughout the war and, while he himself may not have operated at the highest level in diplomatic terms, he was able to initiate conversations between parties much further up the chain of command.

While Bewley posed his own problems for Bryan and G2 abroad, dangers closer to home were becoming apparent, none more so than Herr Hempel and the German Legation on Northumberland Road. Hempel's arrival in Ireland in 1937 was met with considerable fanfare by German nationals living in Ireland. When they arrived at Dún Laoghaire, he and his wife, Eva, were greeted by the German expatriate community and Mrs Hempel was presented with a bouquet of flowers. Before leaving Germany, Hempel had had a private audience with Hitler, who briefed him on his role in Ireland. The conversation was marked by a detailed exchange on Irish–British relations, of which the Führer was said to have extensive knowledge. While never having met Hempel personally, Bryan and G2 were able to compile a comprehensive security profile of him. The Carter tapes reveal that Bryan had built up a clear impression of the German Minister:

I've never met or seen Hempel but to my knowledge Hempel was a shrewd, sensible man whose job it was to keep Ireland neutral until the balloon went up in the west. I suppose he decided that the best way to keep Ireland neutral was by not encouraging rows in Berlin.

While G2 did not place the legation itself under surveillance immediately, it did have a number of opportunities to record the goings-on there. An Garda Síochána was tasked with the protection of German diplomats working under Hempel and intelligence was filtered back to G2 on various diplomats and others who worked in or frequented the legation. Hempel, of course, suspected that the legation was being watched and security was increased. By 1940, the legation had become an important watch post for the Germans. Hempel was routinely updating them on Irish affairs using a secret wireless set at the legation's premises. He reported directly to Berlin on matters such as the weather, crashed German aircraft and the German bombing of Dublin's North Strand in 1941. The transmitter was a necessity for Hempel, since he and other Axis representatives were only dealt with at government functions and only in cases where it was deemed necessary by the rules of diplomacy. He was also isolated from Germany by strict English and Irish censorship, so the wireless set became an important link between the legation and Berlin. However, the Irish and British governments did not share this view. The problem for the British was that, as Ireland was a dominion, the transmitter posed a unique security issue.

It was common practice for wireless sets to be placed secretly in legations – indeed, the British had a wireless set in their Dublin legation. However, speculation and rumours were rife about Hempel's set, and worldwide reports of secret contacts between Berlin and Dublin soon began to filter into the international press. When the issue was reported by newspapers in Washington, it spurred MI5, which had been carrying out its own surveillance in Dublin, to put pressure on G2. Hempel had endeavoured to keep the wireless set hidden – international law on having one was at best obscure. He tried in vain to find alternative means of contacting Germany, but the transmitter was the only feasible method of communication. The alternative was to send sealed mailbags via England and France. Hempel had considered approaching the minister at the Italian legation directly to co-operate on communicating with Berlin, but reconsidered when it became clear that the Italians didn't want to compromise themselves. Instead he assured the Italian Minister Bernardis that messages sent over the wireless from the German Legation travelled via the United States and were secure, but no help was forthcoming. The Italians told Hempel that they would only step in to aid him in rare instances.

In any case it was becoming more and more apparent that Hempel was communicating secretly with Berlin and as time passed it became clear that the authorities in Dublin were going to have to act against him. Hempel was aware that searches had already begun for the source of his broadcasts. Contact between MI5 and G2 on mysterious illicit broadcasts had in fact already been made. In reality it wasn't until a phone call from Guy Liddell to Bryan that G2 became fully aware of the existence of the transmitter in the German Legation. Such naivety was proof that, despite the best efforts of G2, it was impossible to keep abreast of everything that was going on in Dublin. It also became clear that while the British were aware of the transmissions they were not sure of the source. They didn't know if they were from the IRA or from German sources in Ireland. Clearly the extent of espionage and clandestine activity that slipped through the net of both intelligence services was extensive, as Bryan explained:

> [The German Legation] was monitored by us but it was quite a while before we tumbled to the fact that they had a radio, which proves how innocent we were when the war started; however, we were observing them otherwise. They [MI5] knew this traffic was going on at one time. The funny thing is they didn't realise, they must have been as innocent as we were. They didn't realise it was the legation and would be nowhere else. And I remember before bureaucracy and so many things that I could go out and do things myself, looking for a transmitter that was sending diplomatic code 30 miles north of Dublin. The British were worrying about this but didn't refer to the fact that it was in the legation.

Acting on British information about illicit radio traffic, Bryan, with the blessing of Director of Intelligence Liam Archer, travelled to Laytown in County Meath with Dick Green of the Army Signals Corps to trace the source of the transmissions. But this exercise proved futile. The Signals Corps did not have sufficient resources to provide 24-hour monitoring of radio traffic, the very least that would be needed to trace the source of the transmissions. Eventually G2 was bolstered by extra funding and the transfers of two expert army signals men, Captain Sean Nelligan and Captain John Patrick O'Sullivan, from Signals to G2. It was only through 'snifters' (full-time monitoring practices) that it could be confirmed that the wireless set was indeed broadcasting from the German Legation. Archer arranged for a room to be set up in Beggars Bush Barracks to monitor the radio traffic from the legation full time. Sensing that there might be a diplomatic problem if the wireless set was to become known to the British, Archer, alongside the Department of External Affairs, made a conscious decision to keep the British in the dark about it.

According to MI5 surveillance, Hempel had brought the wireless set back with him from a trip to Germany in 1939 and had had it built into a suitcase to hide it from the authorities. The British had erroneously traced the source of suspect transmissions to the Wicklow area. After a time, they were able to triangulate the sources of the transmissions to Dublin, close to the legation. The British Representative in Ireland Sir John Maffey made overtures to the Irish government to try to get them to request British help to deal with the transmitter. To maintain the policy of neutrality the Irish government insisted that any intervention would have to be made through an independent channel. It seemed a stalemate had been reached.

The matter of the transmitter and the danger posed by information leakage from the legation was discussed at the highest levels of the security service. In 1941 a special meeting was convened between the Intelligence Services in Britain and the Government Code and Cypher School (GC&CS) at Bletchley Park to deal with the problem. It was clear that the set was broadcasting on alternate days using high-class German diplomatic cipher. The British recommended that a wireless expert from Britain be allowed to travel to Dublin to deal with the problem.

Dan Bryan was invited to London for a meeting on 11 November 1941 to discuss the issue and to decide who would be sent to Dublin from the British Security Service. It was eventually decided that Lieutenant Colonel Frederick Marrian Stratton would go to Ireland in December 1941 to meet with Bryan, Archer and the G2 Signals Corps. Stratton had a distinguished career as an astrophysicist and Professor of Astrophysics at the University of Cambridge from 1928 to 1947. He also had a brilliant record in Cambridge mathematics as a student and academic and his book *Astronomical Physics*, published in 1925, was the first professional textbook in the field. In addition to his academic prowess, he was also a decorated British Army officer. Stratton had joined the Caius Company of the Cambridge University Rifle Volunteers, which became the Cambridge University Officers' Training Corps, in 1908 and had served with distinction in the British Army Signals Corps in World War I. Stratton's reputation preceded him in the intelligence world. His work in the field of army signals earned him plaudits in France, where he was appointed a knight of the Légion d'honneur in 1919. That same year, on his return to Cambridge following the war, he re-formed the Signals section of the Officers' Training Corps and commanded it until 1928. His work did not go unnoticed by His Majesty King George V and for his military service he was appointed an Officer of the Order of the British Empire (OBE), Military Division in 1929. At the outbreak of hostilities in 1939 Stratton immediately volunteered for service once more, despite being 60 years of age. He was promptly assigned to the Royal Corps of Signals and given a special duties role concerned with radio security. In this unique role Stratton spent the war travelling extensively across the British Empire and the United States.

He met with G2 in 1941 and an agreement was reached that any information from the legation transmitter would be compiled into a report and passed on to him. In return, Stratton would forward any transmissions received from Ireland that G2 had failed to pick up. This in effect opened a channel between G2 and MI5 to work on this specific issue. G2 didn't reveal that the transmissions came from the German Legation, but Stratton was more than aware of the source of the messages. The British toyed with the idea of getting Bryan to copy the cipher books from the legation and forward them to GC&CS, and Bryan suggested jamming the transmission signal, but both ideas were abandoned.

Taoiseach Éamon de Valera, who had a background in mathematics, suggested to Bryan that an attempt might be made to break the code. The issue was discussed at the upper echelons of G2 and Bryan, Archer and de Valera agreed that an attempt should be made. However, G2 did not have the technical expertise to break the high-level diplomatic code that Hempel was using, so it was decided that they would have to second an expert in the field of mathematics into Irish intelligence to break the code. Archer and Bryan approached Dr Richard J. Hayes, who had worked for G2 before being appointed Director of the National Library of Ireland. Hayes was unique in that he was a civilian seconded into G2 and had no military background, but his academic prowess was to stand him in good stead. Hayes and a team of volunteers worked feverishly in 1941 on the legation code and while he could not break it, he was able to obtain a very detailed study of how it worked.

This knowledge would prove to be useful to G2 later in the war.

Throughout the course of the war Hempel would be a significant problem for Bryan and G2, and the legation continued to provide a window for Germany into Ireland. The issue was further complicated by the existence of the land border with Britain that was created by the Irish border. The crisis would reach its highest point in the build-up to Operation Overlord and the D-Day landings. Eventually de Valera's hand was forced and the wireless set was seized by Captain John Patrick O'Sullivan – on orders from Bryan received directly from the government – and kept under lock and key in a Dublin bank.

British and Irish fears in relation to the wireless set were well founded and, indeed, the legation itself and those who visited it during Hempel's tenure were an ongoing security concern for the Irish intelligence service. Hempel was able to use a wide variety of informers and discretionary contacts to build up a very detailed intelligence picture of events in supposedly neutral Ireland. Anti-British sentiment was rife during the war and Hempel received offers of co-operation from various anti-British nationalistic organisations. The Scottish Republican Brotherhood, an organisation that sympathised with its Irish counterparts, contacted Hempel to try to win over his support for the cause of Scottish nationalism. In a detailed request to Hempel, they asked for German planes to drop propaganda pamphlets over Scottish cities and to draw attention in radio broadcasts to a distinct Celtic identity which, they felt, the English were suppressing. They also asked Hempel to demand industrial action in Scotland and to support their ultimate goal of a Scottish republic. Hempel had passed on previous requests, but to avoid drawing any further attention to himself or the legation he asked Berlin to keep the exchanges secret. It's also clear that Hempel passed on messages from British citizens who offered their support to Germany and that such individuals were vetted by the German Foreign Office. Informers also contacted Hempel with technical information about munitions that could be used in the war effort, which Hempel duly passed on to the German Foreign Office.

Perhaps the most peculiar case of a volunteer spy at the legation was that of Sudeten German Oskar Metzke, whose story is still somewhat shrouded in mystery. Metzke was known to Hempel though legation staff member Henning Thomsen. Metzke told Thomsen a strange and complicated tale. He had left Hamburg in 1937 as a stoker on a ship bound for the Balkans. He offered his services to the German Embassy in Belgrade, and then travelled to Switzerland in an attempt to obtain intelligence from the Oerlikon weapons plant there in an effort to show the German Embassy in Belgrade that he was up to the job. The Swiss authorities were soon alerted to his presence and he was arrested. He asked to be repatriated to Germany, but as he was a Czech citizen his request was refused, and he was instead sent to France, where he was given the choice of being sent to a concentration camp or joining the army. He chose to join the army and when France fell to the Germans in 1940, he was evacuated with his unit to England. Here his story took a peculiar turn.

He stole sensitive military documents from the British, claiming that they had been burned in a fire, and in late 1942, he fled to Northern Ireland and tried to bring the documents to Thomsen at the legation in Dublin. It seems Metzke felt that Thomsen and Hempel would be able to send the documents back to Germany. The offer was rejected by the legation, who felt that it would be impossible to pass the information on to Germany. Suspiciously, Metzke had used an alias when contacting the legation and before eventually departing requested money and a role as an agent or spy so that he could make his way back to Germany. Hempel wisely rejected both requests.

As he left, Metzke dropped an envelope on Hempel's table containing sensitive information that he had gathered over the preceding few months. Some of the information was quite stark. Metzke had been able to ascertain that American troops were concentrated in Somerset, Cornwall and Dorset, while the Canadian Army had tanks arriving in Plymouth. He had also gathered intelligence about a factory near Swansea in Wales where the British Army was experimenting with the use of chemicals to produce poison gas. He reported that American troop transports had landed in Londonderry and Larne in Northern Ireland, while US convoys had gathered six miles off the coast of Newfoundland. Three hundred parachutists, who were to be dropped into Czechoslovakia in late January 1943, were being trained in German and Serbian as well as sabotage techniques. Of course, Hempel did not seek out such information, but the incident highlighted the threat of information leakage through the legation that had been feared by both G2 and MI5.

Metzke moved back to the continent, where he became involved in foreign broadcasting, and eventually he came to the attention of the authorities in Berlin. He was accused of high treason, but never returned to Germany to stand trial. Instead, he decided to make his way back to Ireland where he wandered around Munster. On 16 December 1942 Metzke was spotted in Fermoy and Ballyhooley by locals, who immediately felt that the tall, well-built man looked out of place. On 17 December Metzke arrived in Castletownroche and arranged lodgings in a local house. He next called to the local priest Fr James Sheedy, who gave the stranger some money in an act of kindness. Metzke then went to a local grocer to buy bread and cheese. At the grocer's he met the local Garda, Jeremiah O'Sullivan, who suspected that something was out of place and asked Metzke to come to the Garda barracks with him. In the barracks Metzke explained to O'Sullivan that he had come to the town to seek work in the local beet factory. Sensing that all was not as it seemed, O'Sullivan asked Metzke to empty his pockets. Metzke had been carrying maps of the Cork countryside, a fountain pen that doubled as a flashlight and, most sinister of all, a Luger pistol. O'Sullivan left Metzke with his colleague Garda Mannix to report the situation to his superiors. It was a move that gave Metzke time to take a most drastic course of action, as Jeremiah O'Sullivan's son Billy remembered:

> I was a very young boy at the time, but the story was often repeated to me by my father. Oskar Metzke was sitting quietly by the fireplace, when he asked Garda Mannix if he could eat some of his bread and cheese. On receiving permission, he walked over to the table where it lay. He started to eat his frugal meal, then turned his back on the Garda. Seconds later Oskar Metzke was in convulsions, it was obvious that he had swallowed something lethal and my father and Garda Mannix did their utmost to retrieve it from his mouth, but already the German was unconscious. Within a matter of minutes Metzke was dead, but just before he expired,

he received a blessing from the man who only a short time before had been so kind to him, Fr James Sheedy. Dr Jeremiah Foley arrived soon afterwards, but by this time Metzke was beyond all human aid. A post mortem was carried out by the then State Pathologist, Dr John McGrath, and at the subsequent inquest Coroner Nagle of Buttevant revealed that Oskar Metzke had taken a deadly poison, cyanide of potassium.

Metzke was buried in the local church in Castletownroche. A number of years later his body was exhumed and reburied in the German Military Cemetery in Glencree, County Wicklow.

The Metzke affair highlighted how vulnerable Ireland was if the German Legation was to continue to pass information to Nazi Germany. However, such information leakage and volunteer spies were not limited to foreign nationals such as Oskar Metzke. Indeed, Irishmen also offered their services to the German ministers, hoping to aid the IRA and, indirectly, Nazi Germany.

In 1942 Hempel was contacted by IRA volunteers from Northern Ireland who asked for him to arrange passage to Germany for them. They requested that Hempel arrange a U-boat to pick them up off the coast of Ireland and transport them to Germany. Hempel decided not to get involved, but the IRA men continued to try to persuade him to accede to their request. When it became apparent that he could not arrange a U-boat to pick them up, they asked if it were possible to arrange a favourable reception for them by the German Navy if they were to travel there themselves via motorboat. Hempel was partial to the idea of using the IRA men to Germany's advantage and he contacted Berlin to see if they could be used to help bolster German influence over the IRA in Northern Ireland. Hempel was quite happy to offer assistance if they directed their activities against Britain and Northern Ireland, but he was quite explicit that no help should be given to the men to carry out activities in the Irish state and that neutrality should be respected. Hempel needed all the tact and diplomatic skills he had: he didn't want to alienate the IRA or ruin their faith in Nazi Germany as an ally against the British; at the same time, he needed to preserve his unique position in Dublin, and respecting Irish neutrality was central to that role.

He was walking a tightrope. On the one hand he was loyal to Germany, but on the other he had to show respect to the country in which he was living.

Not only had Hempel ample opportunity to benefit from volunteer spies, he was also able to compile profiles and reports on Irish politicians and civil servants, which were of great use to the German High Command in planning its policy on Ireland. Hempel was able to gain insights into the thinking of individuals in the Department of External Affairs, for example Joseph Walshe, who served as Secretary of the department from 1923 to 1946. Hempel told Berlin that he 'worked closely with counterparts in Britain and was sympathetic to Jews having travelled to Palestine with a Jewish friend who paid for his passage'. He also remarked that he was incompetent in running the Department of External Affairs and that de Valera had made excuses and allowances for these shortcomings. Hempel's analysis was compiled from hearsay, press clippings and various other unofficial means and can't be considered an accurate view of Walshe's role in the department during the war.

Hempel was also able to report on Irish officials serving in Madrid, Rome, London, Geneva and Washington. Despite the obvious threat of information leakage posed by Hempel at the legation, the Irish government appreciated his willingness to respect Irish neutrality, at least in an official capacity. Joseph Walshe wrote in a letter John J. Hearne, the Irish High Commissioner to Canada, in 1939:

> The general feeling among our people is anti-Hitler because of his persecution of Christians and Jews. At the same time, the struggle is regarded as essentially one between two imperialisms for which Hitler's antics provide the immediate occasion. Britain's propaganda about small nations is received with scepticism and, as you know, always will be in this country until her new leaf has been turned over a little more completely. The tact of Herr Hempel, the German Minister, has deprived our neutrality of a lot of the problems which would otherwise have made it very difficult to observe. There has been no attempt by submarines against the normal commerce between these two islands, and that is a matter for satisfaction to the British as well as to ourselves. No doubt the British government regret our neutrality for sentimental reasons,

but we believe that they are slowly becoming as convinced as we are that Ireland's neutrality is an advantage for them. It has produced a feeling of contentment in this country, because it is a very clear proof to all shades of Nationalist opinion that our independence is genuine.

Even though most of Hempel's correspondence in relation to Irish diplomats was gleaned from snatches of conversation, press clippings and brief meetings with some of the individuals in question, the German Foreign Ministry and Foreign Minister Joachim von Ribbentrop took it seriously. They also paid close attention to the information gathered from would-be informers and collaborators such as Metzke and the three Northern IRA volunteers. All of this information would play an important role in German policy towards Ireland during the course of the war. Hempel was also, significantly, able to report on the two Irish diplomats who served in Berlin during the war, William Warnock (1938–43) and Con Cremin (1943–5).

Warnock arrived in Berlin as secretary to the Irish Legation in 1938. He was promoted to the role of chargé d'affaires *ad interim* in 1939, in effect succeeding the discredited Charles Bewley. Warnock was seen as a safe pair of hands at what was proving to be a turbulent time diplomatically. Born in Sandymount, Dublin in 1911, Warnock was educated at the High School in Dublin and worked as an Irish teacher there after his graduation from Trinity College Dublin. He was a capable linguist, which was to stand him in good stead when he joined the civil service in 1935. His fluency in German helped him obtain the posting to Berlin, in which he would remain until 1943, at the Irish Legation in the city's Tiergarten.

Initially, Bewley's replacement was to have been Thomas Kiernan, the former Irish High Commissioner in London and Director of Radio Éireann, but Ireland's unusual constitutional position was to make this impossible. Because Ireland was technically still part of the Commonwealth, Kiernan's credentials would have to have been signed by King George VI. The Irish authorities delayed Kiernan's appointment indefinitely (Hempel believed this was being done to avoid confrontation with Britain). Eventually Warnock began to assume the responsibilities of Kiernan's role. The situation left Ireland in a unique position in that Hempel as the Irish representative

outranked his counterpart, Warnock, in Berlin. Kiernan was eventually
sent to the Vatican and Warnock continued in the Berlin role. He was well
received by his German hosts, who remarked on his ability to speak German
and his knowledge of German politics, history and the Nazi regime. Of
course, the Germans watched him closely and read all his outgoing messages to Ireland. Despite this intrusion, Warnock was careful in his wording
of communications and never gave the Germans any hint that he had any
sympathy for the Allied cause. As the war progressed Warnock faced significant difficulties in keeping in touch with the Department of External
Affairs in Dublin, but Irish neutrality ensured that he was treated better
than representatives of other nations:

> We Irish are extremely popular at the moment. Until the last moment
> there were doubts expressed as to whether we would come in on Great
> Britain's side. Once our position had been made clear, our neutral-
> ity was given full publicity over the wireless and in the newspapers.
> Disappointment was felt that the Union of South Africa joined the
> enemy front. That came as somewhat of a surprise, particularly to the
> members of the South African Legation here. So far as I could judge,
> the members of the Legation were, without exception, strongly in favour
> of neutrality. I hope that we shall soon have a more direct way of com-
> municating with you than that through Rome. Our activities are, of
> course, rather curtailed, but even so the closer touch we have with the
> department the more satisfactory for all concerned.

Hempel used his contacts to evaluate Warnock and his successor, Con
Cremin. This helped the Nazi Foreign Office to prepare crucial policy papers
in relation to Ireland and how it could be used strategically in the event of an
invasion of the British mainland. Bryan was aware of this and Irish Military
Intelligence also knew that Warnock's staff had access to his diplomatic
codebook. It was a cause for concern and Bryan and G2 were keen to keep
abreast of the situation.

However, G2 was unaware that plans in relation to Ireland's strategic
importance for a possible invasion of mainland Britain were already under

way. It had become very clear to the Germans that they couldn't invade Ireland unless they claimed that they were doing so to uphold Irish neutrality. In effect, a state of war between Ireland and Britain would have to exist first. Without this important caveat Germany could not make use of any Irish co-operation. If hostilities were to break out between Ireland and Britain, the Germans could intervene and provide weapons and other assistance to the Irish. Therefore, the use of the IRA as a fifth column gained greater significance for the German High Command and it set in motion a number of plans to see if something could be brought to fruition. This happened, of course, via a number of different avenues and would ultimately lead to one of the Nazi regime's must trusted coup d'état experts being brought on to the scene.

Unbeknownst to Bryan and G2, German Foreign Minister Joachim von Ribbentrop and the Foreign Ministry were planning to put one of their most trusted and feared SS officials into a role dealing specifically with Ireland. While Bryan and G2 were trying to deal with the new threat of German spies being sent to Ireland via the O'Donovan link, the exiled IRA Chief of Staff Seán Russell was planning his own return to Ireland via this particular avenue. Russell had caused significant damage before he went to the USA, but now he would give the security services another problem. While he and the IRA had destabilised national security in both England and Ireland with the S-Plan, this time he had German support. Events were about to take a most drastic turn and Bryan, G2 and the whole of Ireland's security apparatus were to be tested in the most extreme fashion possible. Only time would tell if they could withstand the trials that lay ahead.

IV

UPPING THE ANTE

I know, illegally, that you are having another visitor soon. He must know nothing of correspondence between you and me. But you should ask him about me. His answers may interest you. From my knowledge of him, he is far more capable than he appears, and has a long record of successes to his credit.

FRANK RYAN, IRA, TO LEOPOLD H. KERNEY, IRELAND'S
MINISTER TO SPAIN, MADRID, 1942

The year 1940 marked a significant turning point in the war in favour of Germany, the defining event being the fall of France to German forces between May and June. Hitler's Panzer divisions swept into Holland and Belgium through the Ardennes Forest in a move of military genius concocted by General Erich von Manstein and approved by Hitler himself. Unprepared for the invading forces' sheer numbers and completely disbelieving that the Wehrmacht would dare try to penetrate the dense Belgian forests, the French 2 Army, under General Huntziger, was completely overwhelmed. French bombers and the majority of the army were concentrated in Belgium and along the fortifications of the Maginot line, leaving their counterparts further north horribly exposed and vulnerable to what became an insurmountable German attack. Air support from the RAF was also caught unawares and the British were to lose 41 bombers during the fighting. By 13 May the French defences were breached and on 17 June France fell to the German army. The British Expeditionary Force, cornered, outnumbered and with many wounded, were forced to retreat to the coastal village of Dunkirk in northern France. In total, 338,000 troops, a third of them French, had to be evacuated by a combination of the British Navy and pleasure boats from across the English Channel. Speaking about the evacuation in the House of Commons, a chastened Winston Churchill, the British Prime Minister, described the events in Dunkirk 'a colossal military disaster'.

The arrival of German tanks onto French soil for the first time in a generation prompted the flight of the civilian population in a mass evacuation that would become known as l'exode. Huge numbers of refugees flooded onto main roads, where they were attacked by passing German troops and machine-gunned by German Stuka dive bombers. The scenes struck terror in the heart of Europe and it soon became clear that Britain now stood alone against the superior might of the German Wehrmacht. The French government had fled from Paris to Bordeaux on 10 June and, eager to gain a share of the spoils, Mussolini also declared war on France. By the time German tanks rolled into the French capital and paraded up the Champs Élysées it was clear not only the extent of the crushing French defeat but also of how exposed and vulnerable Britain now was. In the following weeks the German army would round up 1.6 million prisoners of war into makeshift camps.

On 17 June, Marshal Philippe Pétain, the French hero of the Battle of Verdun in World War I, agreed to head a new government. He later agreed to form a puppet regime in the spa town of Vichy in southern France, in effect partitioning France. The following day a faint glimmer of hope emerged from a BBC studio in London when General Charles de Gaulle, now exiled in England, broadcast to the French people via the World Service insisting all was not lost and that 'the flame of French resistance must and shall not die'.

With Hitler's focus now on his one remaining enemy – Britain – Ireland was once again of strategic importance to the Führer. By July, detailed directives were issued in relation to attacking Britain on 16 July. This offensive would have to be different from the mainly Panzer-driven onslaught on the continent. It would take the combined might of the Luftwaffe and Kriegsmarine to subdue Britain. Operation Seelöwe (Sealion) was designed as the plan to carry out this objective, and it would involve parachute landings and an amphibious assault on British shores. First, though, Hitler needed to counter the might of the RAF. His aim was to use unremitting attacks to sap the morale of the RAF and the British people. Minesweepers would be used to clear minefields at natural crossing points such as the

Straits of Dover, and heavy artillery would be used along the Atlantic Wall that had been constructed on the French coast. Diversionary tactics to engage the Royal Navy in the North Sea were also mooted.

Though Britain was essentially standing alone against the Nazi threat, it was receiving supplies and military hardware from neutral USA. Hitler was aware of this and instructed Grand Admiral Erich Raeder and his U-boat commander Karl Donitz to target merchant vessels in the Atlantic to sever the USA–Britain link. It was felt that this would leave Britain demoralised and isolated and a swift and decisive victory similar to that in France was envisaged.

For Operation Sealion to be effective, accurate Atlantic weather reports were vital; they would enable the Luftwaffe to plan airborne operations and seaborne landings that could then be scheduled at the best possible time. Ireland's geographical location on the periphery of Western Europe meant that it was back in the Nazis' spotlight. If Germany could gain a foothold in Ireland, it could use it as a back door from which to attack Britain and any advantage that could be gleaned from Irish weather reports now became hugely valuable to the Germans.

By July 1940, the Battle of Britain had begun in earnest, but Germany was also drawing up plans for an invasion of Ireland. Crucial to its plans were a number of espionage missions to be carried out by German spies and also, if possible, by Irish nationals who would be willing to operate inside Ireland to aid the German war machine. While Ireland was the target, it was in Germany that the seeds for these spying missions were sown.

Francis Stuart had been in Germany almost six months when Seán Russell arrived there after his sojourn in the United States. Russell's trip to America had not been without controversy. Upon his arrival he embarked on a propaganda tour with Joseph McGarrity to raise funds and support for a war against the British. He spoke to audiences consisting mainly of members of Clan na Gael, the US sister organisation of the IRB and spiritual successor to the Fenian Brotherhood, and potential financiers. The gatherings also attracted the attention of communists and supporters of fascism and, unbe-knownst to Russell, the US Secret Service, which was able to build a case against Russell based on his public pronouncements of responsibility for the bombing campaign in England. He was swiftly detained in advance of King George VI and Queen Elizabeth's visit to the World Fair in Poughkeepsie, New York. The royal couple had travelled from Canada into the United States to open the British pavilion at the fair and to stir up pro-British sympathy in the build-up to hostilities with Germany. Russell's incarceration garnered huge support for him among the Irish American community and he was soon released on bail, with Joseph McGarrity providing the funds for this.

Russell turned his attention to Germany and became eager to leave the United States before his bail expired. McGarrity contacted a German agent, who relayed a message via the steamship *George Washington*, which was sailing from the United States to Genoa in Italy. Russell's request eventually reached the German consulate in Genoa, was relayed from there to the German Foreign Ministry, and finally went to the Abwehr. The German authorities assured Russell that they would repatriate him to Ireland when the time was right, but first he was to make his way discreetly to Genoa via New York and eventually onward to Germany. Eduard Hempel cautioned against bringing Russell back to Ireland in the long run – he felt that the IRA was not yet a reliable force with which Germany could ally itself. He was also trying to protect his own position; he would have faced expulsion if he were seen to be acting against Irish interests. Ribbentrop and the Foreign Ministry were happy to leave Russell's passage to Germany in the hands of the Abwehr, provided that his mission was of a military and not a political nature. At a meeting of the Foreign Ministry on 28 March 1940, Ribbentrop outlined his renewed intentions for Ireland. Russell would play a significant role.

Russell was welcomed to Germany by the German High Command. They were tantalised at having an Irish leader dedicated to reunification in their midst and eager to exploit such an asset. However, Russell's fate was soon to become entwined with that of a high-ranking SS Brigadef 252hrer whose reputation for ruthlessness preceded him.

In Berlin a sallow-skinned, physically imposing man with a commanding presence and a piercing gaze was relishing his new role as head of the Foreign Office's Irish Bureau. Dr Edmund Veesenmayer was born on 12 November 1904 in Bad Kissingen in Bavaria, southern Germany. Attracted by Hitler's promise of a new Germany, he joined the Nazi Party in February 1932, a year before Hitler's accession to power. Veesenmayer studied international politics at the University of Munich and went on to gain a doctorate in political science. He held a teaching post from 1929 to 1933 before turning his attentions full time to Nazi Party affairs. He was assigned to the German Foreign Ministry in 1933, where he was to remain until 1944. While essentially working under the direction of Ribbentrop at the Foreign Ministry, Veesenmayer also served on the personal staff of SS leader Heinrich Himmler and was described by his peers as a *coup d'état* specialist. As part of his remit in the Foreign Ministry he was assigned oversight of planning in relation to all operations into Ireland between 1940 and 1943.

The Germans' main battle was against the British, and any operations against Ireland must be confined to supporting their primary aim, which was the invasion of the United Kingdom. In the meantime, Irish neutrality was useful to the Germans and any planned operations were to take account of that. Veesenmayer returned from a tour of the Baltic states to take charge of Irish affairs and while the Abwehr initially dealt with Russell the entire operation was under the remit of the Foreign Ministry. One of the first tasks assigned to Russell was to brief another spy who had been selected for a mission to Ireland, Dr Hermann Görtz. Chance events prevented this from happening and Görtz made his way to Ireland by aircraft to be dropped in by parachute in May 1940. His time in Ireland was to be characterised by great misfortune and political intrigue.

In the meantime, to prepare him for operations with the Germans and on Veesenmayer's orders, Russell was trained in sabotage methods by the Foreign Ministry. In the course of his training he observed units in the Brandenburg Regiment working with homemade explosives. Russell was already familiar with such methods but welcomed the training as he was used to more dated arms and ammunition in his IRA activities. Russell struck up an unusual relationship with Veesenmayer, who was impressed by the IRA man's 'traditional' nature, even though Russell wasn't particularly interested in listening to Veesenmayer discuss Nazi propaganda and policy with him. His sole focus was on gaining any advantage he could to remove the British presence from the island of Ireland. Russell lived a very quiet life in Berlin, his only outings being a weekly trip to mass, accompanied by army personnel. His devoutness perhaps contributed to Veesenmayer's view of him as 'straightforward' and 'straight'.

Veesenmayer tried to keep Russell's presence in Berlin under wraps. Russell was only allowed to associate with his Foreign Ministry handler and a few others. However, both Helmut Clissmann and Hoven, now attached to Abwehr II and the Brandenburg Regiment, broke this rule and met several times with Russell, their old acquaintance from Ireland. The Brandenburg unit prided itself on its physical fitness, initiative and high intellectual qualifications. It specialised in sabotage and infiltration and had among its numbers members who were proficient in many languages. The unit saw action in North Africa and the Battle of the Bulge before being disbanded in 1945.

On 25 May 1940, it was decided that Russell would be spirited back to Ireland via U-boat on 6 June and that he would be accompanied by two radio operators. Then he would embark on a sabotage mission. He was given personal radio equipment and demolition materials for the task. The Abwehr arranged for his equipment to be placed in a special case that he could drop into the water before disembarking from the U-boat and rowing to shore in a rubber dinghy. He would then get the IRA to return for the case. Russell's plan was delayed numerous times, mainly because the Abwehr and other branches of the Nazi war machine were occupied with the war in France. After Pétain's surrender they could turn their attention to Russell's mission. Now it was decided that he would be joined by a former colleague in the IRA who had also made his way to Germany. However, his passage was a lot more turbulent than Russell's.

Frank Ryan, even during his lifetime, was a revered IRA figure and his reputation has grown to an almost cult-like status in republican lore. He was born on 11 September 1902 to national schoolteachers Vere and Ann Ryan in Knocklong, County Limerick and attended school across the county bounds in Fermoy, County Cork, where he completed his secondary education in 1921. An outstanding student, he won a scholarship to study at UCD, but he was soon drawn to the republican movement, joining the East Limerick

Brigade of the IRA the same year. Ryan took the anti-Treaty side in the Civil War, was captured by Free State forces and interned in the Curragh Camp until 1923. On his release, he returned to UCD to complete his education, earning a degree in Celtic studies, and at this time he was noted as a gifted orator. After completing his education, he worked for a time as a teacher but was dismissed for participating in a protest against Armistice Day. He worked tirelessly for the republican movement and spoke at many demonstrations and gatherings, frequently getting into clashes with the Gardaí. In 1929, he became editor of *An Phoblacht* and was also involved in the Irish language organisation Conradh na Gaeilge. In 1932, he was jailed for three months for contempt of court and was released just as his former colleagues in Sinn Féin, now members of Fianna Fáil, assumed power under Éamon de Valera. Ryan left the IRA in 1934 following a disagreement over policy and helped set up the left-wing Republican Congress. However, it was a political event abroad that was to shape the rest of his life.

In July 1936, hostilities broke out in Spain between Republicans, loyal to the leftist Popular Front government of the Second Spanish Republic, and Nationalists, comprising monarchists and conservatives led by a military group who counted General Francisco Franco among their number. The Spanish Civil War tore the country apart. When it came to an end in 1939, 500,000 people had been killed and countless others injured. The Nationalists were supported by Mussolini's fascist Italy and Hitler's Nazi Germany, and the Republicans by the Soviet Union and the International Brigades, made up of volunteers from across Europe and the United States. The conflict has been referred to as a dress rehearsal for World War II, such was the level of destruction it wrought, as well as being a proxy war for the dominant ideologies of the day. The war was won by the Nationalists, who went on to rule Spain until Franco's death in 1975.

In 1936 Ryan volunteered to fight with the International Brigades and helped organise other Irishmen to enlist. By 1937 he held the senior role of acting brigadier and took part in the Battle of Jarama, east of Madrid. He was wounded and returned to Ireland, where he was a considerable source of embarrassment for de Valera's government's policy of neutrality. After a period of convalescence Ryan returned to Spain in 1938 and was again wounded and captured by Italian troops, who were fighting on the Nationalist side. Ryan was accused of murder in dubious circumstances, sentenced to death and incarcerated in Burgos prison in extremely tough conditions. After an international campaign his sentence was commuted to life in prison and his plight soon came to the attention of various parties who sought to campaign for his release. In October 1938, the Irish Minister to Spain, Leopold Kerney, visited Burgos prison at de Valera's behest.

Leopold Kerney had a distinguished career in the Irish Diplomatic Service and his intervention in Ryan's case was to save the IRA man's life. Born in 1881 in Carlow, Kerney was brought up in Sandymount and educated at Trinity College Dublin, but he never graduated, instead spending several years travelling abroad. He settled in Paris in 1912 and began his diplomatic career in 1919, when he was appointed commercial representative by Arthur Griffith. In 1935, he moved from Paris to Madrid and was appointed, by de Valera's government, First Minister Plenipotentiary to Spain. His primary objective was to develop trade links between Ireland and Spain, but the Spanish Civil War soon took up the bulk of his time and attention. On de Valera's instructions, Kerney sought to have Ryan released from prison. Writing to Joseph Walshe at the Department of External Affairs in 1939, he described a visit to the prison:

The Central Prison is a palatial-looking building, built about 8 years ago, about 3 miles on the far side of Burgos. The chief warder was at the main gate; he shook hands with me, perhaps mistaking me for some other friend; the director [Antonio Crejo] was awaiting me in his office; I arrived punctually at noon; I formed a very favourable opinion of him; we talked for about 20 minutes and he gave me much useful information. The prison usually holds 1,000 or at the outside 1,500 condemned prisoners; at present there are 4,500; there is no rule of silence; the prisoners spend all day, from 6.30 or 7 a.m. till 8.30 or 9 p.m., in the open court-yard, where their meals are served and where they mix freely with one another until bedtime arrives; they sleep in large dormitories, in each of which there is accommodation for from 100 to 300 men.

During the visit Kerney observed that despite some problems with his heart Ryan seemed in good spirits:

Frank Ryan came into the warder's office when I was there, and we shook hands with each other; the good-hearted warder allowed us to speak in English, and even left the room once or twice during our conversation, which lasted at least an hour, and of course I did not take any notes. He told me the prison doctor had already advised him of my visit. I enquired first about his health, and he said this was excellent, except for his heart; he did not want his family to know about this as it might alarm them needlessly; 4 or 5 years ago he discovered that he had an enlarged heart, but never paid any attention to it until he was in Spain; before the fighting on the Ebro, he was advised by a doctor not to subject it to strain and he had been taking care of himself; recently he had had palpitations, and had been in and out of the infirmary several times, but they were so busy there that he never had his temperature taken, and as soon as his pulse was beating all right out he had to go to make room for others; the assistant doctors were very good, however, and now he was allowed to have longer spells in the infirmary; this meant better food and also less strain, as otherwise he would have to be standing to attention for hours at a time; he thought perhaps I might be able to get some cheese, sausages, &c. sent to him from time to time. He said that a fellow-prisoner, a doctor, had examined him and assured him that the valvular trouble of his heart was not dangerous and could be cured with rest and good food; he said he also had high blood pressure, but remarked laughingly that it was not the prison diet that would make that worse.

At the same time, Russell had been making overtures to the Germans for Ryan's release. Coincidentally, the lawyer Kerney hired to secure Ryan's release happened to have connections to the Abwehr and to Admiral Canaris. Jupp Hoven and Helmut Clissmann also made requests to their superior officers for Ryan's release, saying that it would be advantageous for Germany. Following requests made through a multitude of different avenues,

Franco agreed to release Ryan if an undertaking was given that he would never return to Spain. He was transferred to another prison, then driven to the Spanish border and released under the pretence that he had escaped. From there he was spirited to Paris, where Helmut Clissmann visited him, and was eventually taken to Berlin, where he was reunited with Seán Russell and introduced to Dr Veesenmayer. While Ryan was convalescing in Berlin, Kerney's actions in engineering his release raised suspicions from G2 and Dan Bryan, who began to investigate Kerney more closely.

Veesenmayer decided to add Ryan to the mission that he had sanctioned for Russell. The Germans hoped that Russell and Ryan would travel to Ireland by submarine and that they would liaise with the IRA to help German strategic intentions in relation to Ireland and to help bolster Operation Sealion. This would most likely have been achieved by organising the IRA to create instability in Northern Ireland. Veesenmayer was to finance any such operation by supplying funds to Hempel in the German Legation in Dublin. The mission was codenamed Operation Taube (Dove) and Veesenmayer was able to organise the use of a U-boat and Abwehr support for the operation. Russell and Ryan left Wilhelmshaven U-boat base in Lower Saxony on board U-65, bound for the Kerry coast, on 8 August 1940. They planned to make their way to Tralee before travelling to Dublin. But the mission was doomed. Russell died during the crossing and was buried at sea. He had been suffering from a stomach ulcer, although for many years afterwards rumours persisted about his mysterious death and whether foul play was involved. It is most likely that he died from natural causes – his family confirmed that he had suffered from stomach complaints for many years.

Ryan asked to be taken back to Germany as he didn't consider himself to be a co-organiser of the mission; he was more a subordinate to Russell. During his absence from Berlin, rumours began to circulate in Ireland as to his whereabouts, and G2 was none the wiser. The Abwehr decided to send Elizabeth Clissmann, Helmut's wife, to Madrid to meet with Leopold Kerney to assure him that Ryan was safe in Germany and to get a sense of whether the Irish government suspected a connection between Ryan and the Abwehr. Mrs Clissmann, who knew the Kerney family in Ireland, told the minister that Ryan was in good health (but she didn't disclose where he was); and that Russell had passed away in France. The meeting had the desired effect and the intrigue around Ryan quietly died down. However, Ryan and Veesenmayer's role in affairs between Germany and Ireland had not yet come to a conclusion.

Ryan disembarked from U-65 in Lorient, France, where he was met by Veesenmayer, who was determined to use Ryan as a successor to Russell for another mission like that of Operation Dove. Veesenmayer was impressed by Ryan, whom, he felt, was 'an able politician and fervent nationalist'. He believed that Ryan had a political acumen that far exceeded Russell's, but Veesenmayer didn't fully understand the nuances of politics in Irish republicanism. In fact, Ryan's long absence from the cut and thrust of the IRA, and his left-leaning views, which had won him many enemies on the right in the organisation, made him an unsuitable figure to unite the IRA to work with the Germans. However, Veesenmayer was likely swayed by Ryan's stature as a high-ranking IRA member and he began to groom him for Operation Dove II.

As well as his connections in the IRA Ryan was also well acquainted with members of Fianna Fáil, the Labour Party, the trade unions, the *Irish Press*, the GAA and the Gaelic League. Ryan assured Veesenmayer that he had access to de Valera and the Cabinet through some of his connections. An understanding was reached that anti-British sentiment could be stoked up in Ireland and that any invasion of England would present the IRA with an opportunity to attempt military operations in Northern Ireland. Ryan would ensure that the mission had public support in Ireland and the Germans would ensure the same on their side. Of course, the Germans would only act with the blessing of de Valera, who, Ryan assured them, would be willing to act if he considered it a legitimate risk to take.

In many ways, the mission became a defensive operation rather than an offensive one. Veesenmayer assumed overall control of the mission and the Abwehr would provide technical assistance if needed. In an MI5 interrogation after the war, Kurt Haller, who had worked closely alongside Veesenmayer and others in orchestrating Ryan's release from Burgos, explained how the operation would work. Ryan and Helmut Clissmann would be the mission crew and would be joined by Bruno Rieger, another German who would help operate a wireless transmission set that would be used to communicate with Germany. Rieger would also help re-establish communications between Germany and Abwehr spy Hermann Görtz, whose mission to Ireland had at this stage fallen victim to much misadventure and mishap.

The mission was provided with a more sophisticated wireless transmission set than Russell had had for the initial mission. The exact landing point was undecided, but it was felt that either Tralee or Galway Bay would be an ideal location. When they landed, the group would bury the wireless set, which would be retrieved later. They would then split up and go their separate ways, with Rieger and Clissmann travelling together. They would pose as hikers on a holiday and make their way to Dublin, where they hoped they would be looked after by their contacts. A number of people who might provide lodgings were mentioned, including Ryan's sister Eilis; Nora Connolly, the daughter of 1916 leader James Connolly and founding member, alongside Ryan, of the Republican Congress; and friends of Ryan's, including Moss Twomey, Stephen Hayes, Tom Barry and Seán MacBride. It was simply assumed that these people would be prepared to help; it's unclear if there were any firm arrangements for anyone to provide the men with shelter.

The mission was put on standby during the winter of 1940 and spring of 1941, when Operation Sealion, the planned invasion of Britain, was to take place. During this delay Germany received some scrambled messages from Hermann Görtz in Ireland. The hapless Görtz was asking for money and to be brought back to Germany. Now Ryan's group were given the extra task of bringing money to Görtz. Veesenmayer, eager for the mission to take place, ordered it to go ahead, only to be overruled by Ribbentrop. By the summer of 1941 the Kriegsmarine was under pressure and it became difficult to source a U-boat for the group. The mission then went through various iterations and planning stages, eventually being renamed Operation Sea Eagle. A U-boat could still not be found, so it was decided to obtain a seaplane, which would drop the group at Brandon Bay in County Kerry. But the mission never took place. Operation Barbarossa, the German invasion of Russia, meant that there were no resources for the Irish mission, and it was scrapped. It was also clear by that stage that the IRA was in no position to help the Germans as it had split into a number of feuding factions.

Of course, if the mission had taken place, it was likely that the Irish Coast Watching Service set up by the Defence Forces and working in conjunction with G2 would have been alerted to the arrival of the plane carrying Ryan and his colleagues. According to Prof. Carter's interviews with Dan Bryan, it is clear he was convinced that such a mission would only have succeeded with a lot of good fortune and luck:

> If that plane had flown in over the coast it would have been traced and if it came down it would certainly have not been missed. In my opinion, there was a 75 to 100 per cent chance it would have been noted that it had landed or there would have been a mystery about where it had gone. Then if there had been any mystery about a plane possibly having landed, with the exception of Görtz, the chances of Ryan and Clissmann being able to go to earth when they landed here were very small. They would most likely have been arrested immediately, unless they were very fortunate.

As 1941 progressed Veesenmayer once more turned his attentions to Irish Treaty Ports as an avenue through which to penetrate Ireland. Veesenmayer's original plan had aimed to ensure Irish neutrality and, if possible, stoke up a desire among the Irish to resist any British aggression against Ireland. While Clissmann could concentrate on the political and military side of things, Ryan would be able to make peace between de Valera and those who opposed him in the IRA, essentially creating a pan-nationalist front that would resist the British if they violated Irish neutrality.

During the winter of 1942 and into the following year the U-boat war was proving to be disastrous for the British and there was a palpable fear in Ireland that the British would overrun the Treaty Ports to gain a foothold in the escalating situation. Veesenmayer's Irish bureau suggested that two German divisions be held in reserve near Brest in Brittany in order to counter this potential threat – arms and technical support could be ferried across to Ireland for the Irish to protect themselves from any aggression by the British. The German High Command overruled Veesenmayer as the resources to carry out such a mission were not available and the Kriegsmarine in particular was unable to provide sufficient sea support for the plan to have any realistic chance of success. Veesenmayer suggested that they could drop in arms by air or use blockade runners, but the issue never went any further and the plan was dropped.

By the end of 1942, it had become clear that any plans involving Ryan were no longer possible. Clissmann returned to his work with the Brandenburg Regiment and Ryan was declared unfit for active service. His health had deteriorated and he was unhappy living in Berlin. From October 1940 onwards Helmut Clissmann was detailed to look after Ryan, who was living under the assumed name of Francis (Frank) Richards. The two shared various addresses in Berlin and Ryan kept himself busy by writing articles on Irish affairs. He was paid expenses throughout this period and was generally allowed to move about freely. He was visited regularly by staff from Veesenmayer's Irish bureau, but he grew increasingly forlorn at a lack of Irish companionship and longed to be back at home. He met with Francis Stuart on several occasions and confided in him that he was unaware of the purpose of the German missions which he had been assigned to. During Ryan's time in Berlin Clissmann treated him well and looked after his needs, at one stage even sourcing a hearing aid for him as Ryan was having difficulty hearing in one ear.

Ryan only left Berlin on a few occasions, usually travelling with Clissmann to visit his family in Aachen or in Denmark. When they were in Copenhagen, the pair would meet up with Mrs Clissmann. On one such occasion they were involved in a car accident in which Ryan was badly injured. After convalescing in hospital, Ryan was discharged and returned to Berlin. He spent a considerable amount of time with Francis Stuart, but he didn't partake in any of his broadcasting work. He grew more and more disillusioned with the German plans for Ireland, and while he was perhaps prepared to countenance a German supply of arms to the IRA, or even an invasion in support of defending Irish sovereignty from the British, he would only do so if it upheld and defended Irish neutrality – a view he shared with Helmut Clissmann. Ryan was also growing more and more weary of Veesenmayer, who, he felt, was condescending towards him. By the time

Germany invaded Russia it was clear to him that the war was over, and the tide had permanently turned in favour of the Allies.

By early 1943, two events changed Ryan's life for the worse. First, Helmut Clissmann was reassigned to North Africa, depriving Ryan of his companionship. Second, his health further declined. He suffered a stroke and was again hospitalised and remained ill for the rest of 1943. Despite receiving treatment in various hospitals, he never fully recovered. In early 1944 he was moved to a sanatorium in Dresden, where he died of a cardiac embolism on 10 June 1944, just as American troops were gaining a foothold on the beaches of Normandy. His forecast of the futility of the German war effort post-Operation Barbarossa had proved to be well founded. Ryan was buried in Dresden-Loschwitz cemetery under his alias, Francis Richards, and his body wouldn't be repatriated until after the war. His last few months in Berlin were marked by a considerable decline in his mental health. While he was physically very well looked after, he confided to Francis Stuart that he felt as though he was under house arrest.

After Ryan's death Mrs Clissmann told Veesenmayer, who had since been redeployed to Hungary, that she felt that Ryan's death should not be kept a secret. Thus began a difficult diplomatic exchange of correspondence between Mrs Clissmann, Leopold Kerney and Con Cremin in the Irish Legation in Berlin to repatriate Ryan's remains, but his use of an alias complicated matters.

Eventually the Irish government was informed of Ryan's death but it wasn't until 20 July 1979, after a long campaign spearheaded by his sister Eilis, that his remains were repatriated to Ireland. Frank Ryan's funeral was held in Glasnevin Cemetery and attended by his colleagues in the International Brigades. The service was conducted in Irish by a relative of his, Fr Coyne, and a graveside oration was given in Irish by Con Lehane, former left-wing politician, Clann na Poblachta TD and IRA Army Council member in the 1930s, who reflected that: 'It's impossible to describe the influence that he wielded, it's impossible to describe the popularity Frank had in the city of Dublin among ordinary working people in the years between 1925 and 1932.' His later years in Berlin, however, remained clouded in mystery for many years after he was laid to rest.

Ryan's later years in Berlin were dogged by various diplomatic exchanges between Veesenmayer and others that were a consequence of his initial incarceration. This brought Leopold Kerney's role as Irish Minister in Spain to the attention of Bryan and his colleagues in G2. As early as 1941 there was contact between Veesenmayer and Kerney that may have been initiated by the former Irish Minister in Berlin, Charles Bewley, who was working as a journalist. It is also believed, but unproven, that Bewley had significant contacts with the German establishment. However the initial contact between parties was made, Veesenmayer hoped that Kerney could be used as an informal link between the two governments. Ryan wrote to Kerney in relation to the meeting between Veesenmayer and Kerney in August 1942:

I know, illegally, that you are having another visitor soon. He must know nothing of correspondence between you and me. But you should ask him about me. His answers may interest you. From my knowledge of him, he is far more capable than he appears, and has a long record of successes to his credit. He has been most persistent and successful in preventing dealings with certain people in the little island. His attitude on all questions is that of his chief; hence his insistence that the status quo in the little island is not to be interfered with is significant. He has the extraordinary gift of quickly understanding a small-nation problem: hence, I presume his visit now to you ...

I have never left an opportunity pass of criticising matters like those of Belfast, North Strand (Dublin), the 'City of Bremen', etc., and found him so straightforward in his replies that I found it difficult to maintain the role of a questioner. I think it right to tell you that – to the best of my knowledge (which is fairly good) – he and also the military authorities have relations now only with their own Minister in the little island ...

During the first meeting between Kerney and Veesenmayer, at an open-air café in El Retiro park in Madrid, and at subsequent meetings, they discussed partition and the attitudes of the Irish and British governments, as well as what the mood in Ireland would be if the Germans were successful in the war against the Soviet Union. During the meetings Kerney robustly defended Irish neutrality and in a memo to the Department of External Affairs he outlined his misgivings about Veesenmayer:

> The following is an account of a conversation which I have had with a German, who told me that this was the first visit which he had made to Spain for the past 12 years; he was here under an assumed name, but his real name is Veesenmayer, and I was mindful of the fact that I was in the somewhat delicate position of talking to a gentleman who, if I had looked under the table, might have been capable of disclosing something in the nature of a cloven hoof; however, it seemed to me that some information of value could be obtained by me, and that it was equally important to leave him without any doubt as to Ireland's position of very decided neutrality; I give his statements and my own observations as fully and faithfully as it is possible for me to record them, depending of course on my memory for naturally I did not take any notes.
>
> Veesenmayer is in the confidence of von Ribbentrop, with whom he had business associations before the war; he is a Doctor of Economics, perhaps about 40 years of age, and is a specialist in transport problems, which he says are tremendously difficult; he has no official connections with the Foreign Office, but is one of the original members of the Nazi party; he spoke with every appearance of doing so authoritatively, and I believe that he came to Madrid with the deliberate purpose of making known Germany's attitude in regard to Ireland, and of completing or correcting as far as possible such knowledge as he himself had already obtained in regard to Ireland.

However, despite Kerney's claims of defending Irelands neutrality it's clear that Veesenmayer hoped to persuade Kerney that for Ireland neutrality was only useful up to a point and that it would be better for Ireland to show its allegiance sooner rather than waiting until German victory in the war was assured. Despite the fact that Kerney's memo said he had defended Irish neutrality, the very fact that he was meeting with Veesenmayer raised questions with G2 and with Dan Bryan in particular as to the true nature of Kerney's dealings with the Nazis. To gain a greater insight into the matter,

Bryan sent Joe Healy, another G2 intelligence officer, and Dr Richard Hayes by flying boat from Foynes to interview Leopold Kerney. Their cover stories were plausible: Healy and the other officer were arranging for supplies from the Irish Red Cross to be taken from neutral Portugal to Spanish refugees; Hayes was collecting rare manuscripts for the National Library of Ireland from the archives at Simancas. Bryan felt that he would soon be able to get to the crux of the matter, but he may have been blinded by personal animosity against Kerney.

Kerney hadn't done anything he shouldn't, but he may have been excessively eager to act and failed to check in with his colleague in Dublin in a timely fashion. Healy travelled from Lisbon to Madrid to interview Kerney and found him very personable and pleasant to deal with. He reported to Bryan that the meeting was:

Extremely cordial and expansive – mentioned his annoyance at receiving wire from Ext. Aff. instructing him to give us a friendly reception, asked did they expect he'd receive us with a gun. Lives very well – complains very much about high cost of living at present in Spain.

Healy also said that he had found no evidence that Kerney was acquainted with any elements from either the Axis powers or the British and that his friends and acquaintances appeared to be very much supporters of the Allies. However, it seems that Bryan could not shake off his suspicion of Kerney and his dealings with German elements. It was clear that Kerney had not reported on his meetings with Veesenmayer until well after MI5 had become aware of them. That, coupled with his success at helping engineer the release of Frank Ryan, and his failure to disclose the extent of his contacts with German Intelligence and with Ryan, raised suspicions about his activities. However, his robust defence of neutrality and his misgivings about Veesenmayer's intentions, as articulated in his own correspondence with Dublin, must also be taken into consideration when assessing his role during the period. Kerney was recalled to Dublin in 1943 so that his role in these affairs could be fully assessed. According to the Carter tapes, Bryan personally interviewed Kerney in his office and outlined his reasons for concern:

I have interviewed Mr Kerney in my office when he came back maybe
a year or two afterwards because Kerney had instructions from Mr de
Valera to do anything he possibly could to get Ryan out of prison and
to protect him and to facilitate Ryan. The government was a bit worried
afterwards in view of the way the war went and all that, that Kerney had
taken certain measures in those things. My impression is that Kerney,
who was – this was before the collapse of Europe of course – that Kerney
was excited to get Ryan out and that, but he probably went farther in
his relations with the Germans than the government here was happy
about or it may be that they certainly weren't happy about it as a result
of, partly because of Kerney's insistence that Ryan ended up in Germany,
and there was this suspicion that Ryan, if he wasn't acting against Irish
interests, was at least acting against British interests in Germany and
the government was possibly worried about that.

The meeting came to nought, Kerney, fully exonerated, was sent back to
his post in Madrid shortly afterwards and served out the remainder of his
career in the diplomatic service. He again created a stir in Dublin when he
travelled to Madrid, without government approval, to express his sympathies on the death of Hitler to the German chargé d'affaires. In many ways
Kerney was an independent thinker and was quick to act of his own accord,
traits that he had developed on trade missions in his earlier years, when he
had been less accountable than he was in the diplomatic service. He served
in Madrid until his retirement and died in June 1962. He was buried in
Deansgrange Cemetery and his funeral was attended by former Taoiseach
Éamon de Valera and Minister Frank Aiken.

Ultimately matters in Russia took the war in a different direction and
the intrigue around Ryan and Russell's dealings with Veesenmayer were
no longer relevant. After 1943, Veesenmayer's Irish Bureau was closed and
missions in relation to Ireland were no longer deemed a necessity. In reality there had been much conflict between Veesenmayer and the head of
the Abwehr, Admiral Canaris, who disapproved of Operation Sea Eagle
in particular and who essentially prevented it happening by enforcing a
series of delays. From 1941, Veesenmayer had been attached to the German

diplomatic staff in Zagreb, Croatia and his time was more consumed by this role and less by Ireland. In 1944, Veesenmayer took up a new role as Reich plenipotentiary in Nazi-occupied Hungary, a role in which he would become infamous for the terror he unleashed. Kerney's reference, in his letter to Dublin, to the SS man's 'cloven hoof' would prove very prescient indeed.

The Russell and Ryan operations were a considerable security risk to the state, but they were overcome by a combination of good fortune and by the work done by G2 and others.

While this was going on the Irish security services were stretched to their limit. Admiral Canaris had been using the Abwehr to carry out a number of spying missions to Ireland to link up with the remnants of the IRA that Russell and Ryan had left behind. The spy whom Russell had been detailed to meet but didn't upon his arrival in Berlin in early 1940, Dr Hermann Görtz, was proving to be of particular concern.

V

THE PARACHUTIST

And once there came from out the sky
A most mysterious German spy.
He came not to plunder or to pillage
But said on seeing our sleepy village,
O Gute Nacht Ballivor, Ich werde schlafen Trim.

JOHN QUINN, *GOODNIGHT BALLIVOR,*
I'LL SLEEP IN TRIM (1996)

Francis Stuart's initial trip to Berlin had re-established contacts between the IRA and Nazi Germany and while the Ryan/Russell affair played out in the city, Admiral Wilhelm Canaris was ultimately able to send over a dozen German spies to Ireland to link with the republican movement and to carry out acts of economic and political sabotage. Another crucial element of their work was to gather weather reports and information relating to the sea conditions, which of course were of huge strategic importance in terms of the plans for Operation Sealion. Despite the significance of the mission, the Abwehr's first choice of agent was scarcely a top-level spy.

Ernst Weber-Drohl was a former circus strongman and wrestler, and when he was sent to Ireland on board U-37 he was suffering from arthritis. The landing was planned for Killala Bay on the north Mayo coast, but other sites, such as Clew Bay, Dungarvan Bay and a number of sites in Co. Kerry, were also deemed to be suitable.

The northwest coast was selected because the German could be met in an IRA safe house in Sligo town. Weber-Drohl then travelled to Dublin, where he stayed with Jim O'Donovan and helped him establish a cover address in

London that the IRA could use for communicating with Germany. Weber-Drohl also made contact with Eduard Hempel at the German Legation, but his stay in Ireland was not to last long – he was soon picked up by the Garda Special Branch working with their colleagues in G2. Weber-Drohl's time in Ireland up this this point was a complete failure, although he was able to pave the way for the arrival of another spy, codenamed Dr Schmelzer, who, it was hoped, would work as a link man between the IRA and Nazi Germany. 'Dr Schmelzer' was Dr Hermann Görtz, the German spy whose mission had coincided with Seán Russell's arrival in Berlin in May 1940. In a carefully worded secret Abwehr document given to Prof. Carter by O'Donovan, Weber-Drohl outlined to O'Donovan what preparations should be made for his successor's arrival:

A Dr Schmelzer should come as an American in about a month or so, to Ireland in order to put up a sender [transmitter]. Jim should see, that that man gets a proper room to work in and a good place to put up the sender. Jim should look for a good place to bring this Dr Schmelzer under, so as he will get in no trouble, if possible, Jim should select a few young men to take up and study the Morse code from Dr Schmelzer.

Weber-Drohl was to spend the rest of the war in the internment camp for German prisoners at Custume barracks in Athlone. His presence in Ireland and the furore it raised with G2 and the Gardaí irked Hempel, who warned Berlin that sending any more agents like Weber-Drohl would damage the already delicate diplomatic situation that he found himself in. Little did he know what lay ahead. Hermann Görtz's time in Ireland was to cause Hempel even further distress.

Hermann Görtz was born in Lübeck, northern Germany in 1890, the fourth of seven children. He was descended from Schleswig peasantry on the maternal side of his family – his mother's family hailed from East Friesland – and his maternal grandfather was a director of the county court in Lübeck. His paternal grandfather was a merchant in Bremen, and his own father was a solicitor and notary in Lübeck. Görtz received a classical education, graduating with good grades, then studied law at university in Kiel, eventually earning a doctorate in jurisprudence. He married Ellen Aschenborn in 1916 and the couple had three children, Wiebke, Rolf and Ute. Görtz joined the Nazi Party in 1929 and in 1935 made his first forays into the world of espionage by volunteering for the Abwehr as a civilian. His original plan to join the Luftwaffe had been thwarted after he made a false declaration on his application form and he felt that by volunteering to work for the Abwehr he could curry enough favour to get into the Luftwaffe. A somewhat arrogant man, he attempted to use his role as a solicitor and respected member of society to present himself as an attractvive candidate for the air force, but this plan failed. Such an act was indicative of his arrogance given that he had no background in aviation and assumed his good standing in society would be sufficient to get such a role. In the end Görtz was able to gain an introduction to influential officials in the Reichswehr Ministerium (the Ministry of Defence) and an arrangement was made. If he went to England to spy on the RAF this would be used as a lever to get him into the Luftwaffe – provided, of course, his mission was a success.

Görtz travelled to England in 1935 with his typist, the tall and glamorous 19-year-old Marianne Emig, who had been employed in his solicitor's office. Emig was born in Mainz in 1916 and was 26 years Görtz's junior. The couple's mission was to spy on an RAF base in Kent, and they rented a cottage in Broadstairs, near Manston RAF station at Ramsgate. Görtz aimed to collect enough sensitive information to impress his colleagues in the Abwehr, and he hoped this would be enough to get him into the Luftwaffe. Unfortunately, he and Emig stood out to the bemused public and it wasn't long before the couple raised the suspicions of British airman Kenneth Lewis, whom they had befriended. After a brief trip to Germany, Görtz was arrested at Harwich on suspicion of espionage. His landlady had falsely alerted the police to a burglary, and when his lodgings were raided the police had found incriminating materials, mostly consisting of sketches of Manston RAF base. Görtz's fate was sealed. He was convicted of espionage and sentenced to four years in prison at the Old Bailey in March 1936. He was released in February 1939, just as the IRA was making its initial contact with the Abwehr. Görtz 's first foray into spying was soon to be followed by an even more unfortunate sequel.

In January 1940, Görtz was selected for deployment to Ireland and to complete Ernst Weber-Drohl's abortive mission. Sending Görtz at all was a strange decision; having served a prison sentence in England he was, in his own words, 'already a marked man'. But Görtz was thrilled to be given another opportunity to show his worth to his superiors in the Abwehr. According to an account he gave later:

> My mission was from the Operational Department of the Supreme Command and was to be considered as a strategic support to the activity of the German Navy. The southern and western ports of Ireland were denied to the British by neutral Eire and as things were, the Supreme Command were very satisfied with the result. It had no wish to look for a change, and it was impressed upon me that I must avoid everything which could disturb this favourable situation. On the other hand, there was a national revolutionary body in Ireland the IRA which wanted to fight our common enemy. The Supreme Command wished to make use of this situation and to direct all the energies of these Irish national forces to a point where it became strategically important. This point was for us the Northern Irish harbours.

Görtz's job was to support the navy and help it to prevent the enemy using the northern ports. Görtz, it was hoped, would make contact with the IRA and use them to create instability in Northern Ireland in order to create a bridgehead for an invading German army. He was also tasked with collecting weather reports and general espionage activities. However, there were two fatal flaws in this plan: the IRA had descended into a faction-riven farce that would be completely incapable of mounting an insurrection; and Hermann Görtz himself was not of sound mind. One of the last things he asked for before heading to Ireland was a vial of poison in case he was captured. Remarkably, this didn't ring any alarm bells with his handlers.

The plan was that Görtz would be parachuted into Northern Ireland, where he could link up with a number of IRA men who were expert in guerrilla warfare. A proposed guerrilla campaign involving Görtz and the IRA would then later be supplemented with arms and men from Germany if the possibility were to present itself.

In reality, the mission was a small sideshow for the Abwehr, but Görtz had a penchant for exaggeration and was determined to make something out of the trust that had been placed in him. It was envisaged that while Germany would try to support the IRA in their fight against the common enemy, it wasn't in a position to offer any troops to help either Görtz or the IRA. Görtz wasn't given any specific parameters within which to carry out his mission, but he was given one strict instruction; under no circumstances could he act in any way to cause friction between Germany and the Irish government. Admiral Canaris personally sanctioned Görtz's mission, but it was kept secret from the rest of the German High Command. Delighted with the opportunity to prove himself to his superiors, Görtz set off for Ireland as Seán Russell was travelling to Berlin.

Hermann Görtz left Jever airfield in southern Germany on 5 May 1940, bound for Ireland. After passing unobserved over British airspace – thanks to cloud cover – and entering Irish airspace, he hoped to parachute from the plane and land on farmland in County Tyrone. The farm, which he himself had selected, straddled the border with County Monaghan and the secluded area would provide Görtz with a soft landing. Then he hoped to be picked up by sympathetic republicans. Laragh Castle in County Wicklow, the home of Francis Stuart, was a back-up location should his drop be unsuccessful, but for political reasons he was advised to avoid using this option if at all possible.

Unfortunately for Görtz, the plane, a Heinkel, became hopelessly lost. He and the pilot, Karl Eduard Gartenfeld, knew they were over Ireland, but had no clue exactly where. Görtz had prepared two parachutes for the drop, one for himself and the other for his AFU wireless broadcasting radio. Görtz was to leave the aircraft first, then the pilot would drop the transmitter; but because it was so much lighter it drifted to the ground much more slowly and Görtz never retrieved it.

In reality Görtz was far from Tyrone; he had actually been dropped over the sleepy village of Ballivor in County Meath. As he parachuted gently to the ground in full Luftwaffe uniform, believing – or hoping – that he was landing in Northern Ireland, Görtz felt confident that his outfit would protect him from any ill treatment by the British. He was also carrying papers legitimising him as an officer of the Luftwaffe. Without his radio set and with no food, he found himself lost in the Irish countryside, where he was soon accosted by a pair of local farmers. After gaining his bearings he headed off into the night towards Laragh, where he hoped to find safe lodgings from which he could contact the IRA. However, it wasn't long before his incompetence had raised the suspicions of G2 and the Irish security services, who made him their number one target.

After many trials and tribulations, Görtz made his way to Francis Stuart's house in Wicklow, where he was taken in by Stuart's wife, Iseult, and her mother, Maud Gonne. Iseult went to Switzer's clothing store in Dublin to buy Görtz a suit and some clothes, but this gesture was to prove his undoing. The manager of the store became suspicious that Iseult was buying men's clothes when it was common knowledge that her husband was in Berlin, and he notified the Gardaí, who passed the information to G2. G2 already suspected that a parachutist had entered Ireland illegally because postal censors had intercepted postcards that Görtz had sent to his family in Germany.

In his new civilian clothes, which he hoped would help him blend in, Görtz went to stay with Jim O'Donovan, who was to introduce him to Acting Chief of Staff Stephen Hayes and other members of the IRA. After a period at O'Donovan's house in Shankill, County Dublin, Görtz was moved between a number of houses on Dublin's southside, including addresses in Rathmines and Donnybrook, during which time he met with Stephen Hayes. The meeting didn't go well, and neither man made a good impression on the other. Hayes grossly overexaggerated the IRA's capabilities, while Görtz found Hayes to be lacking any sort of leadership qualities.

At Görtz's request, an IRA team was sent to Carbury bog in County Kildare to retrieve his – missing – transmitter and parachutes, which he had hastily buried. However, gardaí had found one of the parachutes and had immediately briefed G2. Hayes and Görtz arranged to meet again, this time at the house of an IRA sympathiser with German origins, Stephen Carroll-Held, in Templeogue, but Garda Special Branch had already begun to close in on both men. Acting on intelligence from MI5 via the Dublin link, which had been monitoring Carroll-Held and his mistress, G2 was able to ascertain the time and location of the meeting and make plans to apprehend those in attendance. The British contacted Dan Bryan because Liam Archer was on sick leave at a spa in Droitwich in Worcestershire, suffering with rheumatism in his leg. In his absence, Bryan was Acting Chief of Intelligence.

Bryan had his own suspicions that Carroll-Held's house in Templeogue was being used for illicit purposes. An army officer had told Bryan that he had been approached by a businessman living near Carroll-Held's house who said that he felt something suspicious was happening at the property. He told the officer that he was unable to get a radio signal on his FM radio, which he owned for private use. It was discovered that an illegal wireless being operated in the back garden of Carroll-Held's house was in effect blocking the radio signals for all other frequencies in the area, and it transpired that the IRA had provided the transmitter for Görtz to use during his stay. This information, coupled with the MI5 intelligence, gave Bryan and G2 enough information to pass on to the Gardaí, who would carry out a raid on the house. With the plan in place, Bryan settled into bed.

Bryan awoke in the middle of the night to a phone call confirming his suspicion that a spy had landed in Ireland. The Irish authorities would have to act quickly to catch Görtz, but they had the element of surprise on their side. Bryan recalled the phone call in an interview with Prof. Eunan O'Halpin years later:

> The Görtz case as far as I was concerned opened by getting a phone call sometime in the very early hours of the morning. I can't say the date – but it is 1940. The phone call was to go to the house of a person of German origin, but possibly Irish nationality called Held. His father had been a real German. Held's mother was Irish. Once the house was reached it was obvious that a lot of material which it took some time to examine was in the house.

Garda Special Branch had raided the house at 10 p.m. the night before and had broken into a locked room. An officer immediately contacted Bryan to let him know what they had found. Bryan made his way to the house in Templeogue and, on arriving, he discovered Luftwaffe and Nazi paraphernalia, a significant sum of money, and maps that contained military and geographical information on Ireland. Bryan was informed that Görtz and Carroll-Held had been out for a walk during the raid and while Carroll-Held had been arrested on his return, Görtz had escaped into the night. The material found during the raid, coupled with material containing Luftwaffe logos retrieved from Carbury bog, confirmed G2's suspicions that there was an illegal parachutist on the loose in Ireland. Bryan was also horrified to discover documents containing veiled references to Hempel at the German Legation in the house.

Bryan immediately took the documents to Garda headquarters to have photostatic copies made of them, but the machine was cumbersome and the gardaí inexperienced in using it, and it was taking longer than he hoped. If word reached government officials that a German spy had evaded capture, it could have a disastrous impact on security arrangements and particularly on Irish relations with the British. Bryan arranged an emergency meeting with Minister for Defence Oscar Traynor to brief him on the raid. Traynor contacted Minister for Justice Gerald Boland, who arranged for the photostat process to be speeded up and for the documents to be sent to him immediately.

As soon as the documents were copied, Bryan hurriedly took them to the Army Chief of Staff Dan McKenna and briefed him on the deteriorating security situation caused by Görtz's arrival. Then he went to Dublin Castle to brief Garda Commissioner Michael Kinnane, and then to the Department of External Affairs, where he had a hastily arranged meeting with Assistant Secretary General Frederick Boland. (The Secretary General himself was in London.) Bryan stressed the need to act quickly as rumours were already circulating around the city. The British were bound to hear about what had happened, but he was keen to make sure that they didn't receive a distorted version of events, which could perhaps provoke them into unnecessary action. Bryan stressed to Boland the need to inform the British of exactly what had happened in relation to the raid on Carroll-Held's house and the suspicion that a parachutist had successfully evaded the Coast Watching Service, entering the country without their knowledge. Bryan supplied Boland with copies of all the documents that had been seized in the raid and instructed him to forward them to his counterparts in England. As Bryan returned anxiously to his home in Ballsbridge, and Boland rushed the copied documents to British representatives in Dublin, Görtz was on the run. Over the next few days he made his way through ditches and fields back to Laragh Castle, surviving only on wild berries.

Early the next morning Bryan was awoken by another phone call, this time from Frederick Boland in the Department of External Affairs. Boland asked Bryan for a second set of the copied documents to keep at the Department of External Affairs, and a messenger took another set of copies to Dún Laoghaire, where they were put on the next boat to Holyhead. Cecil Liddell arranged for a messenger to collect the documents from Holyhead and they were ferried to MI5 in London.

Of course, news of a German spy spread through Dublin like wildfire and, despite the government's intention not to comment on an ongoing security issue, the matter was raised in the Dáil. In a meeting of the Finance Committee on 15 May 1940, Fine Gael TD Patrick Belton joked about it in an exchange with Fianna Fáil TD and future President of Ireland Erskine Childers: 'Deputy Childers spoke in very general terms. I was waiting to see if he would come down to earth. He did not, because, I suppose, like the parachutist, he did not know where he was going to land.' The affair of the mysterious parachutist was splashed across the local papers, and a statement was made in error in the Dáil that the documents recovered contained an invasion plan for Ireland. Public fear that Ireland could be adversely affected by the war was at an all-time high. The government would have to act quickly to assuage the sense of apprehension that spread over the country.

Meanwhile, the Liddell brothers were visiting Liam Archer at the spa in Droitwich. Guy, who at this stage had risen to be the third most senior officer in MI5, tried to suss out from Archer Irish attitudes to German invasion and whether the Irish would support the British or resist them. Archer flew back to Northern Ireland with British Brigadier Dudley Clarke and on to Dublin, where they attended meetings with de Valera and the Cabinet. Clarke's mission and the subsequent British–Irish meetings appear to have led to many new security arrangements, including greater information-sharing between

Dublin and London. Guy Liddell recorded the meeting with Archer in his diary on 15 May 1940, clearly highlighting the British position:

> I arrived at Droitwich about five o'clock and found Colonel Liam Archer at his clinic. We told him that although it was our original intention to discuss particular cases, recent events in Holland had very much brought home to us the dangers of something similar happening in Eire. There was this probability which had a certain amount of supporting evidence. Archer said that as far as he could see there was nothing to prevent the Germans landing in Eire and he did not see how any resistance could be maintained for more than a week. Archer seemed to think that if the Germans landed in Eire there would be general resentment and a certain amount of resistance, but he thought there might be quite a number of people who would say 'Oh, well, they are here in force, we can't do anything about it' and be prepared just to accept the situation. He was quite emphatic that Eire would be thinking about her independence and that many people would not mind Great Britain getting a licking.

With Archer back in Dublin, attention turned to locating Görtz. The trial of Stephen Carroll-Held, who had been arrested and charged after the raid on his house, garnered more information on the Germans' intentions for Ireland. He was eventually sentenced to five years' imprisonment for his involvement in the Görtz affair, while Iseult Stuart, who herself had also been arrested as part of the hunt for Görtz, was acquitted after a two-day trial, despite the fact that she was clearly guilty of harbouring Görtz. Following Carroll-Held's arrest a series of raids were carried out and 400 IRA men and people thought to be politically suspect were detained. Many of them were placed in makeshift internment camps, including the camp at Custume barracks. While this was happening, de Valera made an appeal to Irishmen to join the army to defend the country from attackers from all quarters:

> I'm sure the deputies will have seen the statements I have recently made on the dangers that threaten our country. These dangers are now obvious

and I only refer to them now that the Dáil and the country may see the urgent necessity for the defence measure which the government is taking. The reservists of the regular army and the first line volunteers are all being called to the colours. A campaign to call thousands more volunteers to the army will at once be undertaken. Those who are willing to give their services to the nation are being registered at once so as to be called up for training the moment we can take them. In view of the dangers that confront us I am sure all our people will be united as one man behind the government, ready to face aggression from whatever quarter it may come.

At the same time, Hempel alerted Berlin that news of the raid on Carroll-Held's house was making headlines across the world and had even been reported in the Washington press. Hempel was keen to avoid any association with Görtz due to the precarious position he found himself in diplomatically.

In the aftermath of the Carroll-Held raid, G2 was able to study some of the material found during the search of the premises, in particular the transmitter and a series of coded messages that Görtz had left behind. The transmitter had been made by a soft-spoken civil servant from County Louth, Anthony (Tony) Deery, to replace the one Görtz had lost parachuting from the Heinkel. Deery, a Post Office telegraphist, was to function as Görtz's radio operator to enable him to communicate with German High Command. The homemade transmitter was similar to the models used by Irish Lights, the oversight body for Irish lighthouses. Bryan had received an earlier tip-off about an IRA attempt to source a similar model from an Irish Lights employee in County Wicklow, so he was familiar with the type found in the Carroll-Held raid. He had sent Commandant Nelligan of the signals section of G2 to deal with the Wicklow transmitter:

Görtz then was after the IRA to get transmitters, radio communications and the IRA found they had a friend, a transmitter on one of the Irish Lights' vessels. They went to this fellow and asked him could he provide them with a transmitter or could he do something and he said he could. He lived in the town of Wicklow next door to a policeman. The Irish

Lights were actually controlled, they still are, by the British government. They're a kind of semi-state service. The Garda regarded this man as kind of a member of the establishment. I sent Commander Nelligan with them to raid this fellow's place. They had the authority to go and raid the place and the Garda that lived next door said 'Oh, he's a very respectable man. He's employed by Irish Lights. He's spending so many days on the ship and then so many ashore, and all that kind of thing. There couldn't be anything wrong with him. He lives next door to me. He's a highly respectable man.' But when Nelligan and the others went up they found he was trying to bring transmitters too.

The transmitter fiasco showed that the IRA was far from an efficient organisation. Bryan correctly surmised that the transmitter that Deery had constructed for Carroll-Held and Görtz could have been put together by anyone with even a passing interest in electronics and a basic competency as an electrician. The fact that the IRA would go to the bother and jeopardy of sourcing one from Wicklow was evidence of how haphazardly it was operating. The IRA had trouble constructing the transmitter themselves because it needed to source special amplifier tubes. This was hugely sensitive – even being seen to purchase them would have been highly suspicious and would have drawn too much attention to whoever made the purchase, even more so following the restrictions and rationing that had been brought in as part of the Emergency Powers Act.

The Carroll-Held raid also shed light on how the Germans were planning to keep their communications with Görtz secret. The Gardaí had confiscated handwritten notes written in code by Görtz which outlined much of the intent behind his mission. Görtz had been entrusted with a very special coding mechanism for enciphering his messages which was Russian in origin but which had been put to special use by the Germans during the war. Indeed, such was the secretive nature of the code that only Görtz had been trusted with using it for his mission. The coding mechanism was extremely intricate, consisting of a polyalphabetic substitution cipher. Crucially, it was later learned, Görtz had memorised the keyword used for deciphering the methods in an effort to thwart the Irish authorities.

As G2 was learning more about the as yet unidentified parachutist, Görtz had successfully trekked back to Laragh Castle, where he was dismayed to find that Iseult Stuart had been arrested. He was greeted at the castle by Helena Moloney, who arranged for him to be taken back to Jim O'Donovan's house in Shankill. Moloney, who was born in Dublin in 1883, came to prominence through her work as an actress, republican, trade unionist and feminist. She had been active in the 1916 Rising and was involved in the same unit of the Irish Citizens Army as fellow Abbey Theatre actor Sean Connolly. The group were active on Easter Monday in the vicinity of Dublin Castle, where Connolly is said to have fired the first shot of the Rising, killing DMP Constable James O'Brien. Moloney first became acquainted with Maud Gonne through the Women's Prisoners' Defence League, the People's Rights Association and the Anti-Partition League. A lifelong advocate of militant Irish republicanism, she was one of many women to harbour the fugitive Nazi spy. As Görtz disappeared into the ether, moving from safe house to safe house in the dead of night, G2 was busy combing the country for any clue that would lead them to the elusive parachutist.

The Görtz affair was compounded by the arrival of new Abwehr spies in June 1940. Walter Simon, travelling under the alias Karl Anderson, arrived in Ireland on 12 June by U-boat, landing in County Kerry. After rowing to shore on Minard beach he made his way to Dingle, the nearest town, and after an alcohol-fuelled tirade in what is today known as Neligan's pub he went to Tralee, where he boarded a train to Dublin. Simon had attracted so much attention that concerned locals had reported him to the Gardaí and he was apprehended by Special Branch detectives when he arrived at Knightsbridge (Heuston) Station in Dublin. He was convicted in the Special Criminal Court under emergency legislation and interned in Custume barracks until the end of the war. The spy who would follow him on 25 June caused considerably more trouble.

While Simon was something of an opportunist, Wilhelm Preetz was a committed Nazi, having joined the party in 1933, and he was only 34 years of age when he arrived in Ireland. At five feet nine inches, with a slender build and light blond hair, he blended in well, but this was not the only reason he was chosen as an agent. He had visited Ireland before, and had married an Irishwoman, Sally Reynolds from Tuam in County Galway, in 1932. Preetz had a mail-order business in Bremen and in January 1939 was selected to go to Ireland under the pretext of selling two newly acquired lines of merchandise (cameras and dental equipment). While the Abwehr provided him with no actual training, it hoped that he would be able to gather crucial weather reports and garner information on troop movements in Northern Ireland. He was given a transmitter to send information back to Germany once he was able to do so.

Preetz was briefed for his mission in Gestapo headquarters in Berlin by his superior officer, Fritz Schmidt, and was given foreign currency by the Bremen Chamber of Commerce at the Gestapo's behest, on the condition that he obtain information for them in Ireland. The Abwehr also instructed Preetz to ascertain the attitude of Irish people towards Hitler and the war and towards the IRA. Preetz compiled a 25-page report on his observations and furnished his Abwehr handlers with it. Delighted by what they saw, they decided to send Preetz back to Ireland for a second mission, but this time they entrusted him with some more specific tasks.

Preetz was asked to go to Dublin to find out all he could about the Vickers Aircraft Company's operations in Ireland, specifically whether Vickers was building aircraft parts in or near Baldonnel and to find out if an aircraft factory was under construction at Baldonnel airport in west Dublin. Vickers was the primary supplier of aircraft and armaments to the RAF and any information on them was of huge interest to the Abwehr. Preetz was also to travel to Kilkishen in west Clare to find out whether an arms factory was being constructed there and, if so, when construction had begun; and to Collinstown near Dublin to find out if work on the aerodrome had started and how long the construction process had been going on. While he was in Ireland it was also expected that he would locate and document as many suitable emergency landing fields as possible. Preetz returned from his mission via Antwerp as a stowaway on a ship, arriving back in Bremen on 6 December 1939. He met his handlers and gave them an oral report on his activities in Ireland. While his mission was largely unsuccessful, he had managed to record a number of landing sites for the Abwehr; however, these turned out to be a number of well-known airports. Despite his lack of success, it was decided to send Preetz back to Ireland for a third time. Neither party suspected that it would be his final trip.

The Abwehr summoned Preetz to Hamburg in January 1940 to meet some officers from Berlin. It was initially planned to train him in the use of explosives and chemicals, but when he refused, they trained him to use a wireless transmitter. Preetz didn't take to the training and the Abwehr realised that he couldn't be trusted with such a mission. In the end, it was decided to send him to Ireland after all – his fluent English and familiarity with Ireland would be useful – but alternative arrangements would be made to operate the transmitter. Preetz was tasked with installing a radio transmitting set in a secret location in Dublin, where he would be joined by a trained operator to help communicate back to Berlin. He was also asked to find a trustworthy Irishman to help him. In the months leading up to his departure in June 1940 he was trained at a farm outside Berlin in how to install the transmitter.

Preetz was to be paid £520 for his trip and was reimbursed £30 he had borrowed from his in-laws on a previous trip. He would also receive a monthly payment of £350, which would be forwarded to his wife in Bremen. Preetz gave the Abwehr three addresses in Ireland where they could contact him if wireless contact failed: the Ormond Hotel on Ormond Quay; the Dublin Hibernian Hotel; and a sweet shop at 32 Park Street. In early June 1940, the final preparations were put in place for Preetz's mission, and the transmitter was delivered to his lodgings on 11 June. Preetz took the afternoon train to Wilhelmshaven, where he was met by a naval lieutenant and escorted to a hotel. The next morning, he was taken by car to a submarine that had been loaded with his transmitter and supplies. The U-boat sank beneath the surface of the North Sea and made its way to Ireland with Preetz on board later that night.

On the night of 25/6 June, Preetz's U-boat surfaced near the Irish coast at Minard, near Dingle, much the same location as where Walter Simon's U-boat had arrived a fortnight earlier. Once on land, Preetz buried his transmitter, hitched a ride from a local farmer in the back of a cattle truck and made his way to Tralee, from where he took a taxi to Limerick. He stayed in Limerick for one night in a hotel paid for out of his spy money and then took the next bus to Dublin. Before he left Limerick, he visited a local department store and bought a suit and aftershave. On arriving in Dublin, he contacted a man named Joe Donohue, a native of Tuam, whom he had met on previous trips to Ireland and whom he trusted. He hoped that Donohue would be able to operate the wireless transmitter for him. The two men bought a second-hand car and Preetz drove back to Dingle two weeks later to dig up the wireless transmitter that he had buried on the beach at Minard. He was relieved to find it was still there and intact. With the radio set in the back of his car he returned to Dublin and set it up at a property at 23 Westland Row, from where he hoped to begin broadcasts back to Germany.

In order to code his messages Preetz was given a particularly detailed method of communicating with his handlers. He had an agreed number – the number 10 – which he would add to the date of any given day. The total would indicate a page in the book *Hide in the Dark* by Francis Noyes Hart. The first three letters of the page would serve as the call letters for both parties in any communications. Once both parties were satisfied the line was secure, messages would be broadcast in Morse code over a high frequency.

Preetz's lifestyle in Dublin proved to be his downfall. His flash lifestyle and dubious contacts soon brought him to the attention of Dan Bryan, Liam Archer and G2, who had been monitoring him on his previous trips to Ireland. His house in Westland Row was also put under radio surveillance by a number of G2 men in the Signals Corps. Bryan and Archer also detailed Luke Patrick Smith, one of their most trusted men, to keep an eye on Preetz's radio traffic and to observe him from a distance and make a note of anyone visiting the house.

Smith was born in Dublin in 1901 and joined the IRA after the Easter Rising. During the War of Independence, he served as an IRA assistant company quartermaster and was involved in an IRA attack on British forces on Terenure Road, Dublin in January 1921. He was a close confidant of IRA Director of Intelligence Michael Collins, who initiated him into the world of intelligence-gathering and surveillance, and was frequently photographed alongside him. During the Truce period Smith continued his IRA service and joined the National Army on 21 July 1922 following the outbreak of the

Civil War. Smith took part in the fighting at the Four Courts at the outbreak of the Civil War in late June/early July 1922 and served throughout
the remainder of the conflict before being demobilised on 7 March 1924.

After the Civil War Luke Smith resumed his role as a second-class library
assistant with the National Library, a role he first took up on 1 January 1921.
He had previously worked at the library as a boy attendant prior to the
outbreak of hostilities against the British in 1916. Through his civilian work
Smith became friendly with the director, Dr Richard Hayes. Like Hayes,
Archer and Bryan, he was seconded back into the National Army via the
Department of Defence at the outbreak of the war. Once back in the army,
Smith was reacquainted with his old colleague Dan Bryan, with whom he
had worked closely in the war against the British. Smith married Mary Anne
Smith, known affectionately as Molly, and after living in various places in
the city, the couple settled in Belton Park Avenue on Dublin's north side.

Smith was tasked with monitoring radio traffic in the city and reporting
any illicit findings to his superior officers. His eldest son, Luke Jr, a former
director of news at RTÉ and one of the inaugural class of studio trainees at
the state broadcaster in 1961, recalled his father 'retiring to the attic to listen
to football matches in England. It wasn't till we were much older that we
realised that he was actually listening to radio traffic and keeping an ear out
for German broadcasts.' Smith also monitored Preetz's house and on one
occasion encouraged Luke Jr to go to the door and knock and ask 'if this is
the house with the apples for sale. Of course, there were no apples for sale
and I got the door slammed in my face.' It was all a ruse, of course; Luke
Sr would get a good look at who answered the door and make a note of it
for a larger intelligence file on the residence, which he would later forward
to Bryan and his superior officers in G2 HQ at the Red House. All of this
helped build a very detailed security picture, which was further bolstered
by the British, who were also monitoring the airwaves. Luke Smith Sr died
on 25 January 1977 and was said to have been on active service until that
day. His expertise had been sought on numerous occasions in relation to
Northern Ireland and emergence of the Provisional IRA.

MI5 had also been keeping tabs on wireless broadcasts from Ireland and
were soon alerted to illicit broadcasts coming from Dublin via Group 1, the

radio security service used for monitoring suspected Abwehr wireless traffic intercepted on monitored frequencies. Guy Liddell noted the intercept in his diary on 27 July 1940 and subsequently made contact with Archer and Bryan about it:

A Group 1 message has been intercepted between Ireland and Germany and refers to a man named Donohue, presumably a German agent, who is coming over here in the course of the next few days. A new branch has been formed in the office called the O Branch, which is to deal with organisation. I should have a lot to do.

During his time in Ireland Preetz had made friends with an Italian national named Staffieri, who soon joined him and Donohue in their illicit dealings. The trio later purchased a flashy Austin car and rented rooms in Great George's Street for partying and entertaining women. They also rented an address on Parkgate, which they were unaware was just a few doors up the street from the Red House, Irish Military Intelligence HQ. In August Preetz upgraded his car to a Chrysler, which didn't go unnoticed by his neighbours on Westland Row. At this stage he was attracting a lot of attention and it wasn't long before G2 put his apartment under 24-hour surveillance. His whirlwind few months in Ireland finally came to an end when he and Donohue were arrested outside their flat on 26 August. When G2 searched the flat they found his transmitter and various other spying materials such as a Morse key and numerous enciphered documents. Among this treasure trove of illegal material were coded requests from the Abwehr for Preetz to find out information on troop movements in Northern Ireland as well as shipping traffic between Ireland and England. Bryan and G2, it seemed, had acted in the nick of time.

Archer wrote to Guy Liddell to tell him that Preetz had been apprehended and the wireless set found. Liddell correctly concluded that Joe Donohue was the Donohue mentioned in the broadcast whom they had intercepted the previous month and about which they had alerted G2. Archer decided to make a full study of the wireless set, to interrogate both Preetz and Donohue and to provide a report to Liddell on the findings. Richard Hayes was called on to carry out both tasks. Hayes was unimpressed with Preetz, whom he found an uncompromising and arrogant man, and not a very intelligent one at that. Donohue, it was felt, was simply going along with Preetz, but it was noted that he was extremely anti-British and was an ardent supporter of Nazi Germany.

After G2 had obtained information from Preetz on his coding methods, he was sent to the internment camp for German prisoners at Custume barracks in Athlone, but to Archer and Bryan's shock, the authorities were instructed not to charge Donohue and to release him immediately. The directive came directly from Minister for Justice Gerald Boland and G2's protests were to no avail. Privately G2 believed that Donohue had got off because of his links to Fianna Fáil in Galway. Bryan felt that the release didn't matter in the long run as Donohue wasn't a major player in the German espionage network. Speaking to Prof. Carter in her taped conversations, Bryan revealed that when Donohue tried to relocate to England, G2 alerted the British about his past activities:

> But the thing about it was the authorities here released Donohue from internment, probably the Department of Justice said he was of no importance, he was only with Preetz. We wouldn't have done that kind of thing, after a period. And then Donohue went off to work in England, having nothing to do here, and by some process, he probably talked in England. The British authorities picked Donohue up in England and said, 'Oh you were the one who was in western Ireland with this man Preetz' and interned him in England. I mean he was an idiot to go to England, but the Gardaí and the Department of Justice acted very much on their own accord and didn't understand the international situation. They didn't keep Donohue for the whole war and after a year or two they let him out.

After dealing with Preetz and Donohue, G2 and the Gardaí turned their attention to Staffieri and the rest of the duo's Italian accomplices. Working in conjunction with the Department of External Affairs, raids were carried out among the Italian community living in Dublin to root out any supporters of Preetz who might have slipped through the net.

Having successfully apprehended the Italian nationals who had been working alongside Preetz and Donohue, G2's energies turned back to Hermann Görtz, who had all but disappeared following the raid on Stephen Carroll-Held's house in Templeogue. Tracing Görtz and incarcerating him was becoming more and more of an issue as the days and months of 1940 went by. Ireland's policy of neutrality was coming under greater scrutiny from all quarters. Little did de Valera, Bryan and G2 know that Ireland would soon suffer death and destruction at the hands of Göring's dreaded Luftwaffe. De Valera thought that he had until this point spared the country from the horrors of the war, but he would learn to his cost that no country was safe from the destruction of Hitler's forces.

VI

NEUTRALITY UNDER PRESSURE

Word came through from headquarters that we were to get ourselves over to the North Strand, a bomb had dropped and there was devastation over there.

ALEC KING, HEAD OF NO. 6 AIR RAID PRECAUTIONS

(ARP) DEPOT

As early as August 1940, it became clear that Ireland's strategic position in the Atlantic was going to cause problems in relation to German aggression. Cargo ships sailing to the British mainland were being routinely targeted off the Irish coast during the Battle of the Atlantic, which proved to be the longest battle of the war. In total 36,200 naval crew and 36,000 merchant seamen were lost on the Allied side; 3,500 merchant vessels and 175 warships were sunk; and 741 RAF aircraft destroyed. The figures were equally stark on the Axis side: 30,000 U-boat sailors killed, and 783 U-boats and 47 other warships lost. Churchill himself was gravely concerned, later writing, 'the only thing that ever really frightened me during the war was the U-boat peril'.

On 20 August 1940 Ireland had its first glimpse of the Battle of the Atlantic when a German bomber in pursuit of the SS *Macville* strafed Blackrock Island, County Mayo, damaging several lantern panes and the roof of the lighthouse. While there were no casualties, it was a sign of things to come.

The sleepy village of Campile, County Wexford lay along the main railway line from Rosslare to Cork where a viaduct crossed the famed River

Barrow. Until the night of 26 August 1940, the village was best known as the location of a camp used by the United Irishmen during the 1798 rebellion. The main employer in the area was the Shelburne Co-op and to the local people the war was of little concern. But everything changed at 1.30 p.m. that day, when Hitler's Luftwaffe rained bombs on the defenceless village. Locals initially thought the aircraft was targeting the railway line, but it soon became apparent that they had a different target. The Luftwaffe dropped their lethal payload directly on the Shelburne Co-op, killing three local women, Mary Ellen Kent (aged 35), Kathleen Kent (25) and Kathleen Hurley (25). All three worked in the Co-op and lived locally. Mary Ellen oversaw the staff restaurant, while Kathleen Kent was in charge of the drapery section. The three women didn't stand a chance – one of the bombs scored a direct hit on the building while they were inside, and no one could have survived the firestorm that followed.

Shortly after the explosion members of the LDF rushed to the scene to search the debris for any survivors. They removed the bodies and set about trying to put out the fire. It wasn't long before eyewitnesses began to tell the LDF men of the events that had led up to the bombing. A lone plane had been spotted 10 minutes before the bombing, circling high above the town as if it was observing the area. Five bombs in total were dropped, one incendiary and four explosives. One of the bombs failed to explode and was later taken into military possession. Members of the LDF had noticed that it bore German army markings, and this information was conveyed to Military Intelligence. In the maelstrom that followed, two little girls named McCrohane suffered facial injuries from shattered glass. They were found shortly afterwards running along a local road crying for their father. In a cruel twist of fate, the bombs had been dropped during the Co-op's lunch hour, and all 40 staff were out of the building except for the three women who were killed. The manager of the Co-op, Simon Murphy, had been chatting to the local priest when he noticed the plane circling above them:

A plane appeared overhead. It looked very large and foreign. I went in to my luncheon and thought no more about the plane. I was inside the restaurant for about three minutes when there was a terrible crash, and

I next found myself standing in the yard, having been blown backwards through the window. There were clouds of dust, debris and falling stones and debris accompanied by the shrieking of women. Persons who ran into the cold storage department of the creamery to take shelter found that the plant had been put out of action and they had to leave owing to escaping ammonia gas and rush outside to a field where they lay down. All was quiet for a few minutes then one of the stores burst into flames. With a number of other men in the field I hurriedly collected about twenty-five extinguishers to fight the blaze.

It later emerged that Kathleen Kent would have been out of the building on her lunch only she was delayed in dealing with a customer. Kathleen Hurley had only returned from holidays the day before the plane struck.

Local eyewitnesses had spotted a distinctive German cross on the body of the aircraft, which distinguished it as a Luftwaffe plane. This, coupled with evidence from the unexploded bomb, confirmed that it was a Luftwaffe attack. De Valera issued a public statement on the bombing via the Government Information Bureau:

A bomber aircraft of German Nationality flew over the area of Campile, Ballynitty, Bannow and Duncormick Co. Wexford between 2 o clock and 3 o clock this afternoon. Bombs were dropped at each of these points. The co-operative creamery at Campile was wrecked. Three girls were killed, one injured by fallen masonry. The Irish Chargé d'Affairs in Berlin has been instructed to make a protest to the German government and to claim full reparation.

Privately, de Valera contacted Mr Murphy at the creamery to convey his and the government's deepest sympathies to the parents and relatives of the three women who had been killed. It wasn't long before rumours began to circulate as to why Campile had been attacked. While it was likely that the aircraft was simply lost, believing it was over Northern Ireland or Wales, the theory that the bombing was a warning shot from the Germans began to gather currency. Following the evacuation of Dunkirk a few months earlier, German forces had found butter boxes from the Shelburne Co-op, and many people believed that the bombing was retaliation against Ireland for supplying the British Army with food. Others felt that the bombing was a direct warning to de Valera to strictly observe his policy of neutrality and to not supply the British in any way.

The creamery had been supplying food to civilians on the British mainland, so this could have been a reason for targeting it. It had also recently installed German machinery, so it was entirely plausible that the Germans knew what the creamery was capable of supplying in terms of aid to the British. The German government paid the Irish government £9,000 compensation in 1943 for what they claimed was a navigational error, but the incident is still shrouded in mystery and there is still no definitive answer to why the Luftwaffe targeted Campile. What is certain is that the bombing initiated an increasingly difficult task for de Valera and G2 – maintaining neutrality in the face of increased German aggression towards Ireland.

Towards the end of 1940, the Luftwaffe again violated Irish airspace. On 20 December 1940, shortly after seven o'clock, residents of Dún Laoghaire in south Dublin noticed what they thought were flares in the sky above the coastal town. They soon realised that these were bombs when they began exploding upon impact. One of the bombs fell on Sandycove railway station, injuring three people. The same day bombs fell in the townland of Shantough near Carrickmacross, County Monaghan. The bombing coincided with Luftwaffe attacks on Liverpool and may have been due to navigational errors by Luftwaffe pilots. However, Military Intelligence soon noticed increasing numbers of aircraft making deep penetrations into Irish airspace and subsequent protests were made by the government in relation to this brazen violation of Irish neutrality.

As 1940 ended, intelligence circles were deeply apprehensive about what the new year would bring. On New Year's Day tensions increased yet again when eight German bombs fell on Duleek and Julianstown, County Meath. Miraculously, despite the number of bombs that were dropped, there were no fatalities. The following morning, shortly after six o'clock, two bombs were dropped in Terenure, County Dublin, destroying several houses and injuring seven people. Two unexploded bombs fell on waste ground near

Fortfield Road, Dublin. The Luftwaffe also dropped bombs on Ballymurrin, County Wexford. Incendiary devices fell on the Curragh Racecourse and in County Wicklow. Three members of the Shannon family, sisters Mary Ellen (aged 40), Brigid (38) and their niece Kathleen (16) lost their lives in a bombing incident in Knockroe near Borris in County Carlow.

The Dublin bombings caused no fatalities but there was considerable damage done to property. Two bombs had been dropped in Rathdown Park, one creating a large crater and the other damaging several houses in the area. The bombings continued into the morning of 3 January, when bombs fell on houses in Dublin's Donore Terrace on the South Circular Road. There were no fatalities, but three houses were destroyed and over 50 others were damaged, including a church, a synagogue and a primary school. In total 20 people were injured. Such was the volume and frequency of the bombing raids that G2 began to suspect that they were a deliberate act of war designed to entice Ireland into the conflict. Dan Bryan's suspicions were raised by the fact that the bombings had taken place following the Irish authorities' refusal to allow Hempel to increase his staff at the German Legation.

Hempel's plan to increase his staff led to a real concern in G2 that he would bring intelligence officers to work in the legation. Acting on advice from G2, de Valera denied Hempel's request and issued an order that any German staff destined for the legation who attempted to land in contravention of his order be arrested immediately. German Foreign Minister Joachim von Ribbentrop was furious at de Valera's stance and Hempel told Joseph Walshe at the Department of External Affairs that there would be consequences. There were also rumours beginning to circulate that the bombings had been carried out by the British using captured German military hardware to increase pressure on Ireland to enter the war and give access to the Treaty Ports. Indeed, German propaganda radio broadcasts had hinted at such a possibility and figures such as William Joyce – the infamous Lord Haw-Haw – were quick to make such connections, however spurious they were.

Suspicions deepened further on 5 May 1941 when bombs were dropped near Glengad Head, Malin, County Donegal. Although the event went largely unnoticed by the public, it is remembered locally and was noted

The town of Gowran, County Kilkenny, in the early 20th century
(© *National Library of Ireland*).

Colonel Dan Bryan,
Director of Irish Military
Intelligence (known as
G2) 1941–52 (*courtesy of
Professor Carolle Carter*).

Colonel Bryan in later life, taken in the early 1970s (*courtesy of Professor Carolle Carter*).

Lieutenant General Liam Archer, Director of Irish Military Intelligence (G2) 1932–41 (© *Wikimedia Commons*).

An Emergency-era Éire sign in Dalkey, Dublin (© *Sir Anto/Alamy Stock Photo*).

Dr Richard J. Hayes: librarian, G2 agent and codebreaker (*courtesy of the Hayes family*).

Professor Carolle J. Carter and Dr Hayes in the early 1970s
(*courtesy of Professor Carolle Carter*).

Stephen Hayes (left), one of three wartime IRA chiefs of staff
(© *Topfoto*).

A G2 Officer wearing the parachute of German intelligence spy John Francis O'Reilly (© *National Archives, London*).

O'Reilly's radio set, taken from MI5 files (© *National Archives, London*).

The Shoes on the Danube Bank, a memorial to murdered Hungarian Jews in Budapest (© *Koba Samurkasov/Alamy Stock Photo*).

Commandant James Power of G2, pictured in the early 1970s at the entrance to the internment camp for German spies at Custume barracks, Athlone (*courtesy of Professor Carolle Carter*).

Some of the tapes recorded by Prof. Carter during her research trips to Ireland in 1969 and 1970.

Prof. Carter and author Marc Mc Menamin at Stanford University, California, in 2021.

by Military Intelligence. While tension was running high, the number of casualties were low and it was generally believed that the bombings were caused by navigational errors due to Luftwaffe aircraft falsely believing they were flying over Northern Ireland or Wales or Liverpool. Indeed, the government itself believed that the attacks were made in error and it attributed the Dublin attacks to navigational errors caused by bad weather – there had been heavy snow in the Dublin area on 1 January. Minister for Defence Frank Aiken acknowledged at Cabinet that the planes were German and that a complaint had been lodged with the German authorities. But this was in reality the calm before the storm.

The tension that had been building during previous bomb attacks had largely gone unnoticed by most of the residents of Dublin. As May drew to a close, and as people went about their business preparing for the upcoming bank holiday weekend, they were blissfully unaware of the onslaught that would be unleashed on the city by the Luftwaffe. Early on the morning of 31 May, Hitler's forces launched their most deadly attack of the war on Irish soil. Army intelligence had received reports the previous night of German aircraft overflying the east coast and breaching Irish airspace. Just after midnight, army searchlights were activated in the city to detect any bombers flying over Dublin. G2 was particularly concerned by reports of explosions out at sea, which indicated that bombs were being dumped. Fears grew that Dublin might be targeted – mistakenly or otherwise – once more. Anti-aircraft gunners were ordered to begin firing to deter any suspect aircraft that might stray over the city. Despite all the precautions, G2's worst fears were realised.

At 1.30 a.m. reports began to filter through that bombs had been dropped on North Richmond Street and Rutland Place, and another was reported to have landed in the Phoenix Park near the zoo. Initial reports suggested that while the zoo buildings had been damaged, no staff or animals had been hurt. In Áras an Uachtaráin President Douglas Hyde was awoken by the sound of the explosions shattering the windows of the presidential residence. Worse was to follow. Shortly after 2 a.m. a German landmine was dropped on North Strand Road between the historic Five Lamps and Newcomen Bridge. The explosion wrought utter destruction, ripping through buildings and leaving a trail of ruin in its wake. As the dust settled, the emergency services raced to the scene to try to help survivors and recover the bodies of the dead. The LDF cordoned off the area around the North Strand as mobile units of St John Ambulance treated survivors. The more severely injured were rushed immediately to the Mater Hospital.

The LDF, the Fire Brigade, Civil Defence and many local civilians clawed desperately through the rubble to find the bodies of the deceased. Initial reports suggested that 27 people had died, but it later emerged that there had been 29 fatalities and over 90 people had been injured. Such was the destruction that over 400 people were left homeless. One of the most horrific incidents of the bombing was the deaths of the entire Browne family of 24 North Strand Road. Harry and Mary Browne and their children, Maureen, Ann, Edward and Angela, as well as Harry's 75-year-old mother, Mary, all perished in the attack. Harry was a member of the LDF and had gone out to help as the first bombs fell. Then he decided to return to his home to be with his family. The house suffered a direct hit and Harry was found partially clothed with the door knocker of his house in his hand. The funerals of the Browne family were the first of the 29 that followed. They were interred at their home place, Drumcooley, near Edenderry, County Offaly.

On 5 June 1941 Taoiseach Éamon de Valera rose to his feet in Dáil Éireann to extend his sympathy to the families of all those who died in North Strand and to assure the public that his government would seek answers from the German government:

> Members of the Dáil desire to be directly associated with the expression of sympathy already tendered by the government on behalf of the nation to the great number of our citizens [1,584] who have been so cruelly bereaved by the recent bombing. Although a complete survey has not yet been possible, the latest report which I have received is that 27 persons were killed outright or subsequently died; 45 were wounded or received other serious bodily injury and are still in hospital; 25 houses were completely destroyed and 300 so damaged as to be unfit for habitation, leaving many hundreds of our people homeless. It has been for all our citizens an occasion of profound sorrow in which the members of this

House have fully shared. [Members rose in their places.] The Dáil will also desire to be associated with the expression of sincere thanks which has gone out from the government and from our whole community to the several voluntary organisations the devoted exertions of whose members helped to confine the extent of the disaster and have mitigated the sufferings of those affected by it. As I have already informed the public, a protest has been made to the German government. The Dáil will not expect me, at the moment, to say more on this.

The same day de Valera attended the funerals of 12 of those killed, who were buried by Dublin Corporation at a public funeral held at the Church of St Laurence O'Toole, Seville Place. Archbishop McQuaid led the mourners in prayer as the city tried to come to terms with the tragic events.

Thoughts in government turned to the reasons for the bombing. Speculation was rife that perhaps it was another case of a lost aircraft, but there were also whisperings of something more sinister. Was it a warning to Dublin to stick to its policy of neutrality? After all, there had been reports of Ireland's favourable attitude towards the Allies. De Valera instructed the Irish Ambassador in Berlin, William Warnock, to make a firm protest to the German authorities. The German government did accept responsibility and offered to pay compensation. Warnock later told Joseph Walshe at the Department of External Affairs that the Germans had assured him that the bombing was accidental:

As, however, the Irish government state that, according to their investigations, the bombs dropped on Dublin are of German origin, and, further, as, owing to the very strong wind prevailing in high altitude on the night of May 30th–May 31st, other German aircraft, without noticing it, may also have reached the east coast of Ireland through having been blown off their course, the possibility cannot be excluded that such aeroplane(s) dropped the bombs.

In the circumstances, the German government does not hesitate to express their sincere regret to the Irish government. In view of the friendly relations existing between Germany and Ireland, the German government are further prepared to pay compensation for the deplorable loss of life and injury to persons and property. While reserving the question of the payment of compensation for agreement at a later date, the German government ask the Irish government, on their part, to continue to do everything necessary to clear up the matter. On the German side, the strictest instructions have been issued once more to prevent the possibility of similar incidents in the future.

Dan Bryan had his own theory. He believed that the bombing was accidental but that it had been caused, not by the weather, but by unintended radio interference from the British. Bryan was referring to what subsequently became known as the Battle of the Beams.

By the time of the North Strand bombing, radio navigation for flying had reached a level of sophistication that enabled the Luftwaffe to bomb with increasing accuracy during the night. In an effort to thwart this, British scientists had developed methods of jamming radio signals to Luftwaffe aircraft. This was widely in use by the British Air Ministry at the time of the Dublin attacks. The concept of using a 'beam' to aid navigation had its origins in the early 1930s, and it was used to assist landing without any outside help. The process involved two directional radio signals that were aimed to the left and right of a runway's midline. Aircraft radio operators listened to these signals and sent a Morse code signal into the two beams to distinguish left and right. The system made it possible to land safely during the night. Göring took the concept a step further with the Luftwaffe, using large antennae that provided greater accuracy at longer ranges. These were named Knickebein and X-Gerät and were used to devasting effect in German bombing raids during the Blitz.

Such was the devastating accuracy of German bombing raids in British cities that MI5 made a concerted effort to glean information about how the German system worked. To counter it, the British began sending their own Morse code signals to trick German aircraft into believing they were centred when in fact they were totally off course. This method was so effective that the Germans believed the British were able to bend radio signals. To counter the British, the Germans invented a new system, Y-Gerät, which operated in a different way, but the British soon rendered this system useless. The Germans soon became convinced that the British would successfully be able to jam their transmissions no matter what innovations they came up with.

Bryan believed that the jamming of Luftwaffe radio signals by the British had caused the Germans to bomb Dublin, and that it may also have explained many of the other bombing incidents around the country during the previous year. He outlined this point to Prof. Carter during one of their many taped interviews:

> You know that the Germans bombed Dublin. My assumption is that the Germans were lost. They were being directed by a German beam and the British bent the beam and misdirected them. I think they were lost.

British Prime Minister Winston Churchill held the same view:

> On the very first night when the Germans had committed themselves to the 'Y apparatus' our new counter measures came into action against them. The success of our efforts was evident from the acrimonious remarks heard passing between the pathfinding aircraft and their controlling ground stations by our listening instruments. The faith of the enemy air crews in their new device was thus shattered at the outset and after many failures the method was abandoned. The bombing of Dublin on May 30th 1941, may well have been an unforeseen and unintended result of our interference with 'Y'.

Bryan had to keep his counsel on these matters and it was only in later years that he voiced his opinion. After the war the West German government accepted responsibility for the North Strand bombing and by 1958 it had paid Ireland £327,000 in compensation, using Marshall Aid funds. While the West German government had accepted responsibility for the bombing, neither Austria nor East Germany ever made any such admission or made any reparations. Despite Bryan's and G2's assumption that the bombing raids were due to forced navigational errors, a cloud of controversy continued to hang over the affair.

The Luftwaffe dropped bombs over Irish towns on two further occasions in 1941. In June, Arklow in County Wicklow was bombed in a raid that caused damage but no casualties. The final bombing incident took place on 24 July in Dundalk, County Louth, when the Luftwaffe dropped bombs that caused minor damage to houses but no casualties. Much of the uncertainty around the reasons for the bombings were fuelled by propagandists such as Lord Haw-Haw, who regularly cited Dublin as a target over the airwaves. In one radio broadcast he had mentioned Dublin's Amiens Street train station as a possible target and its proximity to the North Strand only served to fuel fears that the attack had been deliberate. He also claimed that Dundalk was a possible bombing target because it served as a shipping point for cattle going to Britain.

Another possible reason for the bombings was the perceived favourable treatment given to downed Allied aircraft. It is also possible that a highly clandestine agreement between Ireland and Britain had irked the Germans to the point of engaging in attacks on Irish soil. In January 1941 a meeting took place in Dublin between Taoiseach Éamon de Valera and the British Representative Sir John Maffey, at which it was agreed that flying boats based at RAF Castle Archdale on Lough Erne, County Fermanagh would be permitted to fly across a four-mile stretch of Irish airspace from Belleek, County Fermanagh to Ballyshannon, County Donegal, thus avoiding having to fly north through Northern Ireland and out to sea.

This major concession to the Allies became known as the Donegal Air Corridor and it allowed the British to extend their patrols westwards by at least 100 miles, giving them a greater advantage in the Battle of the Atlantic. While the agreement was top secret, it was more than obvious to local people in south Donegal/west Fermanagh, who often witnessed Catalina and Sunderland planes flying over the area. The Donegal corridor was a great success for the Allies and flying boats were able to provide air support for shipping convoys as far as away as the Bay of Biscay, the North Sea and Gibraltar. Flying boats from Lough Erne sank at least nine U-boats and damaged many more stationed at the Kriegsmarine base at Brest in north-western France.

It is clear that Hitler was aware that flying boats were using Irish airspace over Donegal, and Lord Haw-Haw made a pointed reference to 'the swans of Lough Erne' in his radio broadcasts. Indeed, just four days before the North Strand bombing, a Lough Erne flying boat had perhaps its greatest success of the war. On 26 May 1941 the crew of a Catalina flying boat based at Lough Erne and piloted by Ensign Tuck Smith spotted the famous German battleship the *Bismarck* in a gap in the clouds while on patrol 350 nautical miles west of Brest. Despite heavy enemy gunfire, Smith continued to keep the *Bismarck* under surveillance. He then directed other aircraft and gunships to the area before being relieved due to fuel shortage and returning to base. The *Bismarck* was subsequently sunk, giving the British a decisive victory in the ongoing Battle of the Atlantic. The British Board of the Admiralty subsequently issued congratulations to all those involved:

Their Lordships congratulate C.-in-C., Home Fleet, and all concerned in the unrelenting pursuit and successful destruction of the enemy's most powerful warship. The loss of HMS *Hood* and her company, which is so deeply regretted, has thus been avenged and the Atlantic made more secure for our trade and that of our allies. From the information at present available to Their Lordships there can be no doubt that had it not been for the gallantry, skill, and devotion to duty of the Fleet Air Arm in both *Victorious* and *Ark Royal*, our object might not have been achieved.

G2 worked in close conjunction with its counterparts in the Allied forces. Any crashed Allied aircraft were promptly reported to Military Intelligence and efforts were made to spirit surviving servicemen into Northern Ireland and to recover the remains of any dead servicemen. On 21 March 1941 Catalina AM 265 crashed near Aunagh Hill, Glenade on the Leitrim/ Donegal border near the town of Kinlough. Local LDF at Kinlough promptly contacted the army barracks in Manorhamilton, County Leitrim, which relayed news of the crash to G2 in Athlone. Dan Bryan promptly dispatched Commandant James Power from Athlone along with an attachment from Finner Camp (between Ballyshannon and Bundoran) to investigate the crash and, if possible, to help any survivors. Sadly, the plane had been rendered an inferno by the crash, due to the fact that it been carrying depth charges to deploy against U-boats, and there were no survivors. The LDF carried the bodies down from the mountain and laid them out in the parish hall in Kinlough. Shortly afterwards arrangements were made to contact the British Representative Sir John Maffey to have the bodies repatriated. Incidents such as this were a common occurrence and stood in stark contrast to how Axis crashes were dealt with by the Irish authorities.

This contrast is probably best exemplified by the crashing of a Luftwaffe Heinkel 111H-5 at Tacumshane, Lady's Island, County Wexford on 3 March 1941. The bomber, piloted by Lieutenant Alfred Henzl, had been hit by enemy fire near St George's Channel during an attack on an Allied convoy during the Battle of the Atlantic. One engine had been badly damaged and the rear gunner had been killed in the gun battle. Henzl knew that he had to make an emergency landing and had the option of landing in either Britain or Ireland. Naturally he was going to choose neutral Ireland as he believed he and the crew would receive favourable treatment if they survived the landing. The crew estimated that they had enough fuel to make it to County Wexford and picked out an area near Rostoonstown Strand where they could make an emergency landing. After successfully landing the damaged aircraft, Henzl and the crew set up the plane's machine gun and attempted to destroy the aircraft to get rid of any sensitive information.

The plane had been observed entering Irish airspace by the Coast Watching Service, which promptly alerted the Gardaí and LDF. When the Irish authorities arrived on the scene, they requested the Germans stop firing at the plane, an order that the Germans ignored. After the firing stopped, the Germans were promptly placed in custody and taken to Wexford army barracks. A local solicitor and priest, who were fluent in German, made arrangements for the Germans to phone Hempel at the German Legation to inform him of their crash landing. The men were then transferred to the Curragh Camp in County Kildare where they were interned for the rest of the war at 'K-Lines', or the No. 2 Interment Camp, as it was officially known. K-Lines was a newly constructed barbed-wire camp at the Curragh close to Tin Town, the No. 1 Internment Camp, in which members of the IRA were held.

The favourable treatment given to the Allies and the treatment of the Germans was not lost on Hempel, who regularly kept Ribbentrop informed of events in Ireland. With uncertainty around the reasons for the bombings on neutral Ireland still very much an open wound, tensions were further heightened by the arrival of another German spy in the country in March 1941.

Amid all the chaos of the bombing raids on Ireland, both North and South, on 12 March 1941 a thin, wiry man named Günther Schütz gently parachuted into a field in County Wexford. Schütz had been sent by the Abwehr to engage in economic espionage and to observe British convoy movements. His handlers were keen to find out any information that might be of use in relation to Northern Ireland. Schütz was flown to Ireland on board a Heinkel aircraft piloted by the same man who had dropped Hermann Görtz the previous year. Schütz was given a fake alias and documentation identifying him as a South African national named Hans Marschner. He also had with him a unique coding mechanism involving a series of microdots that he intended to use to communicate with his handlers in Berlin. This process of encryption involved minimising written messages to the size of punctuation marks which could then be viewed using a microscope. Schütz's instructions for his spying mission were concealed in the punctuation of various innocuous newspaper adverts for aspirin and articles with a botanical theme.

Much like Görtz, Schütz's arrival into Ireland was haphazard. He was originally to have been dropped in County Kildare, but navigational errors had led the plane to County Wicklow. His troubles soon got worse when he began to draw attention to himself in the Wicklow countryside. Signs identifying local areas had been removed during the war and locals in the area around Taghmon, where Schütz found himself, soon began to grow suspicious at the German asking them for directions. Early on the morning after he landed, Schütz was apprehended by gardaí and transferred to Mountjoy prison. His microscope and advertisements were taken to be analysed by Dr Richard Hayes and Colonel Éamon de Buitléar, who also both interrogated Schütz at length about the reasons for his mission. Hayes broke the microdot system, and the information was shared by Dan Bryan with his counterparts in MI5 and the Office of Strategic Services (OSS), the USA's wartime intelligence service and precursor to the Central Intelligence

Agency (CIA). While such material was obviously of great use to the Allies and was much appreciated, Bryan was receiving little information in return, much to this dismay of others in G2, particularly de Buitléar. The "22 men", as Bryan often called them, still harboured huge distaste for the British following the War of Independence, yet Bryan was determined to share any relevant information – he knew it was more beneficial to do so than to attempt to go it alone on security matters. The microdot system was completely unknown to the Allies at the time, so Hayes's success at breaking it was an important cryptographical breakthrough. Given such an important contribution to the war effort, the lack of a two-way flow of information from the OSS and MI5 was noted by many of Bryan's detractors.

The Schütz affair came to the attention of the British and was raised by the British Representative Sir John Maffey with Joseph Walshe at the Department of External Affairs. Walshe later informed the Taoiseach about his conversation with Maffey:

> He [Maffey] then asked about the parachutist who was captured a few days ago. I had made enquiries from Col. Archer and Chief Supt. Carroll, and I gave him the following information:- The prisoner's name was Hans Marschner [Günther Schütz's alias]. He was born at Schwidnitz in 1912. His father was a chemist. He went to England in April, 1939, and worked in the dispensary attached to the German Hospital in London … In the course of further conversation, and in reply to questions by Sir John Maffey, I told him that Marschner disavowed any intention of interfering with our neutrality or giving any information about Ireland, and that his purpose was to get to England where he would use his set for some purpose unknown. Generally, the prisoner did not show much intelligence. His English was good on the whole. His authorities seemed to have deceived him into believing that getting back to Germany (via Lisbon) was a relatively easy task. I remarked to Maffey how exceedingly difficult it was for a foreigner to escape notice in Ireland … Maffey agreed, and commended the watchfulness of the Guards in all cases which in any way had come under his notice.

While Maffey had been placated, the Schütz affair was to take another drastic turn, one that reflected badly on the intelligence services. On 15 February 1942, Schütz escaped from Mountjoy. He had managed to acquire women's clothing and make-up by fooling the prison governor into believing they were to be used as gifts for his wife in Germany. Once his disguise was complete, he was able to file the bars off his cell using a file he had acquired in the prison workshop, and then descended over the prison wall using curtain ties. He then made his way to the houses of various IRA members who provided him with lodgings as he evaded the authorities. The whole incident was highly embarrassing for the Irish authorities and further bolstered the British perception that the Irish were unable to deal with the security situation. Schütz was finally apprehended on 30 April 1942 after a huge manhunt. He was arrested in the home of Caitlín Brugha, the widow of the famous republican Cathal Brugha, who had been hiding Schütz in a concealed room in her house. Schütz was taken to Arbour Hill and then to a newly constructed prison camp for German internees in Custume barracks in Athlone.

Bryan was astonished that Schütz had been given such a sophisticated microdot coding system when the Abwehr had tasked him with mundane economic espionage:

> The funny thing about Schütz was that, we didn't find out until afterwards. Schütz had the most elementary instructions as to economic intelligence he was to do. In microdots on one piece of paper. What amazed me was … why was it necessary for this type of thing … that he was to get answers to the most elementary conditions in Belfast.

The Schütz affair had temporarily shifted the authorities' focus away from finding Hermann Görtz, who was continuing to cause embarrassment to Bryan and G2. Görtz had been on the run for almost a year by the time Schütz arrived in Ireland. His interactions and multiple escape attempts from Ireland in the interim had been a major concern to Bryan and his colleagues.

Görtz successfully evaded capture for most of 1940 and 1941, and his continued freedom was a source of both embarrassment and intrigue.

Following the raid on Stephen Carroll-Held's house, Görtz had first made his way back to Laragh in County Wicklow and was then moved around various IRA safe houses throughout Dublin. While it seemed obvious that Görtz would have dealings with the IRA, it was his liaisons with people from mainstream Irish society that raised eyebrows and led to mutterings that his freedom had been sanctioned at a higher level. Görtz was alleged to have had unofficial meetings with members of Dáil Éireann up to and including government ministers such as Dr Jim Ryan, the Minister for Agriculture, and TDs such as Christopher Byrne. Görtz also stayed with a prominent physician in Blackrock, who treated him for an ongoing ulcer problem. Görtz's luck began to run out in early 1941 when it became obvious to his Abwehr spymasters that the IRA was incapable of aiding them in any way in the ongoing war against the British.

Realising that his mission to Ireland had been an abject failure, Görtz made several attempts to escape the country. After a failed attempt to get dropped off on Inishduff Island in County Donegal, Görtz tried to flee to France via boat from Fenit, County Kerry. Although gardaí managed to arrest the crew, Görtz himself slipped away with the help of a sympathetic Garda named James Crofton. Crofton was an IRA plant in the Garda Special Branch and was a close confidant of IRA Chief of Staff Stephen Hayes. (There were so many IRA plants in Special Branch that even a brother-in-law of Hayes, Larry de Lacey, was working in the unit as a mole.) Crofton had a seafaring background, and the idea was for the pair to escape to Germany via motorboat and for Crofton to act as Hayes's representative to the Germans. Crofton, while a member of the Garda Special Branch, was not attached to the political Special Branch.

The caper nearly paid off and Crofton had managed to fool the Gardaí into letting himself and Görtz away on the boat. The escape attempt was only scuppered when Florrie O'Donoghue, who had been in charge of the Munster region, recognised Crofton and instructed the local LDF to arrest him. Görtz, however, managed to run away before he could also be apprehended. O'Donoghue liaised with Archer and Bryan on what had happened in Fenit and alerted them to the fact that Görtz had escaped yet again. Crofton was dismissed from the Gardaí and sentenced to five years' imprisonment for his role in the events.

Throughout the entire year that Görtz had been on the run he had been blessed with good fortune and for a time Dan Bryan even suspected that he had managed to escape back to Germany, which he alludes to in the tapes:

He [Görtz] was lucky. The first thing that happened with Görtz was; we assumed and he disappeared for some time, that he had got out of the country. We couldn't, you see, account for just how he did get out but we thought he did with hostages. Of course, he was lying exceedingly low. Now he was resting down by Brittas Bay. If he was in some chalet down there – I mean that kind of place somebody could go down, unusual people would go and stay there and they'd just say, 'Oh, he's unusual,' and not pay much attention to him. If he went to live some place down near Cong, somewhere, the neighbours would immediately be trying to find out who he was. But in Brittas Bay or down those places, they're used to that kind of person. They don't pay so much attention.

Görtz made a further attempt to escape from Brittas Bay on 13 August 1941 by motor boat but had to return to shore when his engine flooded. He tried again in September, but this again ended in failure. Görtz made one final escape attempt on 20 September 1941 by motorboat, but again to no avail. Realising that he was not going to escape, Görtz returned to Dublin, where he relied on the charity of two sisters, Marie and Bridie Farrell, who kept Görtz in their house at 7 Spencer Villas in Glenageary, near Dún Laoghaire, County Dublin. (The house was being kept under surveillance by G2.) Görtz introduced himself to the new Chief of Staff of the IRA, Pearse Paul Kelly, also known as Paul Kelso, a native of Dungannon, County Tyrone and a hard-line republican. Stephen Hayes had been relieved of his role due to the ongoing and farcical Görtz situation. Indeed, Görtz blamed Hayes for his arrest and this antipathy for Hayes was also felt by Kelly and others in the IRA who suspected Hayes of being a Garda informer. Hayes was arrested by the IRA and an internal investigation was carried out. During his interrogation at 20 Castlewood Park in Rathmines, in his own words, 'all they did was beat the hell outta me', but he managed to escape, presenting himself in a dishevelled state at Rathmines Garda station.

It was decided to move Görtz one last time to a safe house at 1 Blackheath Park in Clontarf. Pearse Paul Kelly was suspicious of the house and suspected that it was being watched by G2 and the Garda Special Branch. However, unknown to both Kelly and Görtz, an acquaintance of Görtz's named Joseph Andrews had already informed the Gardaí that Görtz would be staying in the house. The net was closing in faster than either Görtz or Kelly could have possibly imagined. Görtz was at this stage highly paranoid that he was going to be captured, and he left the house on 17 September but returned after a few weeks. He was convinced that MI5 had bugged the house, but it was the Irish authorities who were about to capture him.

On 27 November the house was raided by the Garda Special Branch, Görtz was arrested under the Special Powers Act and taken to Arbour Hill Prison. The arrest had occurred by accident – gardaí had actually been raiding the house next door when they heard strange noises coming from the neighbouring house. Pearse Kelly was also arrested and sent to the Curragh to be interned with other IRA prisoners. Kelly became the Officer Commanding of IRA internees and had considerable success in improving the conditions of prisoners by ending physical punishments, increasing education and starting concerts and sporting activities in the camp. He was released in 1946 and became a journalist with the *Irish Independent*. In 1958 he was appointed editor of the *Evening Herald* and in 1961 he became Head of News at RTÉ. Kelly died in Dublin in 1974 aged 57.

During the raid in Clontarf, gardaí stumbled on a treasure trove of incriminating material relating to Görtz, including a diary written on sheafs of paper in which he had described his escapades in meticulous detail. While the authorities didn't find any useful material relating to the Abwehr, they did gain a good insight into Görtz's mindset. They also found a sum of money in addition to Görtz 's Wehrmacht identity card and a picture of Frank Ryan. In the German Legation, Hempel made a decision to avoid any contact with Görtz in case it brought any negative publicity on him and the legation. Despite this best efforts Görtz eventually contacted Hempel from prison requesting his help. In the meantime, Bryan had arranged for Görtz to be interrogated by Dr Richard Hayes in an effort to decode a series of messages that had been found during the raids on Carroll-Held's house the previous year. While in custody, Görtz continued to insist his name was Heinz Kruse, an alias he had concocted to keep his true identity secret. Despite his protestations, G2 didn't believe his story added up.

News of Görtz's arrest filtered back to his handlers in Germany, who were infuriated at his arrest and the fact that he was 'interfering' with the Irish government. They concluded that Görtz must have lost all logic and reason to have strayed so far from his mission parameters. Indeed, Görtz's frayed mental state provided Hempel with the perfect cover. In a meeting with Joseph Walshe from the Department of External Affairs he stuck rigidly to prepared scripts, insisting that Görtz was acting of his own volition in Ireland, due in a large part to personal anxiety and a disturbed mental state. When Edmund Veesenmayer heard of Görtz's arrest, it was decided with the Abwehr and the Foreign Ministry to concoct a cover story that Görtz was an agent sent to England on a mission who had been delayed in Ireland. In reality the Foreign Ministry was glad that Görtz was behind bars as it relieved them of the problem of wondering what he was up to and worrying, given his erratic state of mind, that he might do something irrational.

While Bryan had successfully dealt with Görtz and Schütz, the American diplomatic presence in Ireland was starting to pose its own issues for G2. While the USA had an official diplomatic presence in Ireland, Bryan became concerned by the issue of Allied spies operating in the country. It was widely feared that the American security services were sending spies into Ireland under the cover of their diplomatic mission to Dublin. There were also reports filtering through of the presence of US engineers in Northern Ireland, which soon began to concern Bryan and G2. It was suspected that these engineers had a military background, but the Irish authorities were being largely kept in the dark by both the British and Northern Ireland governments and by the American authorities. While the USA remained out of the war, it was becoming increasingly likely that tensions in the east might force it to enter, especially in light of increased Japanese aggression in the Pacific. Sure enough, these fears would be realised.

On 17 September 1940, Hirohito's Japan entered the war, signing the Tripartite Pact with Germany and Italy to further bolster the Axis threat. The US policy of isolation was soon to be met with a devasting attack in the east, and Ireland and G2 would almost immediately come under renewed pressure from many quarters. With the war going firmly in Hitler's favour, it seemed that all hope was lost. Bryan and his colleagues in G2 were Ireland's last line of defence and the future and security of the nation rested on their shoulders. Ireland was now at its most vulnerable, insecure and unable to distinguish friend from foe.

VII

OUR FRIENDS AND ALLIES?

We do not question the Irish government's efforts to stop Axis spy activity. But it would be a mistake to think that the Axis powers will not exploit the conditions in Ireland, as they have in other countries.

CORDELL HULL, 47TH UNITED STATES
SECRETARY OF STATE (1933–44)

The USA was isolated, content to keep out of any future conflict – that much was clear. The high casualty rate of World War I coupled with the economic turmoil unleashed by the Wall Street Crash and subsequent Great Depression had firmly pushed American foreign policy towards isolationism. It was a world view that was widely supported by the American people and unlikely to be abandoned in the short term as the conflict in Europe raged. The whole isolationist project was deeply ingrained in the American psyche, stretching back to the presidency of George Washington, who in his farewell address urged his American countrymen to avoid entanglement in European conflicts:

Why forgo the advantages of so peculiar a situation? Why quit our own to stand upon foreign ground? Why, by interweaving our destiny with that of any part of Europe, entangle our peace and prosperity in the toils of European ambition, rivalship, interest, humour or caprice?

Washington's words provided succour to those who in the 1930s advocated a policy of non-involvement in European wars. This was largely augmented by the expanse of the Atlantic Ocean; however, technological advances made this seemingly unbridgeable divide smaller. US intervention in World War I under President Woodrow Wilson in order, as he saw it, to help maintain world order was considered to have been foolhardy and it was widely felt that the USA's high casualty rate outweighed the benefits. The isolationist movement in the United States was a broad church, crossing both ideological and party divides. It had the support of conservatives, liberals, Democrats and Republicans as well as peace activists like Fr Charles Edward Coughlin, who often addressed the matter on public radio. It was widely supported by prominent business owners and by celebrity figures such as the aviator Charles Lindbergh, who said in 1941 that 'the United States ought to fight any nation that attempted to meddle in the affairs of the western hemisphere. However ... American soldiers ought not to have to "fight everybody in the world who prefers some other system of life to ours".

Such was the determination of the American body politic to avoid another war that it seemed unlikely that the rise of Adolf Hitler and Japanese expansion in the east would deter the nation from its policy of isolationism. The US Congress passed a series of Neutrality Acts, the first of which, enacted in 1935, sought to prohibit 'the export of arms, ammunition, and implements of war from the United States to foreign nations at war and requir[e] arms manufacturers in the United States to apply for an export license'. Much to the dismay of its allies in Europe, it seemed that any US involvement in World War II was a distant and remote possibility.

Nazi Germany was acutely aware that any involvement by the USA in the war would be disastrous for Germany. As a result, Hitler instructed Admiral Canaris to avoid doing anything that would spur the USA into the war on the Allied side or to encourage it to give aid to Britain. The Führer's concerns were well founded. The Abwehr had been conducting operations in the USA well before the outbreak of the war in Europe, something the American intelligence services were aware of. Throughout the late 1930s and until the summer of 1940, Abwehr agents in the United States were sending intelligence relating to the US Navy, including blueprints of ships, aircraft carriers and destroyers, back to their handlers in Germany. They also reported widely on Anglo-American arms deals and on shipping convoys and ship movements along the entire eastern seaboard. On 8 June 1940, Hitler personally instructed

Canaris to discontinue any subversive activities in the USA. However, by late 1941 geopolitics would have changed utterly. On 27 September 1940, Hitler sent Foreign Minister Joachim von Ribbentrop to Japan to sign the Tripartite Pact between Germany, Italy and Japan, which sought to deter the USA entering the war to aid the British. This was to have mutual benefit for the three nations; it sought to aid Germany and Italy in their North African and Mediterranean campaigns and to weaken British colonies in Southeast Asia, clearing the way for Japanese invasion. It was the calm before the storm.

By September 1941, the Japanese began expanding southwards into Indochina, provoking the USA, the UK and other Western powers into freezing Japanese assets and placing economic sanctions on the regime. Encouraged by German support for any declaration of war on the USA, the Japanese made their intentions to attack the US Pacific fleet known to Hitler and Ribbentrop in November 1941. Within a month they had launched a deadly attack on an unsuspecting US Navy. On the morning of 7 December 1941, the Imperial Japanese Naval Air Service attacked the United States naval base at Pearl Harbor on the island of Oahu, Hawaii. Its goal was to destroy or damage as much of the US fleet as possible to prevent it responding to Japanese operations taking place in US, Dutch and British territories in Southeast Asia on the same day. The United States was convulsed in shock and outrage. The following day, Congress declared war on the Empire of Japan, bringing the United States into a global war for the second time in the twentieth century.

Almost immediately, Ireland and its strategic location came into renewed focus for the American authorities. Along the western approaches to Europe there would be a roughly 700-mile-long roughly rectangular area, including Ireland, within which safe passage for wartime shipping and supplies to Britain could be assured. President Roosevelt was a critic of Irish neutrality, even though America itself had been neutral up to this point, a fact that wasn't lost on G2, which was adamant that Ireland would not to be bullied into entering the war. As Douglas Gageby later said:

The Americans, of course, were neutral, until they were bombed into the war. They did very well out of their neutrality, you know; they got all the British destroyers and got various free bases, British gold and assets abroad just vanished. They were doing alright and suddenly they come into the war and 'Ireland must come in!' Cowardly! Ridiculous! You know? Bastards, you know! The only person who went willingly into the war was, the only country surely, was Britain.

The USA's attitude was largely driven by American press reports that Hempel had had a secret radio in the German Legation in Dublin; and speculation was rife that the IRA could be used as a fifth column with which to help attack Britain. The ongoing security situation in relation to Hermann Görtz and the other German spies only served to add fuel to the fire. Before the Japanese attack on Pearl Harbor the USA had prevented its ships entering the war zone along the western approaches, despite Irish fears that this would damage US–Irish trade. This policy made it extremely difficult for Americans to travel to Ireland and US–Irish relations further deteriorated.

In December 1941, President Roosevelt sent US Under Secretary for War Robert P. Patterson to Ireland. Patterson's role at the War Department was to oversee the mobilisation of the armed forces before and during the USA's involvement in World War II. His visit to Ireland left him dismayed and disheartened by Ireland's policy of neutrality. By the time of the attack on Pearl Harbor, Patterson commanded a staff of 1,136 people, of whom 257 were military officers and the remainder civilians. Patterson briefed his superiors in Washington that matters in Ireland were grave from a security point of view and that the country posed a security risk for the Allies, largely due to the issue of the Treaty Ports and ongoing issues with German parachutists. However, US discontent with Irish neutrality stretched back much further to the outbreak of the war, a time when the USA itself was unaligned in the conflict. US–Irish relations was to prove yet another serious security challenge for Bryan and his colleagues in G2.

Disharmony between the USA and Ireland owed much from a diplomatic point of view to the American representative in Ireland, David Gray, who had done much to undermine relations between the two countries from the moment he arrived. Officially styled Envoy Extraordinary and Minister Plenipotentiary to Ireland, Gray succeeded John Clarence Cudahy in the role on 16 February 1940, presenting his credentials to President Douglas Hyde at Áras an Uachtaráin on 15 April. Gray's appointment was controversial and drew accusations of nepotism – he was an uncle through marriage of First Lady Eleanor Roosevelt, which essentially gave Gray a direct line to the White House. Despite the curious nature of his appointment, Gray's academic credentials and war record could not be gainsaid. Gray, who was originally from Buffalo in New York State, had served with the American Expeditionary Forces in France in World War I and was highly decorated, being awarded both the Croix de Guerre and the Légion d'honneur. After the war he graduated with a PhD from Bowdoin College in Brunswick, Maine in 1925.

Gray proved obstinate in relation to Irish neutrality and his relationship with Taoiseach Éamon de Valera got off to a bad start when in one of their first meetings he accused him of collaborating with the Germans. Privately he considered de Valera self-obsessed and unlikely to do business on anything but his own terms. President Roosevelt himself disapproved of Irish neutrality and had communicated his views to the Irish Ambassador in the USA, Robert Brennan. Gray, as a member of the Roosevelt family, reiterated those views in his diplomatic role and sought, at Roosevelt's behest, to persuade de Valera to enter the war on the Allied side. Much to de Valera's discontent, Gray was prepared to work with the British to achieve this objective. Gray often spoke scathingly of de Valera in private correspondence with Roosevelt, referring to him as neither 'Pro German nor Anti British but Pro de Valera'. In one particularly withering letter he lambasted what he considered de Valera's self-importance:

> Since that time there is no record of his having done what was generous or noble or wise, only what he believed served 'the Cause' ... he regarded himself as 'the Cause' ... What was good for de Valera became good for Ireland. There was no honest view other than his ... he dedicated himself to justifying his mistakes and making them stand in history as not being mistakes.

His paranoia that the Irish were secretly pro-Nazi was obvious to de Valera and his officials and did much to damage relations between the two nations. Indeed, Gray had in May 1940 gone as far as to wire the American Secretary of State, Cordell Hull, to outline his views on Ireland. Gray doubted the ability of the Irish Army to deal with an Axis parachute invasion, particularly if it was coupled with a seaborne invasion or carried out with the aid of a fifth column like the IRA. Hull told Gray to contact de Valera and to reiterate that Ireland enjoyed a unique place in American hearts and that the USA would assist Ireland in some ways, but only within the limits of Irish neutrality. It was felt that any overt statement that Ireland was important to US interests would be counter-productive and could put Irish safety from Axis attack in extreme peril.

Matters reached another critical point when Irish Ambassador to Washington Robert Brennan attempted to purchase artillery, armoured cars and anti-aircraft guns from the United States in 1940. The weapons were supplemented by a request for Lee–Enfield rifles, which were intended to bolster Irish security back home. However, the plan ran into problems with the Americans. De Valera requested help with the purchase, but David Gray felt that it wasn't wise to help Ireland defend its neutrality. In the end the shipment of rifles went to Canada, the Americans taking the view that if the British wanted Ireland to have guns, they could have provided them themselves; and any American intervention would have eroded confidence in the special relationship between the USA and the UK. But the British didn't have a problem with the Irish receiving weapons as long as it didn't affect supplies to the UK. Gray continued to apply pressure to de Valera in relation to the British use of Treaty Ports as well as myriad other issues, which further damaged the relationship between the two men.

Gray even went as far as to tell de Valera that the Irish were enjoying national security and a lack of rationing at the expense of the Allies, and that if he didn't consider entering the war on the Allied side there might be a change in public opinion towards the Irish in the United States. Gray's views irritated de Valera. He felt offended that America, which had been neutral until the Japanese attack, would deny the right of Ireland to also be neutral. It was a charge that Gray denied and he reminded de Valera that all Irish rights were dependent on American public opinion. These angry exchanges only served to make de Valera double down on the policy of neutrality, which, he believed, was essential to protect Irish sovereignty. Gray's intransigence neglected to account for the fact that Ireland had virtually no air force and had no protection whatsoever in the event of an Axis air raid.

In March 1941, Frank Aiken, the Defence Minister, travelled to Washington on a diplomatic mission to state the Irish case in relation to its neutrality and retention of the Treaty Ports and to seek support to procure arms for defence purposes. During the visit he met with both President Roosevelt and Secretary Hull. Gray was suspicious of Aiken from the outset due to his background in the IRA and role as former Chief of Staff as well as his strong anti-British views. He believed the true intent of Aiken's mission was to elicit support for Irish neutrality from the President using the lever of Irish sentiment. In any case, whatever Aiken's intent, he was unsuccessful in convincing Roosevelt that the Irish had anything to fear with regard to a British invasion to seize the Treaty Ports, although he seemed to gain some assurances as regards the ill-fated Canadian arms. Aiken described his visit to the Oval Office in a dictated report to the Taoiseach in August 1941:

> The interview, which was scheduled to last 10 minutes, lasted three-quarters of an hour, although we were interrupted every few minutes after the 10 had elapsed by the President's secretary coming in with remarks to the President about various engagements, &c. &c. The interview was finally terminated in the presence of three or four negros who entered and placed the President's lunch on the table. Towards the conclusion of the interview, I asked the President if I might report that we had his sympathy in our stand against aggression. He said, German aggression? surely. I said, British aggression too. He said, nonsense, there is no fear of a British aggression. I said we had asked the British officially for assurance that they would not attack us and that they had refused to give it to us. He again said, nonsense. The British have no thought of attacking you and I am certain Churchill would tell me so. I said, Mr President, will you ask Mr Churchill, and he said yes. We wound up the interview by asking him to let us have a definite reply on the question of arms and ships and the assurance from Mr Churchill within a few days. He promised to let us have the reply and we bade him good-bye.

Aiken also met with Secretary Hull, who treated the minister to a long lecture on his dislike of Hitler, how he had foreseen what was coming with Germany and how he had tried to persuade other countries of what was going to happen. Aiken gave Hull a letter from de Valera outlining his view that it was hard to 'get the British to do the proper thing'. Hull complimented Ireland and informed Aiken of his view that the Germans and Japanese were waging a war of total conquest and he intended to get 35 or 40 countries together in a broad programme of co-operation. A few weeks later Hull contacted Gray in Dublin and informed him of Aiken's hostility towards the British and his view that Aiken was ignorant of the fact that future Irish security and safety depended squarely on an Allied victory. Hull also told Gray that while they didn't question Ireland's right to stay neutral, he believed that Ireland's request for arms would have to be met through co-operation with Britain and other democracies supporting the Allies.

Pressure from the USA was to continue after the attack on Pearl Harbor, albeit in more subtle ways. At Christmas 1941 Cordell Hull gave Robert Brennan a message to pass to de Valera. In the communication Hull outlined the differences between neutrality and giving encouragement to Germany and reiterated that the current freedoms enjoyed by Ireland could only continue if there was a united front against Hitler's policies of enslavement and conquest. This essentially amounted to a final push by Roosevelt to get de Valera to co-operate in a more satisfactory manner with the United States. Having reached the end of his tether with Gray, de Valera told Hull that Ireland would defend itself if there was a German attack and would continue to request arms from the United States. Roosevelt would later claim that de Valera had 'his head in the clouds'.

The true extent of American neutrality before it entered the war was evidenced by the fact that the Americans had flown hundreds of technicians and workmen to offer support to the British in building military bases in Northern Ireland, in particular Belfast and Londonderry. They had also sent workmen to Scotland. Hull was less than helpful when the presence of these workmen was queried by Robert Brennan. He told the Irish Ambassador that it was none of his business; seeing as the British had sovereignty of Northern Ireland, it was a matter for them. US technicians had begun arriving in Northern Ireland from the summer of 1941, and de Valera was irked that he had not been informed, if only as a matter of courtesy.

The Irish government, through Articles 2 and 3 of the 1937 Constitution, laid claim to the entire island of Ireland and de Valera personally viewed partition as an injustice as bad as anything that could be perpetrated by the Germans or anyone else. Hull witheringly informed de Valera that if he cared so much about the six counties of Northern Ireland he should have protested when they were attacked by the Luftwaffe in April and May 1941. The statement infuriated de Valera – he had made a formal protest to Berlin and had condemned the attack outright in a speech in Castlebar, County Mayo on 20 April 1941:

> In the past, and probably in the present, too, a number of them did not see eye to eye with us politically, but they are our people – we are one and the same people – and their sorrows in the present instance are also our sorrows; and I want to say to them that any help we can give to them in the present time we will give to them wholeheartedly, believing that were the circumstances reversed they would also give us their help wholeheartedly.

Aiken had also weighed in on the Belfast Blitz from Boston, stating that 'the people of Belfast are Irish too'. Brennan argued that the American presence in Northern Ireland was tantamount to an acceptance by the Americans of partition. The British argued that American technicians were privately employed and their presence in Ulster didn't therefore constitute a breach of either American or Irish sovereignty and neutrality.

Bryan and his colleagues kept their own counsel on the arrival of American technicians in Northern Ireland, but they believed that they were there because it had become inevitable that the USA would enter the war. Bryan, speaking in the Carter tapes, believed that it was only a matter of time before the USA was goaded into action:

> They were military bases in anticipation of America entering the war. I suppose what they were building at the time were facilities for the

British, at Derry, because the convoys and the destroyers and all that
sort of thing were coming into Derry. They're in my mind mainly in
connection with Derry. But they were also going on in Scotland and
probably in Belfast, but it's in Derry I think mainly.

The influx of American troops on to the island of Ireland brought with
it its own security issues for Bryan and G2. On occasion American soldiers
ventured as far as Dublin to socialise and often their exploits were monitored by the security service. During one such trip an American soldier
visited a bridge tournament in Dublin and became heavily intoxicated. In a
fit of rage, he stabbed his opponent in the chest with a standard issue army
knife. In the same taped interview Bryan recalled the incident and the major
security issue it raised:

> There was a bridge conference in Dublin. An American soldier came
> down here from Northern Ireland, got a lot to drink, ran amok, assaulted
> and knifed one of the people at the tournament. Before he was arrested,
> he was on his way back over the border.

Bryan believed that the American soldier could easily have murdered
his victim, but instead of facing arrest and prosecution for the crime he
was spirited back over the border by the Garda Special Branch. Despite the
fact that the tournament was attended by people from all over Ireland the
incident was never reported in any papers. The affair gave a true reflection
of the nature of Ireland's attitude to the Americans.

The extent to which the Irish took a softly-softly approach to the USA
in relation to neutrality is quite stark; however, there were occasions when
the Irish applied a rigidity that served to irk the Americans. This is perhaps
best illustrated by the arrival in Ireland of two high-ranking American personalities at the midpoint of the war. In November 1942, First Lady Eleanor
Roosevelt paid a visit to Northern Ireland en route to England to boost
morale among US troops stationed there. She was welcomed enthusiastically by the Prime Minister of Northern Ireland, John Miller Andrews, who
publicly extolled the bravery of American troops in the Pacific and North

Africa. Andrews patriotically referred to Northern Ireland and America as 'comrades in arms' in front of a crowd of 25 journalists from the White House Press Corps, who had accompanied the First Lady on her trip.

Despite the triumphalism of Mrs Roosevelt's trip to the North, she had to transit through the South of Ireland, having been forced by bad weather into an impromptu landing at Foynes, County Limerick. Her brief sojourn in the Irish Free State was very different from her visit to the North. Foynes flying boat base was deemed a safe landing site as it had been in regular use for transatlantic flights – most planes had until now lacked sufficient flying range for non-stop transatlantic flights. News of Mrs Roosevelt's impromptu landing in Foynes reached an American diplomat in Cork via diplomatic cable. He promptly told a colleague in Cork to see if he could come and meet the First Lady. Both Americans had served in Russia and they conversed in Russian in order to keep the sensitive matter under wraps. They and the First Lady were astonished when G2 arrived at Foynes – which led the Americans to believe that G2 had been monitoring their communications. Mrs Roosevelt was also irked by the fact that some of the military personnel accompanying her were forced to change into civilian clothes when on Irish soil in order to comply with the rules of neutrality.

The second incident involved a plane crash that took place in early 1943. While the plane was unarmed, the chief passenger was of huge importance. On 15 January 1943 a B-17 Flying Fortress codenamed 'Stinky' carrying Major General Jacob Devers crash landed in Athenry, County Galway. Devers was a high-ranking member of the American forces who was later to hold the rank of Commanding General of the United States Armored Force and also became a four-star general. Also on board was Major General Edward Hale Brooks, who would go on to play an important role in the Normandy landings. The Flying Fortress had been trying to find a safe place to land as it was running low on fuel, but the terrain near Athenry made this impossible and with the fuel almost empty it was decided to crash-land the aircraft.

Devers and his crew had left Gibraltar earlier in the day en route to England but had lost their way near the Bay of Biscay. The Flying Fortress was soon desperately off course, despite navigational signals being sent by the RAF to help redirect them. Captain Thomas Hulings had been directed by Major General Devers to position the aircraft far out into the Atlantic to avoid German forces near Brest off the coast of Brittany in France, and this took the aircraft into Irish airspace. Hulings had spotted a strip of land along the Dublin–Galway railway line where he felt that he could make a safe landing. After circling Athenry for 15 minutes the Flying Fortress's fuel tanks were empty and Hullings landed the plane with an almighty crash, sending debris flying through the air.

The ferocious sound of the crash startled students in the local agricultural college as well as members of the LDF, who immediately rushed to the site. Devers managed to crawl to safety through the rear section of the plane and although the aircraft was severely damaged, amazingly the entire crew had survived unscathed. As Devers got to his feet, he was greeted by the muzzle of a rifle held by a young LDF recruit, who started at the American in disbelief. Devers dusted himself off and dryly remarked to the young LDF recruit, 'Son, point that thing away. It might go off and hurt someone.' Such was the commotion that the Dublin–Galway train stopped so its passengers could get a closer look at what was going on. A crowd soon gathered and when Devers explained that he was on a friendly mission, he and the other survivors were brought to the nearby Railway Hotel, where they were treated to a lavish meal and reception which Devers insisted on paying for. During the meal Devers received a phone call from David Gray, who assured him that all would be well and not to discuss the matter in too much detail over the phone. Devers turned over custody of the Flying Fortress to the townspeople and he and his men made their way to Northern Ireland, where they were greeted at the border by British officials and then re-routed to London. Four months later Devers was appointed overall commander of US army forces in Europe.

The incident is still celebrated in Athenry today and many of the relatives on either side of the Atlantic are still in touch. Despite his joviality, Hempel was apoplectic with rage when he heard about the favouritism shown towards the Americans. One of the passengers on the train happened to be a German national who knew Hempel, and he later told him what had happened. The man in question, Hans Becker, was unknown to the security forces, and according to Dan Bryan G2 had no evidence that he was involved in espionage. The tapes reveal that:

Becker was a fella who was here during the war. We've never associated him with anything – espionage or nefarious activities of any kind – but he was isolated here during the war. I don't know what brought him here but he ran German language classes here and even during the war they were very successful. He must have been in some way associated, interested, in Irish studies because I think he went to the Irish-speaking areas and he moved around the country a lot. Although there was never any evidence ever that he had anything to do with German intelligence or espionage or anything else, he attracted attention. But nothing was ever proven.

Furious at being told about the incident second-hand, Hempel drove to Athenry to inspect the aircraft himself. In a fit of rage, he promptly informed de Valera that under the 1907 Hague Convention Ireland was strictly bound by the rules of neutrality in wartime. In order to placate Hempel, the Irish government told him that the plane had been converted to civilian use to ferry passengers from Canada to Britain and therefore neutrality hadn't been breached; and the Swedish government had released a German aircraft in similar circumstances. The ruse seemed to work and Hempel was pacified. In reality it may have been Hempel's own precarious position that persuaded him to drop the matter.

Despite the Roosevelt incident, Ireland's relationship with the United States was more than clear, but the American Ambassador was still not convinced of Ireland's commitment to the Allies. David Gray's views were also largely out of step with the OSS. Shortly after its formation, the OSS sent four agents to Ireland to report on what was happening there and to gather intelligence in relation to Ireland's ability to deal with Axis spies. Not much is known about one of the spies, but the other three left accounts of their activities in Ireland in interviews, published articles or, in the case of one of them, a book. Ervin Ross 'Spike' Marlin was the OSS agent in charge sent to Ireland during the war and was appointed under the cover of working at the embassy as Gray's 'special assistant'. He was recruited for the role by Whitney Shepardson, chief of the British branch of the OSS, whose wife knew Marlin from their days as students at Trinity College Dublin. Marlin was well acquainted with Irish affairs, having studied at Trinity from 1929 to 1932, graduating with a BA in history. He married Hilda van Stockum in Dublin on 27 June 1932.

Marlin didn't do much to hide his true role at the embassy and it was clear to many from the outset that he was a member of the OSS. Despite this no moves were made by the Irish authorities to expel Marlin, who kept his handler, Colonel David K. E. Bruce, informed of his observations and findings in Ireland. Bruce headed the European branch of the OSS from a base in London and co-ordinated espionage activities behind enemy lines for the US Armed Forces branches. He also helped carry out other OSS functions, including propaganda, subversion and post-war planning. Marlin had a good working relationship with G2 and worked well with Dan Bryan, who supplied him with information that was fed back into the OSS.

One piece of intelligence that was passed on was the total number of IRA men – almost 3,000 – who were interned in Ireland. Information such as this helped persuade Marlin that Irish security was adequate to rebuff any German threats. Bryan also supplied Marlin with information on radio interceptions, submarine and aeroplane sightings, and the names and addresses of American nationals with whom captured German spies had been communicating. The OSS prepared index cards for everyone mentioned in the reports, and Bryan and his colleagues in G2 passed on so much information that the cards soon numbered over 4,000. Marlin never shared any similar information with Bryan; and Bryan never asked him. He assumed that the information flow was one-way.

Marlin was one small part of a large intelligence network operating in Ireland at various different levels. Bryan reveals in the tapes that co-operating with Marlin was simply part of the bigger picture:

There was much contact going on, not between my department and the US but between External Affairs and the US for some years and there were people in the OSS who had been in the diplomatic service during the war. There was a man called Hugh Wilson, who was a well-known diplomat. He was OSS for a while. There were always Americans coming and going and they were encouraged to come here, and political Americans as well as official Americans. The head of the OSS was Bill

Donovan and he had a brother who was a Dominican priest and religion always counts in Ireland. There were always people like that coming and going and seeing our people in External Affairs. External Affairs agreed that Spike Marlin, who had been a student in Trinity College, could come in and go around and around the country. It was a year before Marlin was officially accredited to me so to speak and when he was accredited it was a result of a visit made here by David Bruce.

The working relationship between Marlin and Bryan was so good that they were to remain friends long after the war.

Marlin was soon joined in Ireland by a second OSS spy named Roland Blenner-Hassett, an Irish American with roots in County Kerry. Blenner-Hassett was dispatched to follow up on reports gathered by Robert P. Patterson that Kerry, in particular the Tralee area and the Dingle peninsula, was a hive of German spy activity. This was perhaps a reference to the ill-fated missions of Walter Simon and Wilhelm Preetz. Blenner-Hassett knew the area well. He had emigrated from Tralee to the USA in 1920 to study at Harvard, where he earned a doctorate in philology, and his cover in Kerry was that he was working as a folklore collector. However, he stood out like a sore thumb and the locals soon got wind of his true profession. After four months he requested a transfer out of Ireland because his cover had been blown and because he had no information to gather and report on. Both Blenner-Hassett and Marlin were satisfied that G2 was doing a good job in relation to security matters and that it was doing all it could to apprehend any German spies entering Ireland. Marlin also expressed his view that the IRA was not a serious threat as a fifth column: 'The IRA … in Eire completely lacks anything resembling cohesion, organisation or discipline.'

These views brought Marlin into direct conflict with Gray, who was determined to find fault with the Irish authorities even if there was no reason to do so. Gray wanted Marlin to leave Ireland because he felt undermined by Marlin's good working relationship with Bryan and G2. Colonel Bruce visited Marlin in Dublin in early 1943 and met with Bryan, other members of G2 and the Garda Special Branch. Bryan provided Bruce and the OSS

with information on German spies and the code and ciphers they were
using as well as technical information, supplied by Dr Richard Hayes of the
National Library, on how to break them. Gray was adamant that only he
should be the direct conduit between the USA and Ireland and as a result
it was decided that Marlin would be transferred to the OSS London Office,
where he would maintain contact with Bryan through John Belton of the
Irish Legation in London. Marlin would make occasional visits to Dublin
to liaise with Bryan on matters of mutual concern. After the war he was
transferred to Montreal. An ardent believer that Ireland should enter the
war on the Allied side, Marlin still maintained friendly relations with the
authorities for many years after the war. Joseph Walshe at the Department
of External Affairs wrote to Marlin expressing his warm wishes shortly after
Marlin's departure from Dublin:

> I know you always held tenaciously, and strongly expressed the view, that
> we were wrong to be neutral. But some day I hope to convince you that,
> notwithstanding an increased friendliness in our relations with Britain
> (one of the astonishing results of the war in this part of the world), we
> could never quite resign ourselves to the possibilities and consequences
> of the inevitable re-occupation by British forces. If you, as an American,
> could imagine your feelings were the British still occupying the State of
> Massachusetts, you would be making a good approach to realising the
> Irish attitude. In a people which so narrowly escaped absorption, the
> strongest of all desires is to assert and defend its national distinctiveness.
> We are ready to make any sacrifices and to suffer any obloquy to remain
> Irish and to keep our independence, and I believe that your government,
> once that fundamental principle is accepted by them, will find us ready
> to take part wholeheartedly in devising an international organisation
> for the common good of all peoples.

> I hope that, when the war is over, you and your family will be able to
> take a long holiday in this country, and I can assure you that you will
> be most heartily welcomed.

A third OSS agent, Martin S. Quigley, was sent to Ireland in 1943 to evaluate Irish neutrality and to make clandestine reports back to Washington on
what he saw and observed. Quigley's cover story was that he was working for
the film industry at the behest of Will H. Hays, then President of the Motion
Picture Producers and Distributors of America. Quigley was assigned to the
office of Dr Richard Francis Hayes, the Irish National Film Censor (not to
be confused with Dr Richard J. Hayes the codebreaker and Director of the
National Library of Ireland). Richard F. Hayes, a former TD and veteran of
the 1916 Rising, served as film censor from 1941 to 1954 and also had a stint as
Director of the Abbey Theatre. A devout Catholic, he infamously censored
elements of Walt Disney's 1940 film *Fantasia* owing to what he described as
the films 'materialistic portrayal of the origins of life'.

Quigley was the only OSS agent to remain in Ireland without having
his cover blown; however, Dan Bryan was suspicious of him and had him
under constant observation by G2 officers. Despite the level of scrutiny
he was under, Quigley managed to report regularly back to Washington,
although much of the material he observed was routine and mundane. He
found Hayes's taste in film and aversion to risqué films typical of the Irish
Catholic mindset. In case of an emergency, the OSS in Washington gave
Quigley a means of identifying himself to the American Legation; he was to
approach the legation and ask, 'Do you happen to know where the Gallow
Glasses originated?', to which he would receive the answer 'The Hebrides'.
Quigley was given a largely free role in Ireland and was to maintain his
cover at all costs. He described his role in detail as outlined to him by the
OSS in a subsequent memoir:

> Your territory is Ireland. You will not be the only OSS representative
> in Ireland, but you will not report to any other representative there. It
> would be well for you to confine yourself in the beginning very carefully
> to the direct and pressing interests of the association. You will be expected
> to move slowly and cautiously with your work for the office [the OSS].

During his time in Ireland, Quigley observed that the country was neutral in name alone and that it had made a number of important contributions

to the war effort without seeking reward or notoriety. He also noted how Ireland was genuine in some aspects of its neutrality, given the fact that the German and Japanese diplomatic mission were maintained throughout the war. He reported that the German Legation and Hempel in particular were well received in Irish society, especially by the press; but that Japanese consular staff suddenly became *persona non grata* after the attack on Pearl Harbor. Quigley said that some Irish people appeared to be pro-German, but that this may have been more to do with a deep-seated hatred of the British rather than, for example, any feelings of anti-Semitism. This was hardly a surprise, given that the War of Independence was still alive in Irish popular memory and many of the political class were veterans of that campaign. He estimated that there were never more than a few thousand pro-German Irish people in Ireland and that this dwindled considerably when the truth about the Nazis' activities became more widely known. Among those who publicly espoused pro-German and anti-Semitic views were members of the political class.

In 1943, Laois TD Oliver J. Flanagan publicly decried the Emergency Powers Act brought in to deal with the IRA, saying that such powers should instead be used against the Jewish community in Ireland.

> I have seen that most of these Emergency Acts were always directed against Republicanism. How is it that we do not see any of these Acts directed against the Jews, who crucified Our Saviour 1900 years ago, and who are crucifying us every day in the week? How is it that we do not see them directed against the Masonic Order? How is it that the IRA is considered an illegal organisation while the Masonic Order is not considered an illegal organisation?

Dan Breen, TD for Tipperary, was infamous for his pro-Axis views. Breen, whose life has been largely eulogised, was notoriously involved in the ambush at Soloheadbeg that resulted in the murder of two RIC men. In 1943 Breen sent birthday wishes to Hitler, expressing his hope that Hitler would live long to 'lead Europe on the road to peace, security and happiness'. Notwithstanding the few pro-German exceptions, Quigley was adamant that there was no pro-Japanese sentiment. This can perhaps be put down to strong historical ties with the USA and sympathy for the USA in the wake of the Pearl Harbor attack.

Quigley was recalled from Ireland in December 1943. Because of Allied successes in the war at this point, it was considered unnecessary to send any more OSS agents back to Ireland, either overtly or covertly. Quigley left the OSS at the end of the war and had a distinguished career as the author of several books on the history of motion pictures.

In 1943, Ireland was again targeted by German intelligence agencies. This time it was the Sicherheitsdienst (SD), the intelligence branch of the Schutzstaffel (SS). The SD decided to deploy two Irish nationals, John Francis O'Reilly and John Kenny, who had been living in the Channel Islands.

John Francis O'Reilly, a native of Kilkee, County Clare, was christened by his SD handlers 'Agent V-Mann'. The SD described him as 'an enthusiastic Irish patriot'. Born in August 1916, O'Reilly was the son of RIC constable Bernard O'Reilly, who arrested Sir Roger Casement on Banna Strand on foot of Casement's failed attempt to land arms for the Easter Rising. O'Reilly worked in London until June 1940. Then, while he was on holiday in the Channel Islands, he became embroiled in the German invasion of Jersey, and he eventually made his way to Germany, where he volunteered his services as a spy. He may have simply hoped that he would be sent home to Ireland; it's doubtful that he really believed in any Nazi ideology.

O'Reilly was described by the SD as 'typically Irish looking', a tall man with light red hair, blue eyes and a healthy reddish-brown skin colour. He was said to have been active in the IRA in his youth and maintained a close connection with the movement. This, however, may have been an exaggeration on O'Reilly's part. The SD was satisfied that O'Reilly was 'modest in his way of life and reserved' and that he made 'an excellent and trustworthy impression'.

O'Reilly and Kenny were parachuted into County Clare in December 1943. O'Reilly was carrying a unique new enciphering method based on a code wheel system. The SD hoped that O'Reilly and Kenny – who was tasked with operating the radio set – could obtain information for the purposes of espionage in Northern Ireland. It was particularly interested in any naval and air intelligence O'Reilly could glean in Londonderry, Belfast and, once he had left Ireland, in Liverpool. It was hoped that O'Reilly and Kenny could then travel to Britain. While he was in Ireland O'Reilly would be able to benefit from lodgings offered by his 'considerable' IRA connections. In fact O'Reilly's time in Ireland was fraught with misadventure.

Both men were apprehended within 24 hours of their arrival into Ireland, O'Reilly on 16 December 1943 and Kenny three days later. O'Reilly escaped from jail on 6 July the following year and made his way back to County Clare, but he was again apprehended and reinterned in Arbour Hill Prison. While he was incarcerated, Dan Bryan dispatched Richard Hayes to interrogate him. Hayes found O'Reilly a very unreliable person and disliked him personally – he felt that he was cocky and given to 'red herrings'. Hayes noticed that O'Reilly had been using a code wheel cipher to communicate with his handlers while on the outside and observed some rough work in O'Reilly's cell that he had used to compose messages. Hayes was able to piece these together and ultimately break the code. He passed this information to Dan Bryan, who shared it with Marlin and the Liddells. While the rough work at first seemed to be unimportant, it was later used to great effect in the Battle of the Bulge, after the Germans changed the coding mechanism in relation to tank movements.

Although both O'Reilly and Kenny were captured swiftly and interned in Arbour Hill, and Hayes and Bryan had gleaned crucial information on the O'Reilly cipher, the arrival of the two men in Ireland caused further friction between American envoy David Gray and the Irish government, which prompted Gray to take his most drastic course of action yet.

Gray's discontent with the Irish reached its zenith with what became known as the 'American Note'. In a letter to de Valera written in February 1944, Gray outlined his view that Irish neutrality was operating in favour of the Axis powers and against the United Nations, which, he told the Taoiseach, Ireland relied upon for its security and the maintenance of the Irish economy. Gray argued that neutrality, in addition to Ireland's close geographical proximity to Britain, created the conditions for Axis spies to be able to operate in Ireland at a highly organised level. He added that this was denied to the United States by distance. Gray also referred to the border with Northern Ireland and the fact that its porous nature only exacerbated the problem. Gray's withering criticism also made direct reference to German spies:

Axis agents enjoy almost unrestricted opportunity for bringing military information of vital importance from Great Britain and Northern Ireland into Ireland and from there transmitting it by various routes and methods to Germany ... We request therefore that the Irish government take appropriate steps for the recall of German and Japanese representatives in Ireland. We should be lacking in candour if we did not state our hope that this action will take the form of severance of all diplomatic relations between Ireland and these two countries. You will, of course, readily understand the compelling reasons why we ask as an absolute minimum the removal of these Axis representatives whose presence in Ireland must inevitably be regarded as constituting a danger to the lives of American soldiers and to the success of Allied military operations.

Following delivery of the letter to de Valera, the Department of External Affairs proposed a security conference with MI5 and the OSS. Marlin represented the American side at the conference, alongside Hubert Will, who headed the OSS Counter-Intelligence Section in Europe, while Dan Bryan represented G2 and was accompanied by a representative of the Garda Special Branch. At this point it was officially decided that Marlin would be assigned to Dan Bryan and work with him directly until such time as he was recalled to the United States.

De Valera's deftness at dealing with Gray and the Americans and resisting British claims on the Treaty Ports won him the admiration of much of the Irish public, and this wasn't lost on Bryan and his colleagues in G2. The Carter tapes reveal Bryan's own grudging admiration for the Taoiseach in facing up to Gray:

Mr de Valera's public image was that of Atlas, holding up Ireland but defending it more against the British than Germany. He was a masterful politician, putting him on [a] par with Roosevelt, which was putting him very high. As one of the masterful politicians. He handled that issue very well. On the "22' period and all that, I'm anti de Valera but I'll give him full marks for all that. In a lot of those things his right hand didn't know what his left hand was doing, and as I said to somebody, I was his thumb or first finger for certain purposes.

Gray's mistrust of de Valera was certainly misplaced: G2 was having considerable success in apprehending German spies. The end was in sight, but even though he was behind bars Görtz had been proving that he could be a big problem.

VIII

PRISONERS OF WAR

Our government would, doubtless, be delighted to be rid of both the British and the German internees ... The fact is that the British are expecting more of this country than they do of any other neutral state and, in view of Partition and the recent hostile measures taken against Ireland, it is hard to see why we should meet them in what we know is a quite unprecedented demand.

DR MICHAEL RYNNE, LEGAL ADVISER,
DEPARTMENT OF EXTERNAL AFFAIRS, 1944

Even before Hermann Görtz's arrest in November 1941 the net had already begun to close on the conspirators who had harboured and helped him. In September 1941, Jim O'Donovan had been arrested following a raid on his house in Shankill. The raid was carried out by officers of the Bray Garda district, one of whom, Sergeant Michael Wymes, would later serve as Garda Commissioner from 1968 to 1973. O'Donovan was interned in the Curragh Camp's IRA wing – Tin Town – and released in 1944. He returned to his job in the ESB and died in Dublin in 1979.

On 12 March 1942, Anthony Deery, who had operated Görtz's radio set, was apprehended at an apartment in 47 Upper Clanbrassil Street. During the raid, a series of coded messages were discovered hidden inside a piccolo. These were taken by G2 for further examination by Richard Hayes. Deery himself was interned and released at the end of the war. He returned to his job in the civil service, where he was said by his colleagues to have kept a low profile. He never spoke of his life during the war and lived quietly for the rest of his days.

Görtz himself had been a major thorn in the side of the authorities. Dan Bryan delegated Hayes to personally interrogate him – he felt that Hayes's non-confrontational manner might yield better results than a more aggressive approach. The intervention was very much needed. Görtz had approached the soldiers who were guarding his cell and had tried to manipulate them into passing on coded messages to his supporters on the outside, who in their turn were to bring them to Hempel at the legation. One of those soldiers, a young corporal named Joseph Lynch, continued to pass on messages for Görtz until 1944. While Lynch was eventually discovered and court martialled for his activities, G2 was able to use messages that Görtz tried to smuggle out of Arbour Hill through Sergeant John Power, another young soldier, who, unlike Lynch, immediately brought Görtz's offer to the attention of his superiors. Speaking in the Carter tapes he discusses the incident:

> He [Görtz] offered me £500. You see I was responsible for the posting of sentries and the policing of defence. Well, I mean to a certain extent like, for instance there was a certain post, an elevated post, you know, and they wanted to know if I could have a sentry withdrawn from this post. That was their way of a scheme. So, I told them I couldn't very well do it, that to withdraw the sentry would be very suspicious, that I am willing to help you and now I was offered this money. I was offered £500 so I refused it point blank. I reported it the same evening [to G2]. Word came back to accept any message I got but I refused the money. The thing was that I'd have gotten the £500 at such a place and one thing and another but when I refused, they asked me not to say a word. And I said no, there'd not be another word about it so from that time we went on and I did messages for them and I brought in stuff for them and I went to a certain place in Dublin, did whatever I was instructed to do, went into a café, took out the paper, ordered a cup of coffee. I didn't drink coffee to tell you the truth, but I ordered a coffee in a certain café in Dublin, had a cigarette, read the paper, and when I left, I walked up to the manager and I said 'Are you the manager?' and he says 'I am' and 'You are Mr Power?' and I says 'I am' and he says 'I have a message for

you' so he gives me this parcel. It was coming up to Christmas, you know anyway, the parcel contained all this drilling material.

Sergeant Power was able to keep the ruse going for a considerable period of time and in so doing he was able to help G2 thwart any escape attempts that Görtz was planning. It also gave them greater insight into the networks within which Görtz was working and those outside the jail who were sympathetic to him and willing to aid him. Soon Bryan's attention turned towards breaking the codes found in the Carroll-Held raid and he enlisted Dr Hayes to take on this most important task.

Richard Hayes knew that in order to get any information from Görtz he needed to take a discreet approach. Posing as a Nazi sympathiser to gain Görtz's trust, Hayes eventually coaxed him into divulging some information about his coding system. Both Hayes and Colonel de Buitléar held numerous interrogation sessions with Görtz in his cell. Eventually Görtz showed both men how the system worked but refused to divulge his keyword. On one occasion he decoded some of the more innocent messages from the Carroll-Held raid in an effort to draw attention away from the true intent of the mission. Hayes was suspicious of Görtz and kept the samples Görtz had shown him for further study.

As Hayes was observing Görtz in his cell, he noticed that Görtz was hiding a bunch of papers in his pocket. After arranging for Görtz to be examined for his ulcer problem Hayes was able to retrieve and copy the papers and discovered that Görtz had been planning an elaborate escape attempt through the roof of his cell. A corrugated iron sheet was placed over the roof of Görtz's cell to thwart his plan. While the intervention certainly worked, it only served to increase Görtz's paranoia. Hayes felt there was merit in continuing to observe Görtz in order to gain more clues that might help him break the code.

Then Colonel de Buitléar noticed that Görtz had been burning papers in the grate of his cell. Thinking these might be of some interest, de Buitléar brought them to Dr Hayes, who took them to Trinity College, where a friend of his in the chemistry faculty suggested they treat the burnt fragments of paper with a chemical solution to render them readable. Hayes applied the solution and mounted the treated fragments on glass plates. By holding the plates over a lightbox, it became possible to read them. Hayes was able to decipher a keyword from the burnt fragments and when he combined this with other clues he had extracted from previous sessions with Görtz he was able to determine that the keyword Görtz was using was 'Cathleen Ni Houlihan'. Soon Hayes also extrapolated other keywords, many of which were the names of members of his family. The code system itself was Russian in origin, similar to the codes that had been procured in Russia by Seán Russell and Gerald Boland in 1925.

Anyone who knew Görtz wouldn't have been surprised at his choice of keyword – Görtz was a huge admirer of Yeats and had spent much of his incarceration translating some of his poetry into German. Despite G2's breakthrough, it was decided to keep Görtz in the dark about Hayes's decoding of his cipher and to see if any more important information about the Abwehr could be got out of him. Görtz's messages were passed on to G2 on a near constant basis, while Görtz believed they were still being smuggled out of the prison to republicans and eventually onwards to Hempel. G2 even communicated back to Görtz posing as the German High Command, asking him to compile a complete 80-page report of his time in Ireland and even promoting him to the rank of major for his work in the country.

In early June 1942, all German prisoners were transferred to a specially constructed internment camp at Custume barracks. The escape of Günther Schütz had raised several security issues and it was felt that it would be much easier to prevent any more escapes from the camp in the midlands. The camp at Athlone was overseen by Commandant James Power, one of the most trusted and able men in G2. Hermann Görtz was transferred there in mid-1943, the last spy to be held in the camp. Almost as soon as he arrived in Athlone Hermann Görtz began to devise methods of smuggling coded messages to his supporters on the outside. He emphatically protested his transfer to Athlone and believed that, given his rank in the Luftwaffe, he was above the prisoners there. In reality his mental health had deteriorated significantly and he had become more and more withdrawn. While G2 assumed it had finally got a handle on Görtz, it soon became clear that others unknown to the authorities had been using his code.

In February 1943 one of the huts in Bletchley Park, the wartime location of the UK's Government Code and Cypher School, intercepted a coded message intended for the SD. The message seemed to come from Ireland. The hut in question was known as 'Illicit Signals Oliver Strachey' and its namesake was one of the most esteemed cryptographers ever.

Oliver Strachey was born on 3 November 1874 into a respected and talented family. His father, Richard, was a colonial administrator and his mother, Jane Maria, a writer and suffragist. Oliver's brother Lytton would go on to be an acclaimed writer; another brother, James, became an editor and psychoanalyst. Strachey's only sister, Dorothy, was also a renowned writer. Oliver was educated at Eton College and from an early age showed a huge talent for music. He studied music in Vienna, then was employed for a while in the East India Company before returning to England. Strachey eventually gave up on his dream of becoming a concert pianist and joined the civil service, entering the Foreign Office in 1915. His intellect was immediately noticed and he was drafted into the War Office and put to work in MI1(b), the cryptological unit, where he worked under Major Malcolm Hay. Strachey was sent to Egypt in 1916, narrowly escaping death when his ship was torpedoed.

In the period between the Armistice that ended World War I and the outbreak of the World War II, Strachey joined the Government Code and Cypher School (GC&CS) as a senior assistant and was given crucial work on American naval codes. He continued to work on this area of cryptography for much of the 1920s and in 1934 he made a crucial breakthrough, cracking a hitherto impenetrable Japanese naval code. In the months that followed, Strachey was also involved in breaking the code being used by the Japanese Foreign Office. By the time World War II broke out, Strachey had been given a key role heading the ISOS section at GC&CS at Bletchley Park. The section dealt specifically with German Abwehr intelligence traffic and German manual hand ciphers, which provided a vital insight into the running of German double agents during the war. Strachey's section had many successes, but the intercepted Dublin message proved to be one of their sternest tests.

Strachey's section managed to decode the message, which was intended for the SD and the Nazi Party in Lisbon. The message originated from the ship SS *Edenvale*, which had in its crew a young cook named Christopher

Eastwood. The message had been made out to a worker named Tomas, who was working for the British intelligence services as a double agent. Instead of taking the message to the Germans, he brought it to the British. The message was being transmitted in the same Russian origin code as the Görtz cipher and it referred to a man named Joseph Andrews. Andrews, it turned out, was the acquaintance of Görtz who had informed on him while he was staying in Clontarf and had, unbeknownst to the authorities, begun using his coding method. The haphazard way of transporting the messages was evident given that the Dublin–Lisbon route operated only once a week and Eastwood was frequently drunk and unreliable.

Nonetheless, the code itself continued to stump Strachey's team at Bletchley Park. They were unaware that Richard Hayes had broken the code in Dublin because there had been a delay in informing Bryan. Colonel de Buitléar had not divulged the breakthrough to Bryan because he felt that he was passing everything on to the British and getting nothing in return. When Bryan was eventually told, he immediately contacted the Liddell brothers, who travelled to Dublin to learn more about Hayes's discovery. Writing in his diary on 24 March 1943, Guy Liddell felt an important breakthrough was about to be made:

> Dan Bryan has just telegraphed to say that the Stephen Carroll-Held cipher has been broken and it may be identical to the one being used by Dr Görtz. Messages we have obtained in Lisbon have been examined and appear to be in the handwriting of Andrews, who met Christopher Eastwood on arrival and there was an exchange of notes. A cipher has been found in Görtz's cell, probably by a servant who is in Dan's employ. Dan has asked us to send over an expert to look at the cipher. Denys Page and Cecil Liddell will probably be going over on Saturday.

The ISOS section at Bletchley were able to provide the keywords to the cipher being used but were unable to decipher the workings of the system. Hayes, on the other hand, had detailed knowledge of the system that the cipher used. With both sides holding two different parts of the puzzle, it made sense to work together.

In advance of their trip to Ireland, the Liddells had sent copies of the Eastwood telegram to Dublin for Hayes to study. Denys Page was one of the most trusted British codebreakers in Bletchley Park during the war. Born in Reading, Berkshire in 1908, Page was a noted academic who had studied classics at Oxford, eventually becoming Regius Professor of Greek and Master of Jesus College, Cambridge. A scholar of Ancient Greek tragedy and poetry, he was recruited by GC&CS and posted to Bletchley Park in 1939. His expertise in German was used by Strachey in Hut 9A of the ISOS section of Bletchley in 1942. Such was his standing in Bletchley Park that following the war he became Deputy Director of GC&CS and was knighted by Queen Elizabeth II for his services to the country.

Page and Cecil Liddell met Hayes in Dublin to discuss Hayes's findings in relation to the Görtz cipher. ISOS had discovered that the cipher was Russian in origin, but it was Hayes who filled in the gaps. Hayes explained how the system worked, and Page, using the keywords, was able to read the messages. Bryan and G2 allowed the messages to continue, letting the British read them, without knowing what the contents were or whether they compromised any Irish individuals. As it happened, the coded messages did contain sensitive information indicating that Görtz had been in contact with General Hugo MacNeill of the 2nd Division of the Irish Army, who was known to hold strongly anti-British views.

MacNeill came from a very strong republican background. He was the nephew of Gaelic scholar Eoin MacNeill, who helped found the Irish Volunteers in 1913. Hugo was immersed in Irish republican ideology from a very young age, having attended St Enda's School in Rathfarnham, County Dublin, where he was taught by future 1916 Rising leader Patrick Pearse. He joined the Free State Army in 1922 and rapidly rose through the ranks, being promoted to the rank of Major General in 1924. In 1940 he was assigned to G1, the training branch of the army, and appointed Assistant Chief of Staff, a role he would hold three times in total during his career. MacNeill had made a number of personal approaches to Hempel at the German Legation for help in the event of an Allied invasion. It came as no surprise to Bryan and his colleagues in intelligence that a man with such strongly anti-British views had met with Görtz. Given the nature of the MacNeill revelations, the

British were impressed by Bryan's willingness to help them.

Guy Liddell in particular was impressed with Hayes's zeal at breaking the code and commented that 'his gifts in this direction amounted almost to genius'. The British were also extremely pleased with Bryan, who had, in their estimation, gone over his colleagues' heads to help them. Liddell recorded the meeting in his diary on 5 April 1943, declaring the Anglo-Irish co-operation a success:

> Cecil Liddell returned last Thursday from Dublin after a most successful visit. He was accompanied by Denys Page. The work on the Stephen Held cipher was done by Dr Richard Hayes, curator of the National Library, who appears to have done an extremely good job. The cipher is a very difficult and complicated one. Messages which refer to the bringing of an agent to Eire and also the planning of an escape by Dr Görtz are of considerable interest. They are written by Andrews the son of a butcher from Rush whose father buys sheep on Lambay Island. His father once asked me to find his son a job in the police. Young Andrews was in touch with Görtz before the latter was in prison and in fact was mainly responsible for the information that was given to the Eire authorities for Görtz's arrest. It is presumed through this association he became acquainted with Görtz cipher. How far he is using it on his own or in collaboration with Görtz is not yet clear. He is in any case somewhat of a double-crosser.

Once MI5 had garnered sufficient information from the Görtz cipher, arrangements were made for Andrews to be arrested. He was detained by the Gardaí in August 1943 and was interned until the end of the war. Christopher Eastwood was also arrested and detained until the end of the war. Meanwhile in Athlone, Görtz was vigorously protesting against his transfer from Arbour Hill and complaining that the Irish authorities were treating him like a criminal rather than a prisoner of war. Görtz threatened multiple times to go on hunger strike if his demands to be brought back to Arbour Hill were not met. In the German Legation Hempel was secretly delighted as he felt having Görtz out of Dublin would quell some of the furore that had arisen around him. Meanwhile, back in Athlone the G2 agent in charge of the German POWs, Commandant James Power, had his hands full with Görtz and his comrades.

Commandant Power was a tall, thin, wiry man who lived most of his life in the Retreat area of Athlone town. As he was based in Athlone, he was given responsibility for running the prisoner of war camp for German spies in Custume barracks and was posted there on 1 June 1942. German spies were interned in special quarters within the barracks where they could be kept away from the prying eyes of the public and the press. Commandant Power had the most access to them and in the tapes outlines how he got the greatest insight into their mindsets:

> I had more access to them than anybody else you see. There was nobody. Like the staff had not the same familiarity with them as I had. I was dealing with them everywhere – in their accounts and buying for them, they were allowed to buy you see, they had a certain amount of cash.

In addition to spending privileges the internees benefited from a newly constructed enlarged living quarters made especially for them in the barracks. Each prisoner was given a six-foot by twelve-foot cell fully furnished with carpets, bookshelves and a comfortable bed. Power saw to it that prisoners were rotated from cell to cell in order to prevent internees getting familiar with their lodgings and formulating any escape plans. Much had been learned from the escapes of Schütz and Görtz. Power had the men locked into their rooms at night and a 24-hour watch was placed on the cells. The prisoners were allowed to congregate in a large common room, where they were provided with a radio to listen to; but they seem to have listened to it less often after Hitler's ill-fated invasion of Russia. Those of the prisoners who were veterans of World War I knew only too well the tenacity of Russian soldiers, and many knew that if Hitler was attacking the east, the war was essentially turning against him. One of the Germans said, 'If seven Russian soldiers had one gun between them, all seven would need to be killed before that gun could be taken.' In addition to the radio set internees also had sporting facilities, baseball being their favourite, and were allowed to engage in gardening. Despite the many concessions there were often arguments between the spies and they complained incessantly to Power, mainly due to having so much idle time.

The spies were allowed to keep any money they had on their person when they were arrested. They also received money from Hempel, which they could spend on extra rations. According to Power in the tapes:

> Some of these fellows, there was money in their possession when they were intercepted. I expect that [Hempel] was where it came from. We never queried. We never queried where it came from … They got a certain amount each month. First of all, they had a certain amount of money coming up out here, you see, but when that money was spent, the German embassy took it over, I think, and they allowed him [Hempel] so much money through our Department of Finance. The Department submitted to us every month a cheque to the value of £3–£5 per man.

Power noted that many of the Germans spent the money they had been sent to Ireland with on a variety of foolish items including expensive gold watches. When they eventually ran out of funds, they had to ask Hempel to provide them with a stipend. The Irish government was willing to accede to this, given that the prisoners were essentially special category internees and were subject to different regulations than IRA internees or ordinary criminals. Power was an avid bridge player and often played with the German internees to size them up. He noted that Görtz gripped his cards nervously and often seemed tense or under pressure. Playing bridge with the internees not only gave Power an impression of the internees' state of mind, it also gave him an insight into an escape attempt that they were planning. The prisoners had painted a large eagle and a swastika on the wall of their recreation room. The purpose of this was to create a diversion while they began digging a tunnel from one of the cells. One of the prisoners would keep an eye on the guards, and Wilhelm Preetz was tasked with bouncing a ball to alert those digging the tunnel when the guards were on their way. But it wasn't long before their escape attempt was thwarted.

From the moment he entered the internment camp in Athlone Görtz carried himself with an air of self-importance. He clearly believed that his rank and his role in the Luftwaffe put him head and shoulders above the rest of the internees. In many ways it's easy to see why, as Wilhelm Preetz, Walter Simon and Ernst Weber-Drohl were little more than con artists and opportunists. Görtz's belligerent attitude towards his fellow internees succeeded in splitting the camp into pro- and anti-Görtz factions. The prisoners were also divided according to whether or not they were members of the Nazi Party or of the military. Despite perhaps having the most in common with each other in the group, Schütz and Görtz clashed regularly, sometimes for the most banal reasons. Görtz frequently berated Schütz for listening to English-language radio broadcasts, something Görtz felt was beneath any self-respecting German. On more than one occasion the animosity between the two descended into violence and Power and his colleagues were forced to break up the mêlée.

Görtz had appointed himself a senior officer in the camp, but it was clear that his mental health was declining. He wrote to the Farrell sisters, two elderly women in Glenageary who had become supporters of his, to persuade them to organise help for him to escape. By 1944 he had become increasingly desperate and paranoid. Much to the dismay of Power and his fellow guards, Görtz declared that he would go on hunger strike until he received a transfer from the prison. He managed to survive 21 days without food, but his health took a turn for the worse and the authorities had to intervene and feed Görtz through a tube. Görtz was transferred back to his cell when he was well enough to leave the prison hospital. In his cell he wrote prolifically, translating more of Yeats's poetry into German, and writing a play about Stephen Hayes, whom he increasingly began to hold responsible for his predicament. Power felt some sympathy for Görtz; he felt he was a lot more pleasant to deal with than the likes of Preetz, who Power felt was no more than a common criminal.

Moving the German prisoners from Dublin to Athlone had for the most part been a success because it had taken them very much out of the spotlight. Commandant Power worked mainly with the German spies, but he also helped retrieve personnel from both Allied and German aircraft that had crash landed in Ireland. Commandant James Power died in 1996 at the age of 101 and was buried in Coosan, County Westmeath alongside his wife,

Frances. Their son, Jim, became a prominent dentist in Dublin but passed away at a relatively young age in 1984. His wife and young family emigrated to the United States and Jim's daughter, Samantha Power, went on to serve as the 28th United States Ambassador to the United Nations from 2013 to 2017. She was a high-ranking foreign policy official and aide during the presidencies of Barack Obama and Joe Biden and is a Pulitzer Prize-winning author. In 2018 she visited the former German internment camp at Custume barracks, retracing her grandfather's footsteps. Samantha had been close to her grandfather when she was growing up and he often told her of his dealings with Görtz and the rest of the German internees: 'I heard a lot about these German prisoners but I knew that Ireland was neutral in the Second World War, so what the hell are a bunch of Germans doing in Athlone? It just seemed very strange.' Power's intrigue was understandable and not surprising. Even today, not much is known about the internment camp and it remains a little-known episode in the history of the war in Ireland.

The German internees in Athlone had certainly been made more comfortable than was normal for Irish prisoners. It was a luxury they had in common with their counterparts in the Luftwaffe who had crash landed in Ireland and were held in the K-Lines camp, the No. 2 Internment Camp, in the Curragh. K-Lines, which was built by the government in 1939, was located on the eastern side of the Curragh, directly opposite the No. 1 Internment Camp, Tin Town, which housed members of the IRA who had been detained under the Emergency Powers Act. The camp derived its legal basis from Emergency Orders K and L in Section 2 of the Act. Section K was to 'Authorise and provide for the detention of persons (other than natural-born Irish citizens) where such detention is, in the opinion of a Minister, necessary or expedient in the interests of the public safety or the preservation of the State'. Section L sought to 'Authorise the arrest without warrant of persons (other than natural-born Irish citizens) whose detention has been ordered or directed by a Minister'. Implementation of the orders fell under the remit of the Minister for Justice, at that time Gerald Boland, and the Minister for Defence, then Oscar Traynor.

De Valera held the External Affairs portfolio during the war and as such also had a direct influence on the detention of foreign nationals. Since members of the Luftwaffe were not perceived to be involved in espionage their detention was treated in a different manner from that of the German spies. K-Lines was used solely for the internment of Axis and Allied forces who crash landed on Irish soil to stop them from returning to their respective countries and rejoining the war effort. Even though the Irish forces showed a certain consideration for Allied airmen, as was demonstrated by the Devers incident, it is clear that much less leniency was initially shown towards their Axis counterparts.

K-Lines was not dissimilar from any other prisoner of war camp that operated throughout Europe during the war. In fact, it was modelled on British POW camps used during the revolutionary period in Ireland. The camp was surrounded by an ominous barbed wire fence, which was secured with an armed gate. Inside that was a strip of grass, then another barbed fence. On the four corners of the perimeter sat guard towers in which a 24-hour armed unit was stationed to deter any escape attempts. Inside the perimeter fence armed guards regularly went on foot patrol to secure the inner compounds and there was a parole hut from where entry and exit to the camp was controlled. German forces were detained in what became known as G Camp and Allied internees in a compound directly opposite that was known as B camp. Unsurprisingly the G stood for German and the B for British – the first Allied servicemen to be detained at K-Lines were British. Both Tin Town and K-Lines were under the stewardship of the LDF, which rotated between the two camps almost daily.

Given that little more than 20 years had passed between the Irish War of Independence and the outbreak of World War II, the relationship between the LDF guards and the IRA was fractious, to say the least. This hardened many of the guards and the initial relationship between the LDF and the German internees was quite fraught. This, however, began to change over a period of time as the LDF began to realise that the Germans held them in far less contempt than did the republican prisoners adjacent to them.

During the war roughly 200 German POWs were held in K-Lines compared with about 40 British servicemen. Initially the internees were held in poor regard by their LDF jailers, who, because they feared that there would be attempts at escape, often treated internees harshly. Much of this attitude derived from the personal attitude of the camp commander, Thomas McNally, and trickled down into the general staff in the camp. This view was also shared by the commandant who shared overall responsibility for both the IRA and Axis camps, James Guiney. The German internees resented their poor treatment and communicated their displeasure to Eduard Hempel at the German Legation. Hempel visited the camp in 1940 and agreed that the prisoners were being treated unduly harshly and that their conditions were uncomfortable to say the least. Following the visit, it was agreed that regulations in the camp would be relaxed, and the German internees were to benefit from much improved conditions.

Hempel made representations to de Valera in his role as Taoiseach and Minister for External Affairs and it was agreed that from October 1940 the prison regime would be relaxed and that German internees would be granted certain privileges. A lot of the concessions can be attributed to the good working relationship that Hempel had with de Valera. German internees were now to be paid an allowance of £3 per week for officers and £2 for other ranks. The German government covered the payments, which were used to buy civilian clothing and food. Prisoners were allowed to attend religious services and were given garden tools to grow their own vegetables. Much like their colleagues in Athlone, they had access to radios to keep up to date with the news and progress of the war and they were also allowed to receive packages and use the mail – but unbeknownst to the prisoners this was censored by G2.

The Germans responded well to the concessions and eventually, as a reward for good behaviour, a parole system was introduced for all ranks. The prisoners would be allowed to leave the compound on day release if they agreed to be back at an appointed time. A written declaration was signed by each internee:

> I hereby promise to be back in the compound at _____ o'clock and, during my absence, not to take part in any activity connected with the war or prejudicial to the interests of the Irish state.

If prisoners agreed to the conditions, they were able to avail of many of the amenities in the Curragh Camp, such as the swimming pool and squash courts. Eventually they were permitted to travel to nearby Newbridge and Kilcullen to go to the cinema. They had to wear civilian clothing and were accompanied by members of the LDF for their own safety. There were many pro-British and anti-German elements in the towns near the camp and it was feared that some of the Germans could be attacked if they provoked the ire of any of the locals. The arrangements seemed to work and the German internees began to appreciate their surroundings more, and thus there was less tension in relation to escape attempts.

As the war progressed the internees' lives improved even further. Their quarters were supplied with additional furnishings; there were electric lights and two wood-burning stoves. Prisoners were also able to avail of showers and toilet facilities and ample hot water was provided for most of the day. In addition to this they were given three meals a day, including a cooked breakfast and roast beef dinners, with bread and butter served with every meal. Prisoners could also look forward to bread and jam with their tea in the evenings. A dessert of creamed rice was also provided most days. Hempel and the British representatives felt that this was more in line with how prisoners should be treated, given that Ireland wasn't a belligerent in the war and that most if not all landings in the country were accidental.

Allied pilots usually ended up landing in Ireland because their aircraft was damaged or due to navigational errors, for example thinking they were over Northern Ireland or the British mainland. It was also preferable for planes to land in neutral Ireland than an enemy country, where they would undoubtedly be treated more harshly. In any case, both Allied and Axis airmen had strict protocols for crash landings. All documents that were thought to be of a sensitive nature were automatically destroyed, as was the aircraft itself. Axis pilots in particular were in a quandary because the closest Axis country was France; travelling to France via England would have been fraught with danger. Therefore, it's likely that many Axis aircrews had already resigned themselves to capture and internment by the Irish before they were caught. Allied airmen were in a different predicament – they only had to make it as far as Northern Ireland in order to be recirculated into the air force. On several occasions, Allied airmen attempted to do this but often without much success given the capability of G2's Coast Watching

Service. Within minutes of any crash landing the local LDF units were on the scene.

The conditions at K-Lines sought to make escape undesirable and coupled with the hardship of making it to France it was largely effective as a deterrent. Bryan and G2 also had a good system put in place to deal with any escape attempts. Many of the towns in Kildare had a large military presence and anything out of the ordinary would have been noticed almost immediately and reported back to the camp via G2. This didn't stop escape attempts being made, and it did not prevent sympathisers on both the Axis and Allied sides helping any escapees, but by and large the camp was secure for the majority of the war and it remained unknown to the general public.

One attempted escape on the evening of 9 February 1942 by RAF airmen led to a rethinking of communications between the Irish and British authorities and any leniency regarding parole. Frederick Boland of External Affairs informed de Valera of the attempted escape and how he felt the matter should be dealt with in secret correspondence dated 24 February 1942:

Sir John Maffey called this morning at my request. I told him that it was proposed to restore parole to the British internees as from tomorrow. I gave him the new form of parole which he scrutinised very carefully, but he did not raise any objection. When I showed him a copy of the old form, he laughed and said that, of course, it did not exclude contacts with British military people for the purpose of effecting escape …

He expressed himself as very satisfied that the whole thing was over, and he wished to thank you for all the interest you personally had taken in the matter. He was very confident that we could maintain a good situation in the future by close co-operation between the department and his office …

Wing Commander Begg [Malcolm G. Begg, British Air Attaché, Dublin 1942–45] had now received direct instructions from the Air Ministry to report once a fortnight on the situation in the camp, and on the relations of the internees with the Irish military authorities. Sir John Maffey had frequently asked for specific instructions of this character for the former Air Attaché, but the Air Ministry had until now maintained this attitude of refusing to recognise an 'internee situation' in relation to this country. He could now rely on Wing Commander Begg to keep both himself and the Air Ministry fully informed of the attitude of the internees. Wing Commander Begg, with his new authority, could also secure an improvement in the men's attitude.

Despite some liberties being taken with parole, it was extended to allow British senior officers the use of a telephone to phone the British Representative, Sir John Maffey, at any time. Both British and German internees were also allowed to visit hotels in neighbouring towns and married men were given extra benefits, being allowed extensive day release to spend time with their wives who had travelled over to see them. Eventually internees were even allowed to visit private homes and to attend local dances and functions in the Kildare area. Race meetings at the Curragh also proved popular with internees and special permission was granted for them to attend the Irish Derby. The British began to look for more concessions, but by the end of 1943 it became clear that the tide in the war was turning and most Allied prisoners were secretly released. Twenty of the Axis prisoners were allowed to relocate to Dublin, where many of them enrolled as students at UCD or Trinity College.

By the time the bulk of the prisoners in both the Curragh and Athlone were serving their sentences, plans had already begun for a renewed assault on Europe by the Allies. Over two years of planning had gone into the invasion of Europe and the British were determined to make up for their chastening defeat at Dunkirk. Emboldened by the USA's entry into the war, it was only a matter of time before the Allies would strike again. The British were apprehensive about mounting an invasion attempt through France, given the Atlantic Wall of defences constructed by Rommel and the resulting German preparedness for any such attack. Efforts had been made to try a softer approach and landings were made in North Africa and in Italy prior to the Normandy invasion. On the eastern front the Russians had gained the upper hand following the Battle of Stalingrad and were slowly grinding their way westwards. This proved to be advantageous to the Allies as it stretched Hitler's resources to the point that it became unsustainable to fight a war on two fronts. In order to make any sort of invasion possible it became clear that disinformation via the Double Cross System would be of huge strategic importance.

The Double Cross System was essentially a stable of double agents, i.e. captured Axis spies who were coerced or persuaded to spy for the British. The system, which was operated by MI5, still remains a textbook example of counter-espionage. By 1944, the Double Cross System had reached such a level of sophistication that it was decided to make it a central tenant of Operation Fortitude, the campaign of deception aimed at making the Germans believe that the widely expected Allied invasion would occur in the Pas-de-Calais region. Agents who were trusted by the Germans and who had now been recruited by the British were entrusted to sow this information among the Abwehr and SD, thus luring the German High Command into a false sense of security. It was also hoped that the deception would create the impression in Berlin that the Normandy landings were merely a diversionary tactic that they could ignore. Much of this deception was entrusted to a double agent named Juan Pujol García, codenamed Garbo, a Barcelona-born veteran of the Spanish Civil War.

In January 1944, Pujol's German handlers told him that they believed the Allies were preparing for a large-scale invasion of Europe and tasked him with keeping them informed of any developments. The planned Allied invasion was codenamed Overlord, and Fortitude was one of its major components. In the first six months of 1944 over 500 radio messages were passed between Pujol and Madrid and redirected to Berlin. These appeared to the Germans to be updates on the preparations for Overlord, but much of the information was false. The fact that Hitler himself was certain that Calais, given the short crossing distance from Dover, was the most likely invasion point made the information more credible. Pujol received an MBE for his work in late 1944 before moving to Venezuela. He died in obscurity in the capital, Caracas, in 1988.

Through his close working relationship with Guy and Cecil Liddell, Dan Bryan and G2 played a significant role in controlling any information leakage that came out of Ireland that could have disrupted the plans for D-Day. Therefore, keeping a tight rein on the German spies in custody in Ireland was essential, given the growing number of American troops stationed in Northern Ireland, particularly in Derry. The case of Andrews and Eastwood and communication via Lisbon using the Görtz code was an important turning point in that it presented an opportunity to derail the Allies' planned invasion of Europe through information leakage. If any sort of information, true or false, was to leak, it could have wreaked havoc with the Allies' plans for strategic deception with regards to the D-Day landings. Bryan's foresight in working with the British, and the collaboration between Richard Hayes and Denys Page, succeeded in closing that avenue and helped pave the way for the D-Day landings in June 1944.

In France, de Gaulle had managed to unite the various resistance groups though his emissary, Jean Moulin, and they pledged their support for the combined American, British and Canadian invasion of Normandy. A tentative date was set for the invasion of 5 June 1944, but one last problem threatened to derail the entire process. Bryan had allowed the Allies to use Irish weather reports to plan the invasion. These would prove crucial in carrying out a successful seaborne invasion of Normandy, given the sheer size of the armada involved.

In Blacksod lighthouse, County Mayo, Irish Coast guardsman and lighthouse keeper Ted Sweeney and his wife, Maureen, had been monitoring a storm that was brewing and estimated that it would make landfall on 5 June before making its way over mainland Europe. As Ted Sweeney telephoned his readings to Dublin, little did he know that the fate of 150,000 Allied troops rested on his shoulders. Over the crackling line, Sweeney heard a voice at the other end and said, 'Blacksod, Blacksod calling ... Here is the weather report for the third of June 1944.' The information was read by G2, which immediately realised the danger involved and passed the weather report on to the Allies. Supreme Allied Commander Dwight D. Eisenhower made the decision to delay the D-Day landings for 24 hours until the storm had passed, thus averting a colossal military disaster.

Ireland had shared meteorological information since independence, but Bryan's willingness to continue to share this information in a climate where there was still residual anti-British sentiment is indicative of his foresight. It is noteworthy that no similar arrangement was in place with the Germans.

The Blacksod reports were an important part of the collective efforts that were the Normandy landings. Ted and Maureen Sweeney and G2 had helped change the course of the war.

IX

ENDGAME

In a state in which all power of decision is concentrated in the hands of one man, the orders of this one man are absolutely binding on all members of the civil service hierarchy. This individual is their sovereign, their 'legibus solutus'.

DR KARL DOETZER, DEFENCE COUNSEL FOR DR EDMUND
VEESENMAYER, 11 MAY 1948

E arly on the morning of 6 June 1944 the largest seaborne invasion in history began. Allied forces from America, Britain, Canada and other nations began their assault on the beaches of Normandy. As the French Resistance sabotaged phone and train lines, the Allied forces launched a deadly assault that aimed to drive the Germans back towards Paris and ultimately to Berlin. With Stalin's forces pressing from the east, Hitler's regime was in its death throes. The Normandy forces made up the greatest armada the world had ever known and the lives of millions across Europe depended on its success. The planning that had gone into the landings had taken years and every measure was taken to ensure they achieved their objectives. In the months leading up to the landings Allied reconnaissance aircraft flew spying missions over northern France to capture photographs of key enemy positions and defences. A team of over 1,700 photo analysts pored over the images and were able to build detailed pictures of French coastal towns such as Saint-Lô, Carenten and Caen.

Many of these coastal towns were crucial strategic targets that the Allies hoped to capture within the first 24 hours of arriving on French soil. From 1942 the BBC had issued a public appeal for postcards and photographs taken by holidaymakers before the war of the coast of Europe as far inland as the Pyrenees. The public duly complied and millions of photographs were sent in, helping the Allied forces create three-dimensional models, which helped in the selection of landing sites. Such was the level of detail that covert operations had even retrieved sand samples and measurements of water levels and beach gradients. All this went into the invasion plans.

From dawn on 6 June, Allied forces began an extensive aerial and naval bombardment of Normandy. An airborne assault involving parachute regiments was followed by the deployment of 24,000 airborne troops. With these troops dropped behind enemy lines, the amphibious assault began. At 6.30 a.m. Allied infantry and armoured divisions began landing on an 80km stretch of the Normandy coast, which had been subdivided into five sectors codenamed Utah, Omaha, Gold, Sword and Juno. In addition to enemy gunfire, they had to contend with strong winds, which had blown troop carriers off course. The coast along the beaches had also been heavily mined by the Germans. Barbed wire fences and tripods made it almost impossible to clear the beaches of incendiary devices. Allied troops met the fiercest resistance on the American beaches of Utah and Omaha, while troops that had landed on the British and Canadian beaches were engaged in house-to-house fighting in many of the heavily fortified coastal towns. While the Allies failed to achieve any of their objectives on the first day of the landings, they did secure enough of a foothold to push forward in the days and weeks ahead. Carentan, Saint-Lô and Caen were liberated in the weeks thereafter and in the following months it became clear that Operation Overlord had been a success. But it had come at a huge cost. At least 10,000 casualties were recorded on 6 June, with 4,414 confirmed deaths. German casualties were estimated at between 4,000 and 9,000 men. The Americans alone had lost 184 Sherman tanks. But Hitler was now fighting a war on two fronts and public opinion was that the odds were firmly stacked against him.

By August 1944, American troops had liberated Paris, ending four years of German occupation. It had been feared that fierce fighting would lead to Paris being destroyed; indeed, Hitler had ordered his generals to leave the city in ruins. However, General Dietrich von Choltitz defied the Führer's orders and handed the city back to the French authorities undamaged. Over the course of the next eight months the Allies made advances in most facets of the war. In April 1945, Hitler's forces attempted a last-ditch offensive in the Ardennes – the Battle of the Bulge – but it was all in vain. The Allies had pushed further up through Italy and had made huge inroads into Germany from the west. By early April 1945, Soviet forces were about to make a final push into Berlin. By 30 April the Reichstag had been captured and Hitler had committed suicide in his bunker. His successor, Grand Admiral Karl Dönitz, instructed Alfred Jodl of the OKW to sign the instruments of surrender on 7 May. The war with Germany was over.

The war had been won at a great cost. An estimated 50 to 80 million lives had been lost, in addition to the genocide of the Holocaust and the first use of nuclear weapons in Hiroshima and Nagasaki in May 1945. The war had lasted a gruelling 2,294 days and had left Europe in ruins.

News of the German surrender was met with jubilation across the world, even in Germany, where people had lived under the brutality of Hitler's totalitarian regime for over a decade. In London huge crowds gathered in Piccadilly Circus and bonfires were lit along the River Thames. Churchill declared that the next day would become known as Victory in Europe Day – VE Day. In New York, Times Square became a focal point of celebrations, with large numbers of people gathering to celebrate.

News of the Allied victory began to filter through to Ireland by two o'clock via BBC radio, but the news was received very differently than in London or New York. While there was undoubtedly great relief and celebration, there were also mixed opinions on the ending of the conflict. Allied flags, including that of the Soviet Union, were flown from the roof of Trinity College with the Irish tricolour positioned much lower than the others. The flags were soon replaced by the American star-spangled banner and the tricolour was burned, while students of the largely Protestant university sang 'God Save the King' and 'Rule Britannia'. A counter-protest was arranged by a number of students at the mainly Catholic UCD, among them a future Taoiseach, the 18-year-old commerce student Charles J. Haughey. Haughey had served in the LDF as a second lieutenant during the war and, like many other students, had taken umbrage at the disrespect shown to the Irish flag.

The counter-demonstration marched to the offices of the *Irish Times* on Fleet Street brandishing a Union flag that had been torn from a lamp post nearby. The flag was set alight at the bottom of Grafton Street and windows were broken at the newspaper's offices – the *Irish Times* had been specifically targeted because it was perceived as pro-British. The group then proceeded to scale the railings of Trinity College when a mêlée broke out and gardaí baton-charged the mob. The *Irish Times* had the last laugh, though – it published pictures of the Allied leaders in a V-shape layout on its front page on VE Day.

It was in this maelstrom of mixed public opinion that the Irish government found itself when the war ended. De Valera's government had to decide what to do with German internees and G2's counsel would be sought on this delicate security issue.

From July to August 1945, military personnel being held at the K-Lines camp in the Curragh were sent back to mainland Europe, as Ireland was bound by international law to do. The Allies viewed the German spies held in Ireland very differently. It was largely felt that they couldn't be released so quickly for security reasons. The British believed that all Germans interned in Ireland should be transferred back to Germany immediately to be debriefed and tried if necessary, in line with the Allied policy of denazification, which sought to purge all remnants of the Nazi regime from German society. The Irish authorities were eager to obtain assurances that these German detainees would not be treated as prisoners of war. Joseph Walshe at the Department of External Affairs communicated this view to the British Representative Sir John Maffey in June 1945 and made his thoughts known in a memorandum to the Taoiseach the same day:

> Sir John Maffey came to see me this morning after his return from London where he had spent a few days. Before going over, we had had one or two talks about the German internees during which I made it clear that, if they were to be repatriated to Germany, they should not be treated as prisoners of war either in transit or on their arrival in Germany.
>
> Maffey told me today that his authorities would endeavour to arrange for the transfer to Germany direct by air. Should that method prove impossible or too inconvenient, the internees would have to be taken through England on their way to Germany but would not be regarded

during the passage as German prisoners. On arrival in the British zone in Germany, they would be treated as ordinary disarmed German service personnel, but, when disbanded, if their homes happened to be in the Russian zone, the British could take no responsibility for their treatment there.

On being questioned, Maffey said that there was no idea of forcing them to go into the Russian zone against their will.

It seems to me that this offer should be accepted. The internees arrived here in the course of war operations, and they must have understood from the beginning that they would be repatriated to Germany at the first opportunity. They can have no objection – and it is unlikely that they will offer any – to going back [to] their own country.

To placate the British, an agreement was reached between the Department of External Affairs and the Department of Justice, via senior civil servant Peter Berry, that German internees would be allowed to move freely around Athlone during the day, provided they spent the night in Custume barracks under armed supervision. Such an arrangement afforded the prisoners greater opportunity to socialise and to hear news of how events were progressing in Germany following the establishment of Allied control of the country.

Görtz used his new-found freedom to spend hours walking around Athlone town and going into cafés and shops. During this time, he befriended some local women, who told him that they had seen Commandant Power in town with Fr Joseph Mulreane, a native of Mullingar, County Westmeath, who had served as chaplain to the International Brigade during the Spanish Civil War. Görtz was eager to speak to Fr Mulreane because his daughter had fled Germany following the Allied invasion and had gone to Spain, where she was working as a maid. Görtz hoped that the priest might be able to find out if his daughter was safe and well. He called at Commandant Power's house on Retreat Road to see if he could arrange the meeting for him. Power reluctantly agreed to facilitate the meeting with the proviso that he be there while it took place. Mulreane agreed to help find Görtz's daughter and during the meeting he relayed to Görtz and Power the appalling conditions in which Germans found themselves following the war. Much of

Berlin lay in ruins and over 600,000 apartments had been destroyed. The city had been divided into four sectors, to be administered jointly by the occupying powers of the USA, Great Britain, France and the Soviet Union. Ordinary Germans were forced to get up at dawn to find wood for fuel and many people had gone as long at three months wearing the same clothes. Mulreane's reports greatly affected Görtz, who began to slide further into depression. As he left Power's house and returned to his lodgings in Athlone, he resolved that he would not return to Germany. It was a promise he was determined to keep at any cost.

Not long after his visit to Power's house Görtz was arrested by the Irish authorities and brought in for questioning. He was asked about his mission to Ireland and what he had been up to in the months following his release. Görtz gave a bogus account of his activities, stating that he had communicated regularly with the Fatherland and had sent and received messages to Berlin using invisible ink. He also tried to claim the credit for the attempts to send Seán Russell and Frank Ryan to Ireland on their abortive missions. Görtz was blissfully unaware that he had already given an accurate account of his activities to Richard Hayes in an 80-page coded report that he mistakenly believed had gone to his handlers in Berlin. Görtz became even more withdrawn and gradually developed a depressive disorder. He became even more determined to avoid returning to Berlin at all costs. As a member of the Wehrmacht during and after World War I, he had been involved in quelling the Spartacist uprising in Berlin in 1919 and believed that he would be treated harshly by the Russians should he be brought back to face trial.

In September 1946, the Irish government had reached a consensus that German spies would be released and that the Irish state would offer them asylum. Most of them returned to Germany over the next few years, but Wilhelm Preetz returned to Tuam, County Galway, where he lived with the local GP, Dr Tubridy, and faded into obscurity, and Günther Schütz married a local woman named Una Mackey whom he had met at a dance in Athlone. However, Görtz continued to be a problem for the government. He had moved to Glenageary, where he was staying with the Farrell sisters and he travelled almost daily to the National Library where he studied volumes of Irish law to find the elusive loophole that would grant him permanent residence in Ireland. On one visit he met with Dr Hayes, who had returned to his role as director of the library. Hayes took Görtz to a café on Nassau Street and told him that he had broken his code and that it was he whom Görtz had been communicating with. Görtz congratulated Hayes, but the revelation only increased his anxiety and his decline into mental instability.

By April 1947 the international political climate had changed dramatically. Following the Nuremberg trials, many of the leading members of the Nazi regime had been executed for crimes against humanity and for genocide, newly constituted crimes that had been defined by Polish lawyer Raphael Lemkin and British lawyer Hersch Lauterpacht. Joachim von Ribbentrop and Hermann Göring were among the many leaders to be sentenced to death during the proceedings. Göring evaded the hangman's rope when he committed suicide by ingesting a phial of cyanide in his cell on 15 October 1946. Görtz held Göring in very high regard and told Schütz that he would rather die like Göring than be taken back to Germany against his will. Both Görtz and Schütz fought against their extradition in a high-profile court case but were only successful in gaining an extension so that they could tidy up their personal affairs. Görtz became increasingly erratic and wrote to Frederick Boland and the Department of External Affairs as well as directly to de Valera to ask for an intervention on his behalf for him to be allowed to stay. The Farrell sisters also wrote to the Taoiseach to petition him to allow Görtz to stay in Ireland. In all likelihood Görtz would have been safe, and it's likely that he would have been granted permission to stay in Germany or could perhaps have relocated to Argentina. Dan Bryan had his own thoughts on why Görtz was so afraid to return to Germany, as the tapes he recorded with Prof. Carter reveal:

He had all these friends here and they regarded him as an immensely important person, on the same scale of importance as the people that were tried at Nuremberg. They only saw what happened here while in terms of world affairs Görtz was a very small person, but they probably kept pushing this idea in his head and there was even some political people here I think, strangely enough on the fringe of the government party, and they encouraged him in this idea. That was one reason it was effective. Another reason it was effective was the failure of his mission. It didn't matter, the war was over. Nobody was going to blame him, but he was probably depressed the whole time because everything went wrong. His mission had completely failed. He had achieved nothing. I would have thought that affected him too. And then, of course, he was depressed about conditions in Germany.

Fearing that his deportation was imminent, Görtz travelled to Frederick Boland's house to ask him to prevent it. Boland explained to Görtz that he should have nothing to fear in returning to Germany; in all likelihood, he would simply be detained for interrogation and then released. Boland's assurances didn't convince Görtz and he returned to Glenageary in a distressed state. On arriving at the house he found a letter instructing him to report to the Aliens Registration Office at Dublin Castle at 10 a.m. on 23 May 1947. Günthur Schütz had received a similar letter. An Allied aircraft had been granted permission to land at Baldonnel aerodrome to fly the spies back to Germany where they would be detained by the provisional government under US General Lucius D. Clay. Görtz duly travelled to Dublin Castle, where he exchanged pleasantries with members of the Gardaí. But before he was called into the office, he took from his breast pocket a vial of cyanide, which he had had since the start of his mission to Ireland. He bit into the capsule and, in a macabre mirror image of his hero Hermann Göring's death, Ireland's most infamous Nazi spy died by poisoning.

Dan Bryan was dismayed when he heard what had happened and cursed the official protocol that had prevented him from visiting Görtz to reassure him that he would come to no harm if he returned to Germany. The Carter tapes reveal his extreme dissatisfaction with the matter:

He had never been back to Germany once he had come here. I still feel that if I had been allowed to see Görtz, to discuss with him, I would have told Görtz, 'It's your duty to go back to Germany and stand by your nation now in her difficulties. If you assure me that there was nothing against you but your activities in Ireland, I would assure you, you would certainly be rounded up for interrogation but that you have nothing further to fear and that there's no reason, and it's your duty to go back to your family' … Görtz would have clicked his heels and said, 'You're right.' I may be wrong about that. It may be a bit egotistical for me to say that, but I feel that. But there were all those people, and even people in official circles here who didn't understand conditions and they in a sense, became mixed up in this. He [Görtz] got mixed up in a kind of row between two departments here, the Department of Justice and the Department of External Affairs. Justice, as the legal custodian and all that, said, 'We're responsible.' External Affairs said, 'We're responsible because we handle international affairs and have some understanding …' and that. When he had been out for some time and when he was re-arrested, the Foreign Office rang me and said, 'Oh we're very much afraid he will injure himself or do something. He's been re-arrested.' I didn't know this at the time. I said I'll go see him. He'd been taken back to Mountjoy. I rang Freddy Boland, whom I think had taken over External Affairs and he said 'Oh, go and see him by all means.' But then I rang Justice and Justice said 'No'. And that's all. If that were published the permanent head of the department would have been looking for my head under the Official Secrets Act or something.

Görtz was buried in Deansgrange Cemetery on 27 May 1947. The funeral was well attended and the Farrell sisters were chief mourners. One of the coffin-bearers was Dan Breen TD, and the coffin was draped in a hand-stitched swastika flag. As the coffin was lowered into the ground there were cries of 'Heil Hitler!' and the fascist salute was given. Ellen Görtz travelled to Ireland to see her husband's grave but made no arrangements to have his body repatriated to Germany. In later years she petitioned the Irish state for the money that Görtz had on him when he was initially arrested, but she was informed that the money had been forfeited to the Irish state. In 1974, Görtz's remains were dug up in the dead of night by a group of former Germany army officers and reinterred in the German Military Cemetery in Glencree, County Wicklow.

Günthur Schütz was eventually deported to Germany but was less apprehensive about being sent home than Görtz had been. He was flown to Frankfurt on a US bomber plane and was questioned in a nearby POW camp. He was asked about Irish neutrality and the purpose of his mission, but the Allies realised that he was a very low-level agent and he was soon released. In 1965 he returned to Ireland and paid a visit to the internment camp in Athlone. He and his wife, Una Mackey, opened a hotel in County Wicklow. He died at his home in Shankill, County Dublin in 1991.

Edmund Veesenmayer, the Nazi official who had overseen much of the Abwehr operations dealing with Ireland, had played a leading role as a member of the German diplomatic staff in Zagreb in what was then Yugoslavia (now Croatia). During his tenure there he was a fearless advocate of Nazi Party policy and was responsible for the persecution of Croatian and Serbian Jews. With Slavko Kvaternik, a leading Croatian fascist, Veesenmayer arranged for the proclamation of an Independent State of Croatia in order to install a puppet regime in the country. In March 1944, Veesenmayer was promoted to the role of SS Brigadeführer, thus becoming a Reich plenipotentiary. He was then sent to Budapest, where he became the leading Nazi official in German-controlled Hungary. Until the Nazi occupation, Hungary had been governed by a legitimate, elected parliament and government. It had had an official opposition, freedom of the press and all the hallmarks of a normal functioning democracy. When Veesenmayer was installed as the de facto leader of the country, he began to strip away all these rights. The Nazis' occupation had been aimed at securing control over Hungary's material and human resources in order to gain final victory in the war. The newly installed puppet government under Veesenmayer attempted to crush the spirit of the Hungarian people by instilling fear into everyday life. It wasn't long before Nazi Party policy in relation to the Jewish community began to be carried out in Hungary, to devastating effect.

On 20 January 1942, Nazi leaders and high-ranking members of the SS held a meeting in the Berlin suburb of Wannsee. The conference had been called by the director of the Reich Main Security Office, Reinhard Heydrich, to deal with the 'Final Solution to the Jewish Question'. The plan involved deporting the Jewish population of German-occupied Europe to Poland, where they would be murdered. Heydrich outlined during the meeting how the plan would unfold and how European Jews would be rounded up. In preparation for the conference, Adolf Eichmann, one of the main architects of the Holocaust and one of Nazi Germany's most feared individuals, drew up a list of the number of Jews in various European countries. Eichmann's list was divided into two distinct groups: countries under direct Nazi control and puppet states, such as Vichy France, and Allied countries or those that had declared themselves neutral – this list included Ireland. Eichmann's list included 2,300 Irish Jews who were scheduled for extermination. The 40,000 Croatian Jews and 742,800 Hungarian Jews on Eichmann's list fell under Veesenmayer's direct remit.

Hungarian Jews had already been persecuted under Nazi anti-Jewish legalisation enacted in 1938, 1939 and 1941. They were now in even greater peril. By 15 May 1944 Veesenmayer had ordered the use of deportation trains in Hungary to transport Jews to extermination camps, and within two months 437,402 Jews from regions outside Budapest had been taken to the camps. On 13 June 1944 Veesenmayer reported to the German Foreign Office that 289,357 Jews in 92 trains of 45 cars each had been transported eastwards across the Carpathian Mountains. Two days later he followed this up with a telegram to Nazi Foreign Minister Joachim von Ribbentrop in which he claimed that 340,000 Jews had been delivered to the Reich and promised that by the end of the year he would reach a target of 900,000 – his contribution to the Final Solution.

Veesenmayer was a Nazi loyalist who excelled at implementing Nazi Party policy in Hungary. In a sense he acted as diplomatic cover for Eichmann's murderous policies, receiving promotion after promotion while at the same time spilling the blood of innocent people. The endgame for Veesenmayer began on 27 August 1944, when Soviet troops crossed the Hungarian border. While Hungary was overwhelmed in the fighting, the Soviets ultimately prevailed, establishing themselves in the country for much of the rest of the century. The last Soviet soldier left Hungary on 19 June 1991.

Veesenmayer was captured and was put on trial for crimes against humanity. He was tried in what became known as the Ministries Trial, the eleventh of twelve trials for war crimes held by US authorities in the aftermath of World War II. These trials took place in Allied-controlled Nuremberg in US military courts, in contrast to the international courts that had tried Nazi leaders such as Hermann Göring and Ribbentrop. The trials were formally known as the Trials of War Criminals before the Nuremberg Military Tribunals, and were also known as the Wilhelmstrasse Trials – the German Foreign Office and Reich Chancellery had been located on Wilhelmstrasse in Berlin. These were unique trials that were convened to try officials of Reich ministries for their responsibility in atrocities carried out during the war. The court was presided over by Judge William C. Christianson of Minnesota, Robert F. Maguire of Oregon and Leon W. Powers of Iowa. Telford Taylor acted as chief counsel for the prosecution and Robert Kempner as chief prosecutor.

The indictments against Veesenmayer and the other defendants were filed on 15 November 1947 and the hearings lasted from 6 January to 18 November 1948. In total 21 defendants were arraigned. The judges presented their findings on 11 April 1949. Edmund Veesenmayer was convicted on six of a possible seven counts: crimes against peace (count 1); taking part in a common plan or conspiracy to commit the aforementioned crimes (count 2); crimes against humanity (count 4); war crimes and crimes against humanity through the plundering and spoilation of the Occupied Territories (count 5); and war crimes and crimes against humanity through the enslavement and deportation of concentration camp prisoners and civilians in the Occupied Territories for slave labour (count 6); membership of a criminal organisation, i.e. the NSDAP and the SS (count 7). His defence counsel, Dr Karl Doetzer, claimed that Veesenmayer was acting under orders dictated solely by the Führer and that at times he had shown consideration towards the Jewish community in Hungary:

> It is certainly correct that in late 1943 my client had a conversation with Prime Minister Tiso by order of Ribbentrop on the Jewish Problem in Slovakia, but, according to the evidence, it is equally clear that this was a camouflage order given to him as a liaison man which did not lead to any measures by the Slovakian State against Slovakian Jews … In this same capacity of a liaison man, Dr Veesenmayer was active in Yugoslavia after the outbreak of the revolt in 1941. On the basis of his findings at the time, he supported a request to evacuate several thousands of male

Jews who were suspected of having collaborated with the rebels, which had previously been submitted to the Foreign Office by Ambassador Benzler, who was Plenipotentiary of the Foreign Office with the German Military Commander. The result of the evidence shows that this suggestion of Benzler's had not been implemented but that the Military Commander, who was solely responsible and competent had these Jews taken as hostages and had them shot to death.

Despite Doetzer's pleas, Veesenmayer was condemned by the fact that while he had been more anonymous than other high-profile Nazi leaders, he had worked closely with Adolf Eichmann in Budapest. As such, he could have easily been sentenced to death, as Ribbentrop and others had been. The weight of evidence against Veesenmayer was considerable and the details about how so many people in Croatia and Hungary met their deaths were horrific. Veesenmayer was sentenced to 20 years' imprisonment on counts six and seven. Of all 21 individuals on trial, only two others received sentences as harsh as Veesenmayer's. His crimes were of the greatest magnitude of any of his co-accused. In his final remarks, Doetzer argued that Veesenmayer's membership of the SS was simply symbolic:

As far as Dr Veesenmayer is accused it is decisive whether or not an honorary leader of the SS – and such was my client according to the allegation of the prosecution themselves – can be a member of an organisation declared as criminal. If the tribunal adheres to the practice of the American Occupying Power in Germany, this question is to be denied without reservation. If not, the prosecution must, in the case of an honorary leader, prove that he was closely connected with the SS. This, however, they did not do. Neither did they show that the defendant Veesenmayer swore the SS oath and paid dues, nor that he did SS duty and wore the SS uniform.

Veesenmayer was sent to serve his prison sentence, but he benefited from a reduction of 10 years shortly thereafter, and in December 1951 he was released following the intervention of the UN High Commissioner in

Germany, John J. McCloy, who granted him a pardon. McCloy also pardoned convicted war criminals Ernst von Weizsäcker, Josef Dietrich and Joachim Peiper, all of whom had been convicted of mass murder for their roles in the Malmedy massacre in Belgium in 1944, in which 84 American prisoners of war were assembled in a field and shot with machine guns, the survivors being shot in the head at close range. McCloy later went on to serve as President of the World Bank, as a member of the Warren Commission investigation into the assassination of President John F. Kennedy and was a senior adviser to every US president from Franklin D. Roosevelt to Ronald Reagan.

With his new-found freedom Edmund Veesenmayer moved to Tehran, where he was employed by a German trading company. He later moved to northern France, eventually retiring to Darmstadt in West Germany, where he died in 1977. He never faced the gallows or firing squad for his activities and he can be considered to have got off lightly for his crimes. In 1961, Veesenmayer took the stand as a defence witness for his former colleague, Adolf Eichmann, who was under trial in Jerusalem for crimes against the Jewish people and against humanity. Eichmann offered the same 'I was only following orders' defence, but while Veesenmayer escaped the hangman's rope, Eichmann was less lucky. He was found guilty, sentenced to death and hanged in Ayalon Prison, Ramla, Israel on 1 June 1962.

In Budapest, along the banks of the River Danube, there is a powerful memorial to fascist terror in the Hungarian capital. *The Shoes on the Danube Bank* is a sculpture of 60 pairs of period-appropriate metal shoes. They represent the 20,000 Hungarian Jews who were murdered by members of the Hungarian Arrow Cross party, the puppet regime over which Veesenmayer presided. Their bodies were cast into the river and carried away by the current. Even today, local people and tourists place flowers among the shoes, determined that the horrors of those years should never be forgotten.

By January 1946, Helmut Clissmann was hoping to join his family in Ireland; they had returned there via England and Denmark. He spent the latter years of the war in North Africa with the Brandenburg Regiment following the failure of his endeavours with Frank Ryan. At the end of the war Clissmann found himself interned by the British as a prisoner of war in the Bad Nenndorf camp and during his incarceration he was tortured by his captors. The camp, or interrogation centre, was notorious for its maltreatment of internees. As early as January 1947 it became evident that prisoners were being treated badly when a number of inmates were taken to a nearby civilian hospital near Bremen suffering from frostbite, malnutrition and physical injuries which seemed to indicate that they had been assaulted.

When two of the prisoners died from their injuries, a complaint was made by British personnel at the hospital and an investigation was launched into the treatment of prisoners by senior British Army officers. A British Labour Party MP visited the camp in March 1947 to carry out an inspection, and while he found no evidence of physical abuse or starvation, he was critical of the poor conditions in which the prisoners were being held. He found that most of the prisoners were kept in solitary confinement in unheated cells at temperatures of minus 10 degrees Celsius. The prisoners had been given extra blankets to compensate for the lack of heating in their cells. However, the investigation carried out by the British Army made several accusations of serious abuse.

The investigation, carried out by Inspector Thomas Hayword of the Metropolitan Police at the behest of the British Army, found that prisoners had been subjected to insufficient clothing, intimidation by the guards, mental and physical torture, arbitrary confinement for long periods without excuse and being locked in punishment cells in bitter winter conditions. It also found that inmates had been forced to scrub the floors of their cells and that they were doused in cold water and denied adequate medical treatment and food supplies. Many of the prisoners also complained that their personal property had been stolen by their captors. The findings of the investigation caused consternation in British political circles and comparisons were drawn between the camps and German concentration camps and the torture methods used by political police forces in Eastern Europe. Eventually the matter was brought before an army court martial and the camp was closed down in July 1947.

During his time in Bad Nenndorf Clissmann was tortured. As he said, 'quite a number of times, you were stood in cold water for twelve hours or you were not allowed to lie down for 24 hours, you had to march round in the room, you could not even sit down.' Clissmann spent a full year in solitary confinement and when he left prison, he weighed only four stone.

Under interrogation by MI5, Clissmann consciously tried to forget information about people he knew who had English addresses lest the authorities question them too. In October 1946 MI5 transferred Clissmann to the Danish authorities, who wanted to question him in relation to his time there with the German Academic Exchange Service. He was held in Denmark until April 1948 and was then transferred to a British clearing camp, where he was detained for six weeks before being released in May 1948. His wife, Budge, set about trying to obtain a visa for him to enter Ireland to be reunited with her and her children. By the time Clissmann was released, his visa for Ireland had been denied due to his role in international intelligence-gathering. He was offered a visa in return for spying on his former colleagues in the Brandenburg Regiment, but he declined. He decided he would get to Ireland by other means. 'I made up my mind I would have to go illegally to Ireland. I walked over the Bavarian mountains into Austria then across into Italy then took a train to Rome. After waiting three weeks there I came by air to Shannon airport.'

Clissmann's trip was not without its problems, and he had to overcome many obstacles to make his way to Shannon. He was accompanied on his walk through the Alps by two young Germans, a Dr Braun and his wife. The Brauns waited in Italy for over nine months for the papers and money needed to continue onward on their journey. Clissmann was much more fortunate, having benefited from an encounter with a chief of police in Ciampino airport in Rome. Since he had entered Italy illegally, the police were not permitted to let him leave the country illegally. Clissmann was able to arrange via his connections in Ireland for the chief of police to issue him with the permission needed to travel over the phone – if it were given in person, the officer would have been obliged to arrest him. This would have been a disaster, since the Italian authorities were on close terms with the Americans and British. It was a clever ploy to ease Clissmann through the airport security and onward to Ireland. Clissmann was stopped at the gate as he went to board the plane, but was able to instruct officials at the gate to call a particular official at police headquarters, who gave the go-ahead for him to board. The aeroplane stopped in France en route to Ireland before eventually touching down at Shannon airport. On disembarking, Clissmann produced his visa and birth certificate and was soon reunited with his wife. Following his return to Ireland, he set himself up as a businessman in the pharmaceutical industry.

Writing from Sligo on 19 October 1948, Clissmann expressed his thanks to Joseph Walshe, who was serving as ambassador at the Holy See, for helping to arrange for the special treatment he was given in Rome:

> Please forgive me for not informing you earlier of my happy arrival in Ireland. The lively spirits of four healthy children with a new victim in their clutches have left me so far, no time for serious pursuits.
>
> The arrangements at Ciampino worked as we had hoped and as there was no passport control whatever at Geneva or Paris the journey was happily, entirely uneventful. The family was at Shannon airport to meet me and I was delighted to find that the children had thrived so well on the Irish air and food. Maeve and Billy Ryan came in their new car at the weekend to welcome me and I have been delighted also with the hearty welcome from so many old friends. Altogether, I think you can imagine how very happy I am to have returned safely to my second homeland.
>
> Your kindly reception and your prompt assistance have moved me so deeply and have been of so much value to me that I find it difficult to express my gratitude adequately. My journey was so risky that I would not have undertaken it if there had been any possibility of returning in a more correct manner. But as things stood, had I not been able to call on your assistance my family and I would have had to reckon with two or three more years of uncertainty and anxiety.
>
> My father-in-law and Budge join me in thanking you most sincerely for the trouble to which you went on mine and their behalf. They send you their friendly regards and very best wishes. Perhaps we may have the pleasure in seeing you on your next visit to Ireland.

In the end Clissmann's old republican connections had served him well. The First Inter-Party Government came to power in October 1948, and it was a Clissmann family friend, Seán MacBride, now the Minister for External Affairs, who had instructed Ambassador Walshe to use his influence to grant Clissmann unhindered passage to Ireland from Rome. On his return to Ireland, Clissmann became an advocate of forging strong cultural links between Germany and Ireland. He became a founding member of the Irish German Society and helped found St Kilian's Deutsche Schule in Dublin.

He made a very positive contribution to Irish life, building on his own experiences of human rights abuses at Bad Nenndorf by helping, with Seán MacBride, to establish the Irish section of Amnesty International. He suffered a stroke in 1987, following which he retired from work to spend more time at home with his family. He visited his home in Aachen every year and spent much of his spare time gardening. He died in 1997. He was interviewed several times on RTÉ television by both John Bowman and Cathal O'Shannon about his life during the war, and his pharmaceutical company is still going strong today.

While Clissmann settled into a life of relative obscurity, Dan Bryan remained doubtful about the German's true intent towards his adopted homeland during the war, outlining the following to Prof. Carter, although his belief was merely his own personal view and is not backed up by any evidence to date:

> Well, you see, my impression is that in the first place Clissmann had a bit of an alibi in that he wasn't originally a Nazi – that he belonged to some organisation that the Nazis looked a bit askance at. When Clissmann got back here Clissmann wanted to sell the idea to the Irish authorities that he wasn't a person directing activities against Ireland, that he was working to preserve Irish neutrality and that if the British and Americans came in here that he was going to get the Germans to help us against them. Now he's putting a gloss on that story – that is my impression. I may be wrong, but I don't think I am in this case. When he came back, he didn't want to be labelled as a Nazi and as a person that was acting against Irish interests.

While Bryan was in an ideal position to ascertain Clissmann's true motives during the war, it is important to consider Clissmann's strenuous denials that he acted in any way against Irish interests, as well as his distinguished contributions to Irish life in the post-war period.

Eduard Hempel was granted asylum in Ireland after the war; his close relationship with Taoiseach Éamon de Valera was probably instrumental in that. Hempel was well regarded by the Irish political establishment as it was perceived that he had afforded more respect to the Irish state than American envoy David Gray. De Valera visited Hempel to express his condolences on Hitler's death, a move that won him widespread condemnation. Hempel returned to Germany in 1949, working with the West German foreign service before retiring in 1951. He retired to the Black Forest and died in November 1971. A delegation from the Irish Embassy in Bonn attended his funeral in recognition of his treatment of Ireland during his tenure in Dublin. His legacy in Ireland remains a contested one. He showed great courtesy to his Irish hosts, but he represented Nazi Germany at the height of its worst excesses. The Hempel residence, Gortleitragh, was destroyed in a fire, reputedly by arson, before being demolished in 1955. A modern apartment block now stands on the site, although a portion of the building's original steps is visible from the street.

In the immediate aftermath of the war, Taoiseach Éamon de Valera made one of his most famous speeches, arguably the most important of his career and one that many characterise as his finest hour. In a well-crafted response to Winston Churchill, de Valera defended Irish neutrality and remarked how Ireland, a small island nation, had for centuries stood alone against aggression. The speech helped galvanise Irish public opinion and served as a riposte to Churchill's characterisation of the Irish 'frolicking with the Germans and Japanese' and his assertion that the British had stood alone against Axis aggression. The speech gained widespread and deserved acclaim but was also successful in redrawing the narrative of the war in Ireland as one of isolationism and neutrality in contrast to the view of collaboration with the British and Americans that had been the general opinion during the war. While this undoubtedly garnered huge popularity for de Valera, it also diminished the role of Dan Bryan and G2 in ensuring that the Irish state was both kept neutral and free from the worst horrors of World War II.

G2 was instrumental in safeguarding the state, in preventing a German invasion or a pre-emptive Allied invasion and in thwarting spying missions by Axis powers. The war period in Ireland was certainly Dan Bryan's finest hour, but as the decade approached its end, he found that his role in G2 became much more confined to domestic matters. Later, the Cold War was to be an active issue for Irish intelligence and he and his colleagues in G2 as well as Dr Richard Hayes sought to build on their experiences of the war to better prepare for any future conflict that Ireland might find itself in. G2 had built strong foundations, ones that would serve the state well in the future, and Bryan and the men of G2 had served the state and the people of Ireland well, despite their heroics being largely invisible to the general public.

X

UNSUNG HEROES

It is about time some of the truth be released to set the record straight.

DR RICHARD J. HAYES, 4 NOVEMBER 1961

The immediate aftermath of World War II saw a reorganisation of G2 to combat the emerging threat of communism. This took place against the backdrop of the Irish state basking in the success of its policy of neutrality. The South had seen innumerable benefits of staying out of the war, especially when things had been so different just north of the border. Nine hundred people had died in the Luftwaffe bombing raid on Belfast in 1941, and there had been enormous damage to property. According to government estimates, some 1,300 houses were destroyed, 5,000 badly damaged and nearly 30,000 slightly damaged; 20,000 required minor repairs. This was minute compared to the destruction that had been visited on major European cities such as Dresden, Coventry and London. Press censorship ensured that most people in Ireland were spared seeing the horrors revealed by the liberation of Nazi concentration camps, though some news did filter through; and de Valera's commiseration with Hempel on the death of Hitler had not been without its critics, especially among the Irish diaspora.

The experience of the war highlighted the inadequacies of Irish intelligence in terms of security, the apprehension of spies, and preparedness. Bryan and his colleagues in G2 advocated for greater funding of G2 to help with internal security. Richard Hayes even wrote to de Valera to ask for funding for a permanent cryptography unit in the Irish Army, a request met with deafening silence.

In February 1948, after 16 years in power, the Fianna Fáil government was replaced by a coalition of Fine Gael, Labour, Clann na Poblachta and others. Initially it was felt that the new government might take a more positive view of security funding than its predecessors, but such optimism was short-lived. Despite the inclusion in the Cabinet of Richard Mulcahy, whom Bryan knew well from their shared military background, things stayed much the same for the next number of years. In many ways the approach to the army almost reverted to a pre-Emergency mentality, much to the dismay of those who had fought to secure neutrality during the war. However, this attitude was to be short-lived and it became necessary for the Irish government to get to grips with the new geopolitical situation.

In 1949 the United States and 11 other Western nations formed the North Atlantic Treaty Organization (NATO) to counter Soviet expansion in Europe. This western bulwark was itself met by an amalgamation of communist-influenced countries coming together in the Warsaw Pact of 1955, which sought to counter Western influence. These two groups initiated a realignment of European countries into opposing factions, setting in motion the Cold War era, which defined much of the rest of the century.

Immediately after the war, the USSR sought to extend its influence across Europe by installing pro-Soviet governments in countries that were within its sphere of influence, mainly those that had been ceded to it by the carve-up of Nazi-occupied countries after the collapse of Hitler's regime. To prevent Soviet influence extending even further, in 1947 the United States introduced the Marshall Plan, a diplomatic initiative designed to offer financial aid to US-friendly nations. These funds were used to rebuild war-damaged economies, but the real motive was to curry favour with and influence the governments that accepted the funds. While Ireland did benefit from Marshall Aid, it chose not to join NATO, mainly due to the ongoing partition of the country. Minister for External Affairs Seán MacBride, who had helped Helmut Clissmann get back to Ireland in 1947, and who was a committed republican, strongly advocated against joining NATO until the issue of partition was dealt with.

The idea that a small island such as Ireland would not join NATO had huge security implications and was met with much derision by G2, but the decision had widespread political backing and was even supported by de Valera from the opposition benches. This difference of opinion was indicative of the mistrust between the intelligence services and politicians that would define much of the rest of the century. The Cabinet considered the army's point of view when it was formulating its decision. Largely drawing from Bryan's pre-war *Fundamental Factors* memorandum, the army argued that Ireland's strategic location in Europe would again become crucial if war broke out between NATO and the Soviet Union. Bryan and his colleagues contended that Ireland's geography made it a certainty that it would be drawn into such a war, and that Ireland was defenceless if it found itself under sustained attack from outside forces.

NATO itself concurred with Bryan's assumption that Ireland would be unable to defend itself in the event of a Soviet assault, but such considerations were largely lost on the political classes, who felt that joining NATO would diminish Irish neutrality. When de Valera returned to power, he made efforts to appease the Americans' distrust of Ireland's refusal to join NATO by seeking defence equipment. Frank Aiken made many overtures to the Americans and tried to persuade them that Ireland was only avoiding joining NATO due to the ongoing issue of partition, but these fell on deaf ears. The Americans continued to be unimpressed by the Irish government's policy. Concessions were, however, made to the Americans, in particular the use of Shannon airport as a major transportation hub for transatlantic flights, something that still has repercussions today. While use was granted to the United States, the Irish government gave assurances that the Soviet Union wouldn't be able to benefit from similar treatment.

The post-war era also ushered in a number of changes to state security that had a profound effect on G2 and how it carried out its operations. The Irish security apparatus had benefited from censorship that had been initiated as part of the overall security policy during the war in Ireland. When this ceased after the war, G2 found its ability to monitor subversive activity severely curtailed. Bryan and his colleagues were no longer able to use wiretaps on phones or to monitor post. This had the effect of cutting the main channels of information that G2 relied on. The government was determined to hand these powers to An Garda Síochána, specifically to the Garda

Commissioner. With its main source of information curtailed, much of G2's remit in the period after the war involved clearing up historical information in relation to Axis spies who had been captured in Ireland. This information was shared via the Dublin link with the Liddells and MI5, who maintained a good working relationship with Dan Bryan following the end of the war.

Cecil Liddell maintained a working brief on Irish affairs, although not to the same extent that he had during the war. When Cecil died in 1952, Bryan passed on his condolences to his brother Guy, who by this stage had risen to the rank of Deputy Director of MI5. Cecil was replaced at the Irish section by Sir Dick White, who had worked on some of the Irish spy cases during the war. White made several trips to Dublin, meeting Bryan and other leading figures in G2 and building up a good working relationship. White had been instrumental in the operation of the Double Cross System and his talents were soon used elsewhere in MI5. After leaving the Irish section he was promoted to the role of Deputy Director General of MI5, eventually succeeding Sir Percy Sillitoe as Director in 1953. In 1956 Prime Minister Anthony Eden moved him to the secret intelligence service, MI6, where he became Director before retiring in 1968. White had held the unique honour of having been head of both MI5 and MI6.

With White's promotion, the Irish section was headed by Brigadier Bill Magan, who was born in County Meath and had served in the British Army in India. Magan had been appointed director of MI5's overseas department in 1951 and had worked in a number of countries, including Malaya (now Malaysia), Kenya, Nyasaland, Borneo and Aden (now Yemen). He was considered a safe pair of hands and was trusted implicitly with Irish affairs by his colleagues. Magan retired from his role in the security service in 1968 and successfully ran a fruit farm in Kent. Despite multiple changes in personnel, the Dublin link between G2 and MI5 endured and both sides worked well with each other, which is in many ways a tribute to the strong foundations laid by Bryan and the Liddells.

Throughout the 1950s information was passed between G2 and MI5 mainly on communist subversives in Ireland. Bryan forwarded samples of Soviet propaganda that had been noted and collected by G2 operatives operating in the state and kept Irish diplomats abreast of communist subversive activity. Writing to Denis R. McDonald at the Mission to the Holy See, he outlined the increasing success with which communism was organising in Ireland:

> I judge the Communists solely from the extent to which they might interfere with Irish defence efforts in a crisis or, still more important, by the extent to which they might use sections of the Irish population in England, America and other countries during a war that would affect Irish interests. Briefly this means, how could Russia in a future conflict, or even in peace time, use the Irish population here, in England or America for anti-British and anti-American propaganda or for sabotage or espionage against these countries. In my opinion, if, as I am convinced, this is the Russian and Communist purpose, they are meeting with a fair measure of success and are improving their potential organisation, while at the same time working on the nationalist and anti-Partition spirit and skilfully selling their propaganda. So far, no information of attempts to use the Irish people for espionage has come to my knowledge. This would, however, only follow after skilful penetration by propaganda etc. The Russians have attempted to use Irish organisations in England for this purpose before and certainly will again.

During the 1950s G2 also built on its relationship with the OSS; which had been stymied in the latter end of the 1940s by David Gray's continuing presence in Dublin. Gray was held in scant regard by many in the Department of External Affairs and by members of G2, who regarded him as almost anti-Irish. Following his departure, it became possible to build on Ireland's political relationship with the USA.

Bryan met with an American military attaché who explained that the USA wanted to scrutinise how the Irish were dealing with communist activities. Bryan felt that the Americans seemed to be more sensitive to the issue of communist activity in Ireland than they had been to German and Japanese spies active during the war. They seemed very determined to curb any communist influence in Western Europe and took the Irish situation very seriously. It was decided then to keep the Americans abreast of any information gathered by G2 to pre-empt any complicated situations that might arise if the Americans were kept in the dark. G2 was able to build on the good relationship it had with the OSS following Gray's departure from Dublin in 1948.

From 1950 onwards the relationship with America developed further from a security perspective when the successor organisation to the OSS, the CIA, approached Dan Bryan about posting a permanent representative to Dublin. It was envisaged that the CIA representative would work closely with G2 on security matters. Bryan declined because he felt it was unnecessary and inappropriate, and the proposed candidate was instead sent to London. The Americans raised the issue again in 1954, explaining that any co-operation between the CIA and G2 would centre on counter-espionage and monitoring suspected communists. They proposed that the link could operate through the American Embassy in London.

Eventually the proposal was pursued through official government channels when CIA Director Allen Dulles wrote to the Minister for External Affairs, Liam Cosgrave, who agreed to the proposed arrangement. Two CIA officers were sent to Dublin from London and worked extremely well with their G2 counterparts. The CIA officers monitored the radical left in Ireland and kept themselves abreast of suspected communist activities in the state. In return for this liaison G2 sought information from the CIA in relation to IRA activities abroad, particularly in the United States. In the event, very little information was passed on, as intelligence of this kind fell under the remit of the FBI, and the CIA was not in a position to divulge anything to G2. Bryan was satisfied that his efforts in investigating communism in Ireland had been of great benefit to state security. This was largely because it negated the need for the British and Americans to establish a covert presence in Ireland. Bryan clashed on various occasions with Minister for External Affairs Seán MacBride, who, as a staunch republican, had issues with British espionage in Ireland.

By 1952 Bryan was coming to the end of his tenure as Director of Intelligence and a much quieter life awaited him. Given his exemplary record during the war, he expected to be appointed to the role of adjutant general of the army – and was bitterly disappointed when he was passed over. His reputation in Intelligence was outstanding, and he had been kept in the role by his superiors as he excelled where it was felt others wouldn't have done as well.

In March 1952 Bryan was appointed to the role of Commandant of the Military College in County Kildare, bringing to an end his tenure as the director of G2. His time at the Military College was a more low-key affair than his role in Intelligence, although he maintained a good working relationship with his colleagues and he was well thought of by his students. During his tenure at the college, he hoped that he would receive a promotion, but this never came to pass. Feeling that his career had run its course, he took early retirement from the army in November 1955. He remained active with the army as a member of the reserve, but only really in a token capacity. In 1965 he was relinquished of his commission and returned to civilian life for the first time since he had travelled to Dublin as a young medical student so many years earlier. He and his wife, Ellen, enjoyed their new-found freedom and were able to entertain friends and socialise more than they had before. He was also able to indulge his passion for military history – in 1949 he had been a founder member of the Military History Society of Ireland.

Bryan felt deeply that military history in Ireland should be given greater emphasis and he lobbied alongside academics Professors Michael Tierney, Gerard Hayes-McCoy and Robert Dudley Edwards for a chair of military history to be established at his alma mater, UCD. While this did not come to pass, Bryan was instrumental in seeing that the Military Archive was organised into a suitable fashion for more widespread consultation. He gave many talks on his time in the IRA in the 1920s and during these he met many of his old colleagues from the War of Independence. He was a founding member of the 1916–1921 Club of veterans of the revolutionary period who would meet up at various venues for historical talks about the era. Membership of the society straddled the Civil War divide and the officer board included, along with Bryan, such luminaries as Richard Mulcahy, Martin Walton, Tom Gunn, Dick Hegarty and Eamon Broy. Bryan talked about his own experiences at the meetings and often gave a very popular talk entitled 'British Intelligence in Ireland 1916–1921'. Meetings like these played a role in ending some Civil War animosities, and at one talk he gave to the society in 1971 he exchanged his chair as Club President and shook hands with his successor, who had been on the opposite side in the Civil War.

Bryan also kept in contact with many of the people he had worked with at the Department of External Affairs and occasionally visited Dr Richard Hayes at his home in Thornfield, Sandymount to reminisce about the old days during the war. When Hayes passed away from lung cancer on 21 January 1976, Bryan was greatly saddened – a further connection with those halcyon days had been lost. The death of his beloved wife, Ellen, on 17 February 1978 was a hammer blow. She had been a constant presence by his side since they married in 1930. Much of Bryan's latter years were passed studying military history. Topics he researched included the Curragh during the Jacobite War, the Battle of Rathmines, the life of Colonel Richard Grace and the Battle of Dungan's Hill. He regularly gave interviews about his time in G2 and often spoke of his exploits on RTÉ radio and television.

By 1985 Bryan's health was deteriorating and he was diagnosed with stomach cancer. He died on 16 June 1985 at his home in Ballsbridge and was buried at Clara graveyard near his family home at Dunbell, County Kilkenny. His funeral mass, held in St Mary's Church, Haddington Road, Ballsbridge, was attended by two former chiefs of staff as well as his old army colleagues and many of the politicians and political figures with whom he had worked during his long tenure in the army. At his family's request the army was not asked to provide military honours at the funeral – Bryan didn't want any pomp. He also asked that the tricolour be draped over his coffin only after his funeral and only in preparation for the journey to Kilkenny. A second mass was held for him in Clara church and celebrated by his cousin Fr John Holohan. The chief mourners were his brothers Michael, Stephen and Paddy and his sisters Mary, Bridget, Nellie and Margaret. His nephews Bartley and John, as well as other family members, were also present. In the days and months that followed his death, many of his former colleagues paid tribute to him and his life of service to the Irish state. One of the most touching tributes came from his former Director of Signals, Colonel E. D. Doyle:

He was a true patriot in the best sense of that term in that he asked for neither reward or publicity ... He only quietly expressed his satisfaction with doing a good job and a vital job right through the last Emergency.

Doyle was glowing in his praise for his old friend, describing him as possessing a keen brain and an unfailing sense of duty. The sitting Chief of Staff of the Defence Forces echoed Colonel Doyle. Bryan, he said, 'would be remembered as an officer of considerable stature and intellectual capacity who contributed significantly to the modern defence forces'.

With Dan Bryan's passing, Ireland lost one of the last links to the secret war that was waged by G2 to keep the country neutral and safe from invasion by Axis and Allied powers during World War II. Ireland had benefited greatly from having such a patriotic and selfless man in post at such a sensitive period in Irish history. The evolution of intelligence in Ireland is largely the story of Dan Bryan and his co-operation and good standing with his peers that allowed him to mastermind the most sophisticated security operation that the Irish state had ever seen. Unfortunately, due to his discreet nature and a similar attitude to public service by many of his colleagues in G2, much of this patriotism has been lost on the Irish public. His legacy, however, was taking G2 through its most difficult and vulnerable period and beginning its evolution into a modern, sophisticated intelligence service that has dealt with many major security threats in the Irish state. The foundations built by Bryan were tested many times, from the Arms Crisis of 1970 through the Troubles in Northern Ireland to more recent threats such as the HSE cyber-attack of 2021. G2 has gone from strength to strength and today is an active component of the Irish state security apparatus. Much of that success was built on the ingenuity of Bryan, the humble farmer's son from County Kilkenny, Ireland's forgotten patriot and an unsung hero who served the state and the Irish people with distinction and honour.

In the years since Bryan's time, G2 has modernised into a sophisticated intelligence network catering for the entire Defence Forces and it was redesignated J2 to refer to the joint intelligence services of the Army, Naval Service and Air Corps. This was the first time intelligence had been given an official name within the army, as until this point G2 had been a purely colloquial moniker.

Monitoring communist activity in Ireland continued for the rest of the Cold War period. A special level of surveillance was kept on the embassies of Eastern Bloc countries and those who worked in them. Often the land border with Northern Ireland was of concern to J2. In November 1983, in a particularly fraught moment for national security, Director of Intelligence Colonel Leo Buckley briefed Peter Barry, the Minister for Foreign Affairs, on the possibility that British/NATO nuclear missiles were being stored on the island of Ireland. The security service believed that nuclear weapons were being stored at underground facilities inside Benbradagh Mountain near Dungiven, County Derry. Buckley believed that US forces were using the mountain as a communication hub for their North Atlantic fleet and that the mountain-based facility was also capable of storing high-grade explosives. This gave rise to the theory that nuclear weapons were being stored there. In a memo to Minister Barry, Buckley outlined that J2's surveillance systems were not sophisticated enough to be able to confirm or deny the presence of nuclear weapons at the location. The British strongly denied that there were any land-based nuclear weapons at the site but refused to deny that they were using air- and sea-based nuclear weapons in the Derry area.

Anxiety around the storage of nuclear weapons in Northern Ireland further plagued J2 during the 1980s. In 1985 it carried out reconnaissance of a British Army barracks at Forkhill, County Armagh, when information was received from local sources that the facility had been converted for nuclear storage. J2 was able to establish that while material was being brought on site at night and that underground bunkers existed in the complex, they were for protection from mortar attacks by the Provisional IRA as opposed to use for nuclear purposes.

Throughout the late 1960s and 1970s Irish Military Intelligence was primarily concerned with the threat of paramilitary organisations in Northern Ireland. This had its genesis in the unrest that erupted in 1969, and from the outbreak of the Troubles J2 officers were regularly sent across the border on intelligence-gathering missions. Indeed, Captain James Kelly, later involved in the Arms Trial of 1970, was present during the Battle of the Bogside, but not in an official capacity. The off-duty captain had been visiting a friend in Derry when the violence erupted. In the wake of the violence in Derry,

Taoiseach Jack Lynch asked J2 to draw up plans for a military intervention in Northern Ireland using guerrilla tactics to protect Catholics from attacks by loyalist mobs. The plan, codenamed Exercise Armageddon, was later deemed unworkable due to fears that it would further escalate tensions and that the army was ill equipped for such an endeavour. The irony that some ministers who had underfunded the army for many years and were now asking the same army to attack another NATO country was not lost on Military Intelligence.

In 1970, the Irish intelligence services became embroiled in Ireland's most infamous political scandal. Intelligence officer Captain James Kelly was implicated in a clandestine operation to import arms into Ireland to help beleaguered nationalists in Belfast and Derry. The plan, which was carried out with the knowledge of Minister for Finance Charles Haughey and Minister for Agriculture Neil Blaney, saw £50,000 of a £100,000 fund diverted to illegally smuggle in arms and ammunition for Citizen Defence committees in Northern Ireland. The operation came to the attention of the Garda Special Branch, which informed Minister for Justice Mícheál Ó Móráin and Taoiseach Jack Lynch, who failed to act promptly. The Special Branch, feeling that the matter wasn't being dealt with quickly enough, leaked the information to the leader of the opposition, Liam Cosgrave, who forced Lynch's hand. Lynch sacked Ministers Haughey and Blaney, and Captain Kelly was forced to resign. The subsequent trial, at which Director of G2 Colonel Michael Hefferon testified, collapsed, resulting in the acquittal of the three men as well as businessman Albert Luykx, who had also been implicated in the scandal. Today the extent to which the entire operation was sanctioned at the highest levels of government is regularly debated and still very much shrouded in mystery.

In more recent times G2 has been involved in monitoring threats from Islamic extremists who seek to exploit Ireland as a platform from which to launch attacks on Britain, in much the same way as Nazi Germany intended to during the war. In 2017, Rachid Redouane, one of the three ISIS terrorists involved in the London Bridge attack, which resulted in the deaths of seven people, was discovered to have been living in Rathmines in Dublin for five years prior to this. When Redouane was shot by the police, he had

Irish identity papers on him. According to former Deputy Director of G2, Retired Lieutenant Colonel Michael C. Murphy, Ireland's present security arrangements in relation to foreign subversive threats are not fit for purpose. Speaking at the McGill Summer School in Glenties, County Donegal in 2020, Murphy said:

I can tell you here today that any expert conducting an inquiry will examine our current intelligence architecture against the reasons for intelligence failure. It will not take them very long to come to the conclusion that this state's counter-terrorism preparation was GROSSLY NEGLIGENT. Our current intelligence structures are not fit for purpose. Not alone does this put the lives of our own people at risk but also those of our close neighbours in the UK, and elsewhere in Europe. However, there is some light beginning to shine. Already the new Taoiseach Leo Varadkar has promised that within 50 days of taking office [2 August] he will have a new Cabinet Security Committee established, similar to COBRA in the UK. Recently we all learned that Mr Varadkar can be a good runner. So, now it will be interesting to see how good he is at getting over obstacles. I say that because if he wishes to implement his proposed changes, he is going to have to get over the many obstacles that will [be] placed in his path by the usual vested interests. I say that because it was reported in 2016 that Mr Simon Coveney, who was then the Minister for Defence, made proposals regarding changing our intelligence structures but was met by fierce opposition by the then Taoiseach, the Minister for Justice, the Department of Justice, and An Garda Síochána. However, another light in recent months is that there appears to be greater awareness of our security inadequacies by a growing number of TDs and Senators. Importantly, among them is the leader of the opposition, Mr Micheál Martin, who has acknowledged that we have a security problem and that we need to consider creating a civilian intelligence agency and rethink how we do security.

Murphy argues that a number of measures are needed to modernise Irish security. He believes strongly that the structures and functions of the

National Security Committee need to be reviewed and recommends the establishment of a National Intelligence Analysis Centre led by a Director for National Intelligence who would advise the government and co-ordinate intelligence across all government departments and agencies. Murphy also advocates the establishment of a civilian intelligence agency and the removal of state security responsibility from the Garda Commissioner based on the present Canadian security model. Doing this will, he believes, address significant security shortcomings in the current Irish intelligence make-up.

Notwithstanding present security difficulties, Irish intelligence has grown substantially over the twentieth century largely due to the strong foundations built by Dan Bryan and his colleagues during the Emergency. While many of the same financing issues persist, J2 is considered one of the most effective and secretive intelligence agencies in the world. It has been successfully involved in peacekeeping duties with the UN, in which it has provided safety and security to Irish troops, but has also used these trips abroad to build up extensive dossiers on subversive forces hostile to Ireland. While the Irish government does not deny the existence of J2, it is rarely mentioned, and the location of its headquarters is unknown to the public, although it is believed that J2 maintain bases in Newbridge, County Kildare as well as at McKee Barracks. J2 also operates a Defence Intelligence section dealing with security and languages at the Military College in the Curragh, County Kildare. A Naval Intelligence Cell and Fishery section is based at Haulbowline Naval Base at Cork Harbour, while the Air Intelligence section is based at Casement Aerodrome in Baldonnel outside Dublin City. The former site of G2 headquarters, the Red House at Montpellier Hill, near the Criminal Courts of Justice, where Dan Bryan masterminded Irish security during World War II and where Dr Richard Hayes broke the infamous Görtz cipher, now lies derelict.

In many ways the Red House characterises the story of Bryan, Hayes and the many other heroes of G2. The building is empty and broken, weeds and grass shooting up through paving stones in the adjoining yard. As of 2021 a sign hand-painted by some local people reading 'community garden' is fixed at the entrance to the compound. Attached to the sign is a request by locals that the area be transformed into a garden for the local community. Little, if anything, is known of the former significance of the derelict building and its crucial role in World War II. Such indifference to the war years in Irish history is unfortunately quite commonplace.

In 2008, one of the many Éire signs that were scattered around the Irish coast was rediscovered after a gorse fire on Bray Head in County Wicklow. The area had become overgrown with gorse bushes that had obscured the sign, which had been long forgotten about locally. The large granite boulders that had been painstakingly put in place during the war were completely submerged under thick bushes, and the bright white paint that had helped illuminate them to belligerent aircraft had long been sullied by 80-odd years of inclement Irish weather. The drought brought on by the hottest summer on record in 2018 provided a natural environment for a gorse fire to spread and soon the area was stripped bare of foliage once again. When local volunteers cleaned down the stones their brilliant white sheen became visible once more against the blackened and scorched earth.

After terrific efforts by volunteers from Greystones all the rocks were cleaned and gorse roots were removed from around their bases before they were repainted with all-weather paint. In the weeks and months that followed the team of volunteers restored the sign to its former glory and the site now intrigues walkers along the Wicklow coastline, prompting questions about the purpose of the signs and reigniting an interest in the story of World War II in Ireland for a younger generation. The Bray Head Éire sign is in many ways a metaphor of what needs to be done on a wider scale in Ireland to promote the legacy of G2 and the defence forces as a whole, and the role they played in ensuring that Irish neutrality and sovereignty were upheld and protected during the course of World War II.

The issue of commemoration of this period has been dealt with in some respects with the construction of the Irish National War Memorial Gardens at Islandbridge in Dublin. The gardens commemorate all Irish people who died during both world wars and although some of the earlier commemorations attracted huge crowds, the gardens, due to fears of republican violence, were never officially opened or dedicated. Such fears were certainly well placed. On Christmas Day 1956 an IRA bomb was placed under the cross of remembrance. A repeat attack was carried out by republicans in October 1958 but fortunately both attacks were unsuccessful and the Wicklow granite stone was able to withstand each blast. Where the IRA had failed, the government succeeded; the gardens were damaged beyond repair by neglect during the 1970s and 1980s, when they were used as a halting site for the Travelling community and a Dublin Corporation rubbish dump for the city's refuse. Sadly, some structural damage remains to this day, although there has been a concerted effort in recent decades to restore the gardens to their former glory. Today they provide a glorious public green space, even if many of those visiting them are largely unaware of their significance.

The Irish state also honoured its commitment to the memory of all those who fought in both wars when a state commemoration was held in 2016 to mark the centenary of the Battle of the Somme. On 18 May 2011 Queen Elizabeth II laid a wreath to honour Ireland's dead of both world wars and the Irish government and people were represented by Taoiseach Enda Kenny and President Mary McAleese. While huge steps have been taken to recognise Ireland's role in World War II, there are still many challenges to official commemoration, among which is the lack of a process to deal with Ireland's militant nationalistic tradition during both the War of Independence and the Troubles in Northern Ireland.

Due to a lack of sufficient measures to deal with the past, most of Irish history is often viewed myopically through the lens of militant republicanism. Men like Dan Bryan and Richard Hayes simply don't fit into the nationalist narrative that the state has been built upon. Sharing security information with the British to counter the mutual threat of Nazism simply doesn't sound as romantic as being part of a flying column engaging in guerrilla warfare in West Cork against the Black and Tans or Auxiliaries. This over-simplification of heroic nationalism has been perpetuated by both of the founding parties, Fine Gael and Fianna Fáil, as their political *raison d'être* since the foundation of the state. Such deference to the militant nationalist tradition is problematic due to the narrow strictures of such an ideology.

In September 1951 a statue of Seán Russell was unveiled in Fairview Park commemorating the former IRA Chief of Staff as well as all those who fought in the IRA during the 1930s and 1940s. The statute was unveiled in front of a huge crowd to rapturous applause, and the event was attended by members of the IRA, along with Sinn Féin, Cumann na mBan, Na Fianna and Clan na Gael. Other attendees included the Transport Workers' Union band, the writer Brendan Behan, and members of Clann na Poblachta, the Labour Party, the trade union movement, Dublin Corporation and the GAA.

Almost immediately the statue began to attract criticism and in 1954 it was vandalised for the first time. The statue has been vandalised many times since by right-wing groups who believe that Russell's dealings with the Soviet Union in the 1920s show that he was a Communist, and by left-wing groups who believe that his dealings with Edmund Veesenmayer during World War II show that he was a fascist. To label Russell a Nazi sympathiser is incorrect and inaccurate; he was purely a militarist who was happy to receive weapons from any quarter. The fact that on his trip to the Soviet Union in the 1920s, which he undertook on de Valera's behalf, he was accompanied by Gerald Boland, who would later serve as Minister for Justice during the war, indicates that he came from the same militant tradition as many of his colleagues who would later oppose him in the ruling Fianna Fáil government.

In many ways Russell was simply carrying on the pure republican tradition in the vein of the 1916 leaders, who also indicated their willingness to collaborate with Germany when they referred to 'gallant allies in Europe' in the 1916 Proclamation. There is simply no evidence that Russell believed in Nazi ideology or was anti-Semitic. Indeed, any anti-Semitic sentiment expressed in Ireland has generally been from mainstream politicians such as Oliver J. Flanagan, whose remarks in the Dáil regarding the Jewish community were so offensive, and Dan Breen, who made no bones about his anti-Semitic views, so much so that he was willing to shoulder the coffin of Hermann Görtz in Deansgrange Cemetery in 1947. However, if Russell was not a Nazi, he was guilty of extraordinary naivety about the brutality of the Nazi regime and the consequences that would have had for Ireland if Germany had won the war. A united Ireland achieved with Nazi assistance must be weighed against the 2,300 Irish Jews who were enumerated on Adolf Eichmann's list of European Jews at the Wannsee Conference. Would Irish unity have been worth the lives of these Irish citizens? While Russell was dead by the time the conference took place, the legacy of his collaboration must be considered, especially in light of the knowledge we have of Nazi atrocities.

Perhaps one of the most poignant memorials to Nazi terror lies at the site of the former village of Oradour-sur-Glane in the Haute-Vienne department in Nouvelle-Aquitaine in west central France. In 1944, just 10 days after the D-Day landings, up to 200 soldiers of the Waffen SS, a unit that included foreign nationals in its ranks, entered the village. Women and children were rounded up and locked into a local church, which was then set alight. The SS men picked off anyone who tried to escape with machine-gun fire. In total 642 men, women and children were killed, along with a small number of Spanish refugees, making this the worst civilian atrocity to take place in France during the war. As they left the village the SS set it on fire, burning it to the ground. In 1946 General Charles de Gaulle ordered that the entire site be preserved as it was, and the 40-acre site now acts as a 'martyred village', a symbol of Nazi terror and a united France opposed to such horrors. In the same year the French National Assembly passed a law classifying Oradour as a historic monument, ensuring that the town be preserved as it was for all time.

Had Russell and Stephen Hayes succeeded in their mission, no matter how noble they believed their intentions were, how many small villages in Ireland could have suffered a similar fate? Stephen Hayes's own words in the Carter tapes back up the assumption that he and others were extraordinarily naive. They also suggest that there were likely no anti-Semitic motives behind working with Germany:

We didn't want the Germans in [invading] as much as the British. If you got the Germans in, in 100 years' time it would, you would, be still trying to get them out. The only thing we needed of them was help.

The anger behind the defacement of the Russell statue is misplaced – Russell simply belonged to the same nationalist tradition that both Fine Gael and Fianna Fáil have sought to eulogise when it was politically expedient to do so. The Seán Russell statue was again defaced as recently as 2020, and the campaign of removing statues associated with colonialism that was largely sparked by the murder of George Floyd in Minneapolis prompted then Taoiseach Leo Varadkar to comment, 'We've a few of our own statues we might need to think about' in reference to the Russell statue.

The Seán Russell statue issue is indicative of a wider problem in relation to the lack of commemoration of Dan Bryan, others in G2, and Richard Hayes. Overtly nationalistic politics in Ireland has written many of the heroes of both world wars out of the historical narrative. This is evident in the fact that while many Irishmen who had fought Nazism were blacklisted by the de Valera government for fighting in British uniforms against Hitler's Germany, numerous IRA men who collaborated with the Nazis returned to the jobs they had held prior to the war without hindrance, retiring on full pensions. While it is unclear why such favourable treatment was offered to these men and others, the fact that they were veterans of the War of Independence cannot be discounted. While Dan Bryan and many others in G2 were also veterans of the same conflict, their role during World War II does not seem to merit the same recognition.

The role of Richard Hayes, a civilian codebreaker, deserves special mention and recognition by the state, which has forgotten him. In 2020 I tried to rectify this historical wrong by campaigning to the Irish government for formal recognition for Hayes's contribution to the state during the war and his crucial role in helping maintain neutrality and protecting Irish sovereignty. This, I thought, was an obvious starting point for the debate; the recognition of Bryan and others could be addressed afterwards. My idea was warmly received by Minister for Arts Josepha Madigan, who enthusiastically championed a state commemoration of Dr Hayes. Unfortunately, the Covid-19 pandemic hindered any real progress and the idea was not as keenly received by Minister Madigan's successor, Minister Catherine Martin, who told me in late 2020 via her private secretary that her department had no interest in any such commemoration:

> I write further to your request for a meeting with Catherine Martin, TD, Minister for Media, Tourism, Art, Culture, Sports and the Gaeltacht, regarding commemoration for Dr Richard J Hayes former Director of the National Library of Ireland. The Minister appreciates your interest in Dr Hayes, however with regard to commemoration, she is currently focused on the Decade of Centenaries Programme and you will

appreciate commemorating the events of 1920–23 are a priority for this department.

Minister for Foreign Affairs and Defence Simon Coveney was equally unenthusiastic about commemorating Hayes, outlining his views to me via email shortly after Minister Martin's response:

> I have consulted with my colleagues in the Military Archives who have confirmed that while Dr Hayes did work with army intelligence on code-breaking, Dr Richard J. Hayes was not a member of the Defence Forces and there are no records to indicate that Dr Hayes served a temporary commission in the Defence Forces. On the basis that Dr Hayes was not a member of the Defence Forces, the question of a military honour does not arise and as such it would not be appropriate for my department to take the lead on any commemorative event. I am sorry the news is not more favourable.

Such views on this period of history are not new, but they do raise the question of how Ireland as a country reckons with the legacy of two world wars and of how it treats the memory of Dr Hayes and Colonel Dan Bryan and the many other brave men of G2 who acted as bulwark against fascism at a time when Irish sovereignty was at its most vulnerable since the foundation of the state.

While Bryan and his colleagues may never receive any official recognition in their own country, their legacy is evident in the standing in which Ireland is held today by members of MI5, the CIA and the security services of other former Allied nations, who recognise the role that Ireland played in defeating Hitler and the Nazi regime. Such esteem was almost immediate and hasn't diminished in the intervening decades.

On 14 May 1945, the first of a fleet of German U-boats made their way up the River Foyle in Derry to the port of Lisahally, where they were formally ordered to surrender by Admiral Sir Max Horton, Commander-in-Chief of the Western Approaches. Standing alongside the British forces, in civilian clothing, was Dan Bryan. His invitation to the surrender was an unofficial recognition of the tremendous role he and G2 had played in defeating Hitler's Nazi forces. It was the most discreet of honours for a most discreet man.

The old falsehood that Ireland was cowardly in its neutrality is slowly but surely being chipped away. With that, at least Bryan, the farmer's son from rural Kilkenny, can take his place in the pantheon of Irish heroes who, while missing from the historical record, loom large across the ages with their selfless deeds and bravery when all other hope was lost. They were and they remain the most decent of men in most indecent times.

XI

EPILOGUE: A JOURNEY WEST

When I envisaged myself sitting down to write the epilogue to this book, I imagined doing so in very different circumstances to those in which I now find myself. My original plan was to travel to California once time allowed, to visit Prof. Carter and to look through her personal collection of archives in relation to Ireland during the Emergency. I'd also hoped to visit the Hoover Institute at Stanford University, which has in its collections a wealth of information regarding the war in Ireland. As it turned out, I was originally able to make it some of the way as far as California – about halfway, to be exact. In early 2021, my partner, Madeleine, and I moved temporarily to Toronto, Canada. Madeleine is a doctor and works delivering care to pre-term infants, and we hoped that the relocation would allow her to take the next steps in her career. I had planned to visit Prof. Carter soon after our arrival here, but the ongoing spectre of Covid-19 restrictions made that impossible. In mid-November 2021 the Biden administration reopened the US border to international visitors, and that finally gave me the opportunity to make my trip out west.

Over the course of the last year, I have been fortunate enough to build up a good professional relationship with Prof. Carter and have enjoyed many Zoom calls with her throughout the pandemic. Her interest in and passion for Irish history have long impressed me, but my greatest admiration is reserved for the remarkable way in which she has preserved the important oral histories of Colonel Dan Bryan and others for over 50 years. World War II and Ireland's participation as a country is one of the most neglected aspects of our small island's history. It seems incredible that one of the most unique oral histories from that time has been preserved far from Irish shores in California, and that is testament to Prof. Carter's standing as a historian and her passion for conserving the past. Getting to meet her and to look through the archive for this book was an honour and a privilege.

As we walked around the campus in Stanford University, I couldn't help but be fascinated by Prof. Carter's recounting of her many extraordinary experiences in Dublin in the 1970s. During her research, she spent many hours with Dan Bryan, Richard Hayes, Douglas Gageby and many others, and she speaks very warmly of those men and their quiet patriotism. The untold story of Bryan and Hayes *et al* has consumed me for the last several years, and perhaps the most personally rewarding moment of this constant research came where Prof. Carter told me that, 'It's a pity you never met Dr Hayes and Dan Bryan; I think they would have really liked you and appreciated what you are doing. You know, they really wanted this story told." Such a compliment was extremely heartening for me, and made me feel that all the work I have carried out thus far has been worthwhile.

If this popular history volume achieves one thing, I hope that it piques the interest of others to further research this too-often neglected period of Irish history. The construction of a political aura of mystique and romanticism has cloaked the revolutionary period of Irish history from 1916 to the end of the Civil War in a shroud of sanitisation, and this has had a detrimental effect on the history of both world wars on the island of Ireland. Does one really have to be valued over the other in order to give the nation a foundation stone on which to build its politics? While the revolutionary period certainly gave birth to the modern Irish state, it has also fostered the spectre of political violence that haunts Ireland to this day. Such fratricidal violence stands in stark contrast to the deeds of Bryan and others who put country before ideology when Ireland was at its most vulnerable. All the gains of the War of Independence would have been for naught had German troops landed on these shores 80 years ago. While the revolutionary period has been commemorated in almost every aspect possible since 2016, and rightly so, the history of both world wars – especially World War II – has been more or less ignored by the state. I couldn't help but notice how things were different in Canada.

On arrival in Toronto and after quarantining, one of the first things I wished to do was to receive my vaccination for Covid-19. I knew virtually nothing about the city and as I made my way along Queen Street, past Nathan Phillips Square to the vaccination centre, I was struck by the sight of the Old City Hall cenotaph that commemorates all Canadians who died during both world wars as well as the Korean War. While the word 'cenotaph' has certain connotations in Ireland and is associated with Remembrance Sunday in London and elsewhere, the origins of the word are in themselves interesting. Originating from the Greek word *kenotaphion* – *kenos*, empty and *taphos*, tomb – it signifies an empty tomb. Fittingly, the inscription on the Toronto cenotaph reads 'To Our Glorious Dead', in memoriam to all those who died and served in both world wars and are buried elsewhere. The Canadian flag flies proudly overhead and the cenotaph is a focal point for any commemorative events and has been for many decades now. Clearly this is much easier given Canada's status as a Commonwealth country and its close ties to the United Kingdom, but there also seems to be a unifying factor here. While Ireland has made large strides in recent years, we are perhaps some way off official recognition of Hayes, Bryan and others. With time, that position will hopefully change.

As I prepared to leave Ireland earlier this year, I found myself in Kilkenny on a research trip for another project. Driving through the rural landscapes of Bennettsbridge and Dunbell reminded me very much of my own home near Ballyshannon. The familiar sight of old homesteads long left empty and derelict by the passage of time dot the landscape, much as they do in rural Donegal. Each of them tells their own story and is part of the collective Irish history that makes up the fabric of our small country. Unaccustomed to the area, I found myself having to stop and ask a local farmer for directions to my destination: Clara graveyard. I had one last thing to do before I closed the book on my own personal journey through this story.

I explained to the farmer that I was looking for the grave of Dan Bryan, and the gentleman soon put me on my way to the small graveyard. Such is the tightknit nature of rural Ireland that I wondered whether some relation of the man might have known Bryan. Perhaps he himself did? I soon found myself in the small graveyard and was struck by the sight of Bryan's final resting place. Such a modest grave for a colossal figure in Irish history. Perhaps it's what he would have wanted and is fitting to the man's nature, but it belies the pivotal role he and others played in charting the course of the nascent Irish state through its most perilous stage of development. The simple stone description reads 'Sacred to the memory of Col. Dan Bryan, Ballsbridge, Dublin'. As I paid my respects to Colonel Bryan, I couldn't help but be struck by the fact that so much of history is circumstance. It, like life itself, is about doing the right thing – if not necessarily the popular thing, as my old friend Gerry Connolly used to say. Dan Bryan certainly lived a remarkable life by those lines; one that straddled the history of the Irish state from Independence until the mid-1980s. History and the crucial decisions that can define a state are often made by those who work quietly in the shadows rather than by those who shout the loudest.

After a moment I walked back to my car, turned the key in the ignition and began to make my way home. Four hours back to Ballyshannon and then soon a short hop across the Atlantic to Canada and on to the next adventure, the next story that piques my interest. Hopefully Prof. Carter was right, and Dan Bryan would have approved of his story being told to a wider audience. As I leave the townlands of rural Kilkenny behind, something tells me that he would have been, and that he and his colleagues would have been more than delighted to be around today to receive the plaudits they so richly deserve.

Viris fortibus non opus est moenibus.

BIBLIOGRAPHY

Primary Sources
Oral History Interviews, Carolle J. Carter – Private Collection:
Colonel Dan Bryan, Dublin, Ireland, August 1969 and August 1971
Helmut Clissmann, Dublin, Ireland, August 1969 and August 1971
Corporal John Dillon, Moate, Ireland, August 1971
Dr Richard J. Hayes, Dublin, August 1969 and August 1971
Stephen Hayes, Enniscorthy, Ireland, August 1969
James O'Donovan, Dublin, Ireland, August 1969
Commandant James Power, Athlone, Ireland, August 1969 and August 1971
Sergeant John Power, Athlone, Ireland, August 1969
Günther Schultz, Arklow, Ireland, August 1969 and August 1971

San José State University:
The Burdick Military History Project, San José State University History
    Department. http://www.sjsu.edu/depts/history
Charles B. Burdick Military History Collection, MSS-2010-03-01, San José State
    University Library Special Collections & Archives
Charles B. Burdick War Poster Collection, MSS-2010-02-02, San José State
    University Library Special Collections & Archives
Hugh T. Carlisle Collection, MSS-2011-09-16, San José State University Library,
    Special Collections & Archives

Documents on Irish Foreign Policy Series:
Fanning, Ronan, et al, (eds). *Documents on Irish Foreign Policy Vol. V: 1937–1939*,
    vol. 5, Royal Irish Academy, Dublin, Ireland, 2006.
Kennedy, Michael, et al, (eds). *Documents on Irish Foreign Policy Vol. VI:
    1939–1941*, vol. 6, Royal Irish Academy, Dublin, Ireland, 2008.
Fanning, Ronan, et al, (eds). *Documents on Irish Foreign Policy Vol. VII: 1941–
    1945*, vol. 7, Royal Irish Academy, Dublin, Ireland, 2010.
Fanning, Ronan, et al, (eds). *Documents on Irish Foreign Policy Vol. VIII: 1945–
    1948*, vol. 8, Royal Irish Academy, Dublin, Ireland, 2012.
Crowe, Caitriona, et al, (eds). *Documents on Irish Foreign Policy Vol. IX: 1948–
    1951*, vol. 9, Royal Irish Academy, Dublin, Ireland, 2014.

Kennedy, Michael, et al, (eds). *Documents on Irish Foreign Policy Vol. X: 1951–1957*, vol. 10, Royal Irish Academy, Dublin, Ireland, 2016.

Hoover Institution on War, Revolution and Peace, Stanford University California, United States of America:
James A. Healy Collection on Irish History

National Library of Ireland:
Dr Richard Hayes Papers – MS 22, 981–22, 984
Florence O'Donoghue Papers – MS 31, 344–31, 351, MS 31,347/4/1
James O'Donovan Papers – MS 21, 155, MS 22, 307

Private Collections:
Prof. Carolle J. Carter (personal archive)
Dr Richard Hayes Papers (family possession)
Brian D. Martin, Interviews with Spike Marlin and Douglas Gageby
Captain John Patrick O'Sullivan Papers (family possession)

National Archives of Ireland:
Department of Foreign Affairs Files:
Parachutists (Joseph Lenihan) – A27
Hermann Görtz –A34
O'Reilly/Kenny – A52 I, A52 II
Bryan – Liddell Correspondence –A60
Francis Stuart – A72
Jewish refugees – D/T S11007B/1
Óbed, Tributh and Gärtner – S/12013
Charles McGuinness – S/12860
Hermann Görtz – S/13301
Hermann Görtz – S/13963

Public Record Office for Northern Ireland:
German U-Boat Surrender Londonderry – CAB/3/G/21
Flying Boats at Killadeas, Lough Erne, Co. Fermanagh – CAB/3/G/6

Irish Military Archives:
Directorate of Irish Military (G2) Intelligence Files:
Joseph Andrews – G2/3261
Sgt Codd – G2/4949
Hermann Görtz – G2/1722

Stephen Hayes – G2/3048
Stephen Held – G2/0077
John Kenny – G2/X/1263
Helena Moloney – G2/3364
James O'Donovan – G2/3783
Maisie O'Mahony – G2/3997
John O'Reilly – G2/3824
Seán Russell – G2/3010
Günther Schütz – G2/X/0703
Walter Simon – G2/0207
Francis and Iseult Stuart – G2/0214
Unland/Wilhelm Preetz – G2/0265
Jan Van Loon – G2/3748
Ernst Weber-Drohl – G2/1928

UCD Archives:
Papers of Frank Aiken (1898–1983) – IE UCDA P104
Memoir of Colonel Daniel Bryan (1900–1985) – IE UCDA P109
Papers of Colonel Daniel Bryan (1900–1985) – IE UCDA P71
Papers of Moss Twomey (1896–1978) – IE UCDA P69
Papers of Éamon de Valera (1882–1975) – IE UCDA P150

National University of Ireland, Galway Archives:
Paper-based material in the collection, relating to the work and interests of Col.
    Éamon de Buitléar and that of his son, Éamon de Buitléar, G48/1

University of Georgia: School of Law Archive:
Doetzer, Karl, 'Closing Statement on Behalf of Dr Edmund Veesenmayer', (1948).
    Trial 11 – Ministries Case. 5.
https://digitalcommons.law.uga.edu/nmt11/5

British National Archives Kew Gardens:
Criminal Files:
Hermann Görtz – CRIM 1/813
Dominions Office Files:
Hermann Görtz – DO 121/86
Reports on German Legation in Dublin – DO 121/87
Foreign Office, Government Code and Cypher School, 1922-1946 Files:
Government Code and Cypher School: ISOS Section and ISK Section: Decrypts
    of German Secret Service (Abwehr and Sicherheitsdienst) Messages (ISOS,
    ISK and other series) – HW19

Travel to Éire: Ewald Heindrich; Helmut Clissmann – FO 940/49
MI5 Records:
Joseph Gerard Andrews – KV2/3119
Hermann Görtz – KV2/1321
Stephen Carroll-Held – KV2/1450
Helmut Clissmann/Elizabeth Clissmann – KV6/81
Karel Richter – KV2/31
O'Reilly and Kenny – KV2/119
Joachim Wilhelm Canaris – KV2/167
Wilhelm Eberhardt Preetz – KV2/1303-6

Newspapers, Magazines and Periodicals:
The Banner
An Cosantóir
Donegal Democrat
History Ireland
Impartial Reporter
Irish Independent
Irish Press
Irish Times
Sunday Chronicle
Sunday Dispatch
Sunday Press
Sunday Tribune
The Bell
The Evening Herald
The Evening Mail
The People

Interviews:
Captain Daniel Ayotis – Irish Military Archives, Dublin
Prof. Carolle J. Carter – Los Altos, California
Brian Costello – Roscommon
Faery Hayes – Dublin
Dr Mark M. Hull – Fort Leavenworth, Kansas
Marcel Krüger – Dundalk
Gerry Long – National Library of Ireland
Michael C. Murphy – Ex Deputy Director Military Intelligence, Dublin
Professor Eunan O'Halpin – Trinity College Dublin
Joe O'Loughlin – Belleek, Co. Fermanagh

Dónall Ó Luanaigh – National Library of Ireland
Professor Gary McGuire – University College Dublin
Christine O'Sullivan – Killarney
Sheila O'Sullivan – Killarney
Dr Chris Smith – Coventry

Parliamentary and Official Publications:
Dáil Debates
Seanad Debates
House of Commons Debates
US House of Representatives Debates
US Senate Debates

Historical Annuals:
Greystones Archaeological and Historical Society:
Scannell, James, Journal Volume 4, 2004 'Major Hermann Goertz and German
    World War 2 Intelligence Gathering in Ireland'.
Journal Volume 5, 2006, 'John Francis O'Reilly and John Kenny: Irishmen Sent
    by the Germans to Spy in Ireland during World War 2'.
Text of Talk Given to Clontarf Historical Society, 13 June 2017: 'Captain Hermann
    Görtz – the German WW2 Intelligence Gatherer who Came in Uniform'.

Media Sources:
RTÉ Documentary on One: *Richard Hayes, Nazi Codebreaker,* 2017
RTÉ Documentary on One: *Codename Paddy O'Brien,* 2007
RTÉ Documentary on One: *Goodnight Ballivor, I'll Sleep in Trim,* 1996
Ireland's Nazis, RTÉ Television, TILE FILMS, 2007
Caught in a Free State, RTÉ Television, 1983

Secondary Sources
Abshagen, Karl, Heinz, *Canaris.* Translated by Alan Houghton Broderick
    (London: Hutchinson and Co., 1956)
Bell, J. Bowyer, *The Secret Army – The IRA 1916–1979* (Dublin: Poolbeg Press,
    1989)
Biddlecombe, Darragh, *Colonel Dan Bryan and the Evolution of Irish Military
    Intelligence, 1919–1945* (Thesis for the Degree of MA, Department of Modern
    History, NUI Maynooth, July 1998)
Blake, John W., *Northern Ireland in the Second World War* (Belfast: Her Majesty's
    Stationery Office, 1956)
Breuer, William B., *The Secret War with Germany* (Shrewsbury: Airlife
    Publishing, 1988)

Carroll, Joseph, *Ireland in the War Years, 1939–1945* (Newton Abbott: David & Charles, 1975)

Carter, Carolle J., *The Shamrock and the Swastika: German Espionage in Ireland in World War II* (Palo Alto, CA: Pacific Book Publishers, 1977)

Cass, Michael (ed.), *Intelligence and Military Operations* (London: Frank Cass, 1990)

Churchill, Sir Winston, *The Second World War*. 5 Vols. (Boston: Houghton Miffin, 1950)

Colvin, Ian, *Chief of Intelligence* (London: Gollancz, 1951)

Coogan, Tim Pat, *The IRA: A History* (New York: Roberts Rinehart, 1994)

Éamon de Valera, The Man Who Was Ireland (New York: Harper Perrenial, 1995)

Cox, Colm, 'Militär Geographiche Angaben über Irland', *An Cosnatór*, March 1975, pp. 80–94

Deacon, Richard, *A History of the British Secret Service* (London: Frederick Muller, 1969)

Duggan, John, *Neutral Ireland and the Third Reich* (Dublin: Lilliput Press, 1989)

'The German Threat – Myth or Reality', *An Cosantóir*, September 1989

Dwyer, T. Ryle, *Irish Neutrality and the USA, 1939-1947* (Dublin: Gill & Macmillan, 1977)

Behind the Green Curtain – Ireland's Phoney Neutrality during World War II (Dublin, Gill & Macmillan, 2009)

Elborn, Geoffrey, *Francis Stuart: A Life* (Dublin: Raven Arts Press, 1990)

Falls, Cyril, *Northern Ireland as an Outpost of Defence* (Belfast: Her Majesty's Stationery Office, 1952)

Farago, Ladislas, *The Game of the Foxes: The Untold Story of German Espionage in the United States and Great Britain during World War II,* (David McKay Co.; Book Club (BCE/BOMC) edition (Jan. 1, 1971))

Ferriter, Diarmaid, *Judging Dev* (Dublin: Royal Irish Academy, 2007)

Fisk, Robert, *In Time of War, Ireland, Ulster and the Price of Neutrality 1939–1945* (London: Hutchinson & Co., 1940)

Fleming, Peter, *Operation Sea Lion* (New York: Simon & Schuster, 1957)

Invasion 1940 (London: Hart-Davis, 1957)

Gellately, Robert, *The Gestapo and German Society* (Oxford: Clarendon Press, 1990)

Girvin, Brian, *The Emergency: Neutral Ireland 1939–1945* (London, Pan Books, 2007)

Hinsley, F.H., & Simkins, C.A.G., *British Intelligence in the Second World War, Vol. 4: Security and Counter Intelligence* (London: H.M.S.O., 1990)

The Trial of German Major War Criminals, Part I, 20 Nov.–1 Dec. 194 (London: His Majesty's Stationery Office, 1946)

Hitler, Adolf, *Mein Kampf* (New York: Reynal and Hitchcock, 1939)

Hull, Cordell, *The Memoirs of Cordell Hull*, The MacMillan Company; Volume 1 + 2 edition (1 Jan., 1948)

Hull, Mark, *Irish Secrets: German Espionage in Ireland 1939–1945* (Dublin and Portland, OR: Irish Academic Press, 2003)

Irving, David, *Hitler's War* (London: Hamish Hamilton, 1978)

Johnson, David Alan, *Germany's Spies and Saboteurs* (Osceola, WI: MBI, 1998)

Kahn, David. *The Codebreakers: The Story of Secret Writing* (New York: David McKay, 1969)

Hitler's Spies (New York: Macmillan, 1978).

Kennedy, Brian, *Dr Hermann Goertz – A German Spy in South County Dublin*, Pub. No. 27, Foxrock Local History Club, 1989

Keogh, Dermot, *Ireland and Europe 1919–1948* (Dublin: Gill & Macmillan, 1994)

'Éamon de Valera and Hitler: An Analysis of the International Reaction Visit of the German Minister, May 1945', *Irish Studies in International Affairs*, Vol. 3, No. 1 (1989)

Twentieth-Century Ireland: Nation and State (Cork: Cork University Press, 1999)

Kilbride-Jones, H.E., 'Adolf Mahr', *Archaeology Ireland*, Vol. 7, No. 3 (Autumn 1993), pp. 29–30

Liddell Hart, B.H. (ed.), *The Other Side of the Hill: Germany's Generals, Their Rise and Fall, With their own Account of Military Events, 1939–1945* (London: Cassell, 1948)

History of the Second World War (London: Cassell, 1970)

Littlejohn, David, *Foreign Legions of the Third Reich*, Vol. 1 (San Jose, CA: Bender Publishing, 1981)

Longford, Lord, & O'Neill, T.P., *Éamon de Valera* (London: Arrow Books, 1970)

Lucas, James, *Hitler's Enforcers* (London: Arms and Armour Press, 1996)

Lysaght, Jim, *Oskar Metzke, The Spy Who Should Not Have Died* (blackwater.ie, accessed online 29/09/2020)

McCullagh, David, *De Valera: Rise 1882–1932* (Gill Books, 2018)

De Valera: Rule 1932–1975 (Gill Books, 2018)

McGarry, Fearghal, *Irish Politics and the Spanish Civil War* (Cork: Cork University Press, 1999)

McGuinness, Charles J., *Nomad* (London: Meuthuen & Company, 1934)

Manning, Maurice, *James Dillon, A Biography* (Dublin: Wolfhound Press, 1999)

Martin, Brian D., *The Role of Irish Military Intelligence during World War Two*, Unpublished Thesis, National University of Ireland Maynooth, August 1994

Masterman, J.C., *The Double-Cross System in the War of 1939–1945* (New Haven and London: Yale University Press, 1972)

Mollet, Ralph, *The German Occupation of Jersey, 1940–1945: Notes on the General Conditions, How the Population Fared* (St Helier: Société Jersiaise, 1954)

Molohan, Cathy, *Germany and Ireland 1945–1955: Two Nations' Friendship* (Dublin: Irish Academic Press, 1999)

Natterstad, J.H., *Francis Stuart* (London: Bucknell University Press, 1969)

Nowlan, Kevin B. & Williams, T. Desmond (eds), *Ireland in the War Years and After, 1939–57* (Dublin: Gill & Macmillan, 1969)

O' Callaghan, Sean, *The Jackboot in Ireland* (London: Allan Wingate Ltd., 1958)

O' Donoghue, David, *Hitler's Irish Voices: The Story of German Radio's Wartime Service* (Belfast: Beyond the Pale, 1998).

The Devil's Deal: the IRA, Nazi Germany and the Double Life of Jim O'Donovan (Belfast: Beyond the Pale, 2010)

O'Halpin, Eunan, 'Aspects of Intelligence', *The Irish Sword,* Vol. XIX, Nos. 75 and 76 (1993–4), pp. 57–65

Defending Ireland (Oxford: Oxford University Press, 1999)

'Army, Politics and Society in Independent Ireland, 1923-1945', in T.G. Frasier and Keith Jeffery (eds), *Men, Women and War* (Dublin: Lilliput Press, 2000)

'MI5's Irish memories', in Brian Girvin and Geoff Roberts (eds), *Ireland in the Second World War* (London: Frank Cass, 2000)

(Ed.), *MI5 and Ireland: The Official History* (Dublin and Portland, OR: Irish Academic Press, 2003)

O' Loughlin, Joe, 'Voices of the Donegal Corridor' (self-published, 2005)

Ó Luanaigh, Dónall, 'Richard James Hayes (1902 -1976)', *Oxford Dictionary of National Biography* (Oxford University Press, 2004)

Paine, Lauran, *The Abwehr: German Military Intelligence in World War Two* (New York: Stein and Day, 1984)

Peszke, Michael Alfred, *Poland's Navy, 1918–1945* (Hippocrene Books, 1999)

Rhodes, James Robert, *Churchill: A Study in Failure* (New York: World, 1970)

Roosevelt, Eleanor, *This I Remember* (New York: Harper and Brothers, 1949)

Roth, Jonathan, *Burdick Military History Project.* Pamphlet. San José, CA: San José State University History Department

Share, Bernard, *The Emergency: Neutral Ireland, 1939–1945* (Dublin: Gill & Macmillan, 1978)

Singh, Simon, *The Codebook: The Science of Secrecy from Ancient Egypt to Quantum Cryptography* (London: Fourth Estate, 1999)

Stephan, Enno, *Spies in Ireland* (London: Macdonald, 1963)

Stuart, Francis, *Black List, Section H* (London: Penguin Books, 1996)

Toomey, Deirdre, 'Stuart, Iseult Lucille Germaine (1894–1954)', *Oxford Dictionary of National Biography* (Oxford University Press, 2004)

Walsh, James P. & Wheeler, Gerald E., *Charles B. Burdick and San José State* (From *War, Revolution and Peace: Essays in Honor of Charles B. Burdick*, pp. 1–8, Remak, Joachim (ed.) (Lanham, MD: University Press of America, Inc., 1987))

Walsh, Maurice, *G2: In Defence of Ireland, Irish Military Intelligence 1918–45* (Cork: Collins Press, 2010)

Weizächer, Ernst Von, *Erinnerungen* (Munich: Paul List Verlag, 1950)

West, Nigel, *MI5* (London: Triad Grafton, 1983)

The Guy Liddell Diaries, Vol. I, 1939–1942, (Oxfordshire: Routledge, 2005)

The Guy Liddell Diaries, Vol. II, 1942–1945, (Oxfordshire: Routledge,2005)

Wheatley, Ronald, *Operation Sea Lion* (London: Oxford University Press, 1958)

Wighton, Charles, & Peis, Gunther, *They Spied on England: Based on German Secret Service War Diary of General von Lahousen* (London: Odhams Press Ltd, 1958)

Zentner & Bedürftig (eds), *The Encyclopaedia of the Third Reich*, Vol. 1 (1991)

INDEX

1916–1921 Club of veterans 191–2

A

Abwehr
  Bletchley Park, ISOS and 149
  Brandenburg Regiment 66, 67, 75
  Clissmann, Elizabeth and 71–2
  Clissmann, Helmut and xvii, 67
  espionage missions to Ireland 81, 82, 94–6
  German diplomatic missions, operatives
    attached to 34
  Görtz and 84, 85, 86, 118, 121
  Hitler's reorganisation of 33
  IRA and 35, 36, 41, 44, 45
  Operation Taube (Dove) 71, 72–3
  post-WWI restrictions 33
  Russell, Seán and 35, 65, 66, 67
  Schütz, Günther and 115, 117
  Stuart, Francis and 44–5
  USA, operations in 124
  Veesenmayer and 174
  see also Canaris, Admiral Wilhelm Franz
Aiken, Frank 7, 80
  Belfast Blitz condemned by 131
  German attacks, complaint lodged about 107
  Hull, Cordell, meeting with 129, 130
  partition, NATO and 187
  Roosevelt, meeting with 129
airmen
  Allied airmen 159–60
  Axis airmen 159
  protocols for crash landings 159
  see also Allied aircraft crashes; Axis aircraft
    crashes
Aliens Registration Office, Dublin Castle 172
Allied aircraft crashes 113–14, 133–4, 157, 159
Allied internees
  release of 161
  see also Curragh Camp
Amnesty International 182
Andrews, John Miller 132–3
Andrews, Joseph 120, 150, 152, 163
Anglo-Irish defence co-operation 11, 152
Anglo-Irish Treaty 4
anti-British sentiment 3, 54, 72, 140, 151, 163
Anti-Partition League 94
anti-Semitism 47–8, 140, 200
Aosdána 45
Arbour Hill Prison 120, 142, 146, 152

Archer, Colonel Liam
  background 7–8
  de Valera, meetings with 90
  Deputy Chief of Staff, promotion to 13
  Director of Intelligence 8, 12, 15, 51
  G2, reorganisation of 8
  German Legation, monitoring of 51–2
  ill health 88
  Liddell, Guy, meetings with 19, 90–1
  Local Defence Force (LDF), intelligence
    section 16
  MI5, co-operation with 18–19, 90
  National Army Signal Corps 8
  Nazi Germany, concerns about 8
  Preetz, monitored by 97
Ardnacrusha hydroelectric scheme 19–20
Ark Royal, HMS (aircraft carrier) 113
Arklow, County Wicklow 112
Arms Trial (1970) 193, 194, 195
Army Comrades Association 7
Atlantic, merchant vessels targeting of 64
Auslands Organisation (AO) 23
  Dublin branch 23
  G2 surveillance of 24
  intelligence transmitted to Nazi High
    Command 24
  Landesgruppen 23
  trade agreements and 23–4
Auxiliary Division of the RIC (ADRIC) 27, 199
Axis aircraft crashes 114, 159

B

Bad Nenndorf (British interrogation centre)
  178–80, 182
Baldonnel airport 95
Ballinderry Sword 21
Ballivor, County Meath 86–7
Ballymurrin, County Wexford 106
Barry, Monty (later O'Donovan) 36
Barry, Tom 25, 26, 27–8, 29, 30, 32
Barry, Tom, Senior 27
Barton-Fraser, Eleanor Mary (later Bryan) 6
BBC
  Allied victory, news of 167
  de Gaulle's broadcast 63
  French coast, appeal for photographs 165–6
  Stuart, Francis, broadcasts from Germany 45
BBC World Service 63
Béaslaí, Piaras 8

Becker, Hans 134–5
Begg, Malcolm G. (British Air Attaché) 160–1
Belton, John 138
Belton, Patrick 90
Berry, Peter 169
Bewley, Charles Henry 59
  anti-Semitic views 47–8
  background 46
  German establishment and 77
  German Foreign Ministry and 48–9
  IRA and 48, 49
  Irish Minister in Berlin 46, 47, 48
  Irish Race Convention, attendance at 46
  Minister to the Holy See 48
  security problems posed by 49
Bismarck (German battleship) 113
Black and Tans 27, 199
Blackrock Island, County Mayo 102
Blacksod Lighhouse, County Mayo 163, 164
Blaney, Neil 195
Blenner-Hassett, Roland (OSS agent) 137
Bletchley Park
  Government Code and Cypher School
    (GC&CS) 52, 53
  ISOS section 149, 150, 151
Bloody Sunday 4
Blueshirts 7, 35
Boland, Frederick 89, 90, 160–1, 171, 172, 173
Boland, Gerald 32, 89, 90, 100, 156
  codes procured by 148
  Soviet Union, visit to 31, 200
Boland, Harry 47
Brandenburg Regiment 66, 67, 75, 178, 180
Brase, Colonel Fritz 22
Breen, Dan 3–4, 140, 200
Brennan, Lieutenant General Michael 8
Brennan, Robert (Irish Ambassador in the USA)
  127, 128, 130–1
Briscoe, Robert 47–8
British Air Ministry 110
British Army
  Badd Nenndorf, investigation into 179
  Forkhill Barracks, County Armagh 194
  Irishmen in 3, 28, 188, 202
  poison gas, experimenting with 55
  prisoners, abuse of 179
  Shelburne Co-op, food supplied by 105
  Signals Corps 52
British Board of the Admiralty 113
British Dominions Office 18
British Expeditionary Force, Dunkirk, retreat
  to 62
British School of Telegraphy 14
Brooks, Major General Edward Hale 133
Browne family 108

Bruce, Colonel David K.E. 136, 137
Brugha, Caitlín 35, 117
Brugha, Cathal 35, 117
Bryan, Colonel Dan xv, 1
  1916–1921 Club of veterans 191–2
  audio tapes of xvi, xviii, xx, 206
  background 1–2
  Becker, Hans, views on 134–5
  'British Intelligence in Ireland 1916–1921'
    191
  CIA proposal 190
  Clara graveyard, burial in 207–8
  Clissman, perception of 182
  Coast Watching Service, importance of
    17–18
  commemoration, lack of 202, 203, 207
  communist subversives, views on 188–9
  de Valera, views on 30
  death 192
  Dublin bombings, theory about 110, 111
  Dublin diplomatic circles, monitoring 45, 46
  Free State, external threats to 8–9
  *Fundamental Factors affecting Irish Defence
    Policy* 8–9, 11, 187
  G2 and 6, 7, 8, 13–14, 88, 193
  German espionage in Ireland 41
  German Legation, transmitter in 51
  Görtz and 88–9, 150, 171–3
  Hayes, Richard J. and 192
  Hempel, security profile of 49
  illicit radio traffic, tracing source of 51
  information leakage, control of 162–3
  IRA and 4, 13, 40, 191
  Ireland's security status 10–11
  Irish Volunteers and 3, 4
  Kerney, Leopold H., investigation of 71, 77,
    78–80
  legacy 203, 208
  Local Defence Force (LDF), intelligence
    section 16
  Luftwaffe bombings, views on 106
  MacBride, Seán, clashes with 190
  marriage 6
  memoir (incomplete) xxi
  MI5, co-operation with 18–19, 52
  Military College, Commandant of 191
  military history, knowledge of 10–11, 191,
    192
  National Army and 4
  NATO, views on 187
  Nazi Germany, concerns about 8
  neutrality, German attitude towards 12
  neutrality recommended by 9
  OSS agent, co-operation with 136–7, 143–4
  Preetz, monitored by 97

pro-Treaty stance 4
reputation 191
retirement 191
Ryan, Frank and 74
safeguarding the Irish state, role in 184
Schütz, microdot coding system and 117
Stuart, Francis, suspicions about 43
Supplemental Intelligence Section (SIS) 16
thesis, Irish security policy and 7
tributes 192–3
U-boats, attendance at surrender of 203–4
US soldier, incident in Dublin 132
US technicians in Northern Ireland 131–2
US-Irish relations, security challenge and
    126
see also G2; Hayes, Richard J.
Bryan, Eleanor Mary (née Barton-Fraser) 6,
    191, 192
Bryan family 2, 192
Bryan, John 2
Bryan, Margaret Mary (née Lanagan) 2
Buckley, Colonel Leo 194
Bunreacht na hÉireann (1937) see Constitution
    of Ireland (1937)
Burdick, Charles B. xvi
Burdick Military History Project xvi

C
Cambridge University Officers' Training Corps
    52
Campile, County Wexford 102–5
Canaris, Admiral Wilhelm Franz
    Abwehr and 33, 70, 80, 81
    espionage missions to Ireland 81, 82, 86
    Görtz's mission sanctioned by 86
    Hitler and 33–4, 124–5
    WWI submarine captain 33
    see also Abwehr
Carroll-Held, Stephen
    coded messages found in house 120–1, 147,
        150
    Gardaí, house raided by 88–9, 92, 93, 101
    Görtz and 87–8
    trial 91
Carter, Carolle J. 205–6
    Bryan, Dan and xviii, 7, 17, 30, 40, 49, 74,
        79–80, 100, 111, 132–3, 143–4, 171–3, 182
    Clissmann, Helmut and xvii, xx, xxi, 25, 182
    Hayes, Richard J. and xvi, 206
    Hayes, Stephen and 201
    O'Donovan, James and 37–8, 80
    Power, James and 146–7
    Shamrock and the Swastika, The xv–xvi
Casement Aerodrome, Baldonnel 197
Casement, Sir Roger 19, 141

Celtic studies, German academics and 22, 25
censorship 12, 14, 50, 139, 185, 187
Central Intelligence Agency (CIA) 115–16, 190
    see also Office of Strategic Services (OSS)
Chamberlain, Neville 39
Childers, Erskine 90
Choltitz, General Dietrich von 166
Churchill, Winston 63, 102, 111, 129, 167, 183
CIA see Central Intelligence Agency
ciphers
    German 52, 53, 99, 138, 141–2, 148, 149
    Görtz cipher 93, 150, 151, 152, 197
    Russian 31, 150
Clan na Gael 32, 64, 200
Clann na Poblachta 76, 186, 200
Clarke, Brigadier Dudley 90–1
Clarke, Kathleen 35
Clay, General Lucius D. 172
Clissmann, Elizabeth (Budge) (née Mulcahy)
    26, 71–2, 75, 76, 180, 181
Clissmann, Helmut
    Abwehr, involvement with xvii, 67
    audio tapes of xvii, xx, xxi, 25, 182
    Brandenburg Regiment 67, 75, 178, 180
    Bryan's perception of 182
    Denmark and 75, 178, 180
    German Academic Exchange Service and
        25–6
    German language classes 26
    Germany, recalled to 27
    internment at Bad Nenndorf camp 178,
        179–80
    IRA contacts 25, 26–7, 181–2
    Ireland, return to 180–2
    Irish German Society and 182
    Irish nationalism, interest in 25
    MacBride, Seán, friendship with 25, 181,
        182, 186
    marriage 26
    MI5, interrogation by 180
    Nazi Party membership 26
    North Africa, reassignment to 76
    Operation Taube (Dove) 72–3
    pharmaceutical company established by 181,
        182
    Ryan, Frank and 70, 71, 75, 178
    St Kilian's Deutsche Schule, Dublin 182
    Stuart, Francis and 45
    Trinity College Dublin and 25
    'Wild Geese in Germany, The' (thesis) 25
Coast Watching Service 6, 16–18, 74, 114,
    159–60
Codebreaker (Mc Menamin) v–vi, xv
codebreakers xx, 151
    see also Bletchley Park; Hayes, Richard J.;
        Page, Denys; Strachey, Oliver

Coffey, Diarmuid 47
Cold War 184, 186, 194
Collins, Michael 4, 8, 14, 30, 36, 97
Collinstown aerodrome 95
communism/communists 185, 186, 188–9, 194
Connolly, James 38, 73
Connolly, Nora 73
Connolly, Sean 94
Conradh na Gaeilge 68
conscription 3
Constitution of Ireland (1937) 45, 46, 131
Cosgrave, Liam 190, 195
Cosgrave, W.T. 3, 6, 12, 30
Costello, Commandant Michael Joe 16
Coughlin, Revd Charles Edward 124
Coveney, Simon 196, 203
Covid-19 pandemic xvii, xix, xx, xxii, 202, 205, 206
Cremin, Cornelius (Con) 59, 60, 76
Criminal Investigations Department (CID) 5
Croatia 81, 174, 175, 177
Crofton, James 118
Cryptography xv, 31, 116, 149, 185
Cumann na nGaedheal 6, 22
Curragh Camp, County Kildare 68
    Allied internees 157, 160–1, 168
    concessions granted to internees 158–9, 161
    escape attempts 160–1
    German internees, concessions granted to 158–9
    Hempel's visit to 158
    internees, harsh treatment of 158
    IRA internees 156, 157
    K-Lines (No. 2 Internment Camp) 114, 156, 157, 160, 168
    Local Defence Force (LDF) and 157–8, 159
    Luftwaffe, members of 156, 157
    parole system 158, 160, 161
    security measures 157
    Tin Town (No. 1 Internment Camp) 114, 120, 145, 156
Curragh Racecourse, County Kildare 106
Custume Barracks, Athlone
    cells, 24-hour watch on 153
    complaints, internees and 154
    concessions, internees and 153, 154, 169
    escape attempts 154
    German internees 83, 91, 94, 100, 117, 153–6, 169
    see also Power, Commandant James
Czechoslovakia 9, 55

D
D-Day 54, 162–3, 201
    see also Normandy landings

Dáil Éireann 3, 4, 34
de Buitléar, Lieutenant Colonel Éamonn 12, 13, 115, 116, 147, 150
de Gaulle, General Charles 63, 163, 201
de Lacey, Larry 118
de Valera, Éamon 1
    Aiken's report 129
    Archer, meetings with 90
    army, neglect of 9–10
    army recruits, appeal for 91–2
    Belfast Blitz condemned by 131
    Bryan's views on 30, 143–4
    Cabinet Committee on National Defence 8
    Constitution of Ireland and 45, 46
    constitutional politics and 32
    cryptography unit, Hayes's request for 185
    External Affairs portfolio 156–7
    Fianna Fáil and 7, 29, 43
    German government, protest made to 109
    German internees, end of war and 168–9
    Gray, David, difficulties with 127, 128, 130, 142–3, 144
    Hempel and 44, 53, 54, 106, 158, 183, 185
    Hitler's death, condolences on 183
    Hull's criticism of 131
    IRA, suppression of 40, 43
    Ireland, dominion status of 45–6
    Irish airspace, flying boats and 112
    Irish neutrality and 10, 20, 101
    Irish Race Convention (1922) 47
    Kerney, Leopold H. and 80
    Luftwaffe bombings in Ireland 104, 108–9
    NATO, views on 187
    perception of 143–4
    post-war defence of Irish neutrality 183
    Roosevelt's perception of 130
    Stuart, Francis and 42, 43
    supporters 42
    Treaty Ports and 10
    US technicians in Northern Ireland 131
    World War II and xxii
de Valera, Lieutenant Rúaidhri 13
Deery, Anthony (Tony) 92, 93, 145
Denmark, Clissmann and 75, 178, 180
Department of External Affairs 6, 18, 58, 60, 69, 145
    Bryan, Dan and 89, 90, 100–1, 192
    German Legation, wireless set in 52
    Görtz and 171, 173
    Gray, David, perception of 189
    Hempel and 106, 121
    Kerney, Leopold H., memo sent by 78
    Luftwaffe bombings 109
    Maffey, Sir John and 116, 168–9
    OSS agent and 138

security conference proposal 143
Stuart, Francis, travel documents for 43
see also Boland, Frederick; Walshe, Joseph
Department of Foreign Affairs xxi, 6
Derry
    Battle of the Bogside xvii, 194–5
    military bases 131–2
    U-boats, surrender 203–4
    US troops in 163
Deutsche Akademischer Austauschdienst 24–5
Devers, Major General Jacob 133–4, 157
Dietrich, Josef 178
Digital Roots Studio, California xix
Disney, Walt, *Fantasia* 139
Doetzer, Karl 165, 176–7
Dominions Office, London 45–6
Donegal Air Corridor 112–13
Dönitz, Grand Admiral Karl 64, 167
Donohue, Joe 97, 99, 100, 101
Donovan, Bill, OSS and 136–7
double agents 149, 150, 162
Double Cross System 162, 188
Doyle, Colonel E.D. 192–3
Dublin
    anti-aircraft gunners 107
    bombings, Bryan's theory about 110, 111
    Luftwaffe bombings 50, 77, 102, 105, 106,
        107–8
Dublin Castle 14, 89, 94
    Aliens Registration Office 172
    Cairo Gang, assassination of 4
Dublin Corporation 109, 199, 200
Duggan, Richard 35–6
Duleek, County Meath 105
Dulles, Allen (CIA Director) 190
Dundalk, County Louth 112
Dwyer, T. Ryle xxi

E

East Germany 111
Easter Rising (1916) 8, 28, 94
    aftermath 2, 3, 31
    execution of leaders 3, 25, 35
    Russell, Seán and 30–1
Eastwood, Christopher 149–50, 151, 152, 163
Edenvale, SS, coded message sent from 149–50
Eichmann, Adolf 175, 177, 178, 200
Éire coastal signs
    Bray Head sign 198
    World War II and 198
Eisenhower, Dwight D. 163
Elizabeth, Empress of Russia 31
Elizabeth II, Queen 151, 199
Emergency
    Bryan, Dan and xviii, 12

coastal and air defence 14
G2 personnel 12–13
Gardaí, killing of 39
German espionage during xv
    see also World War II
Emergency Powers Act (1939) 93, 140, 156
Emig, Marianne 84
espionage
    in Ireland xv–xvi, 41, 51
    see also double agents; Görtz, Hermann;
        Hoven, Joseph; Kenny, John; Marlin,
        Ervin Ross; Metzke, Oskar; O'Reilly, John
        Francis; Pfaus, Oscar C.; Preetz, Wilhelm;
        Quigley, Martin S.; Schütz, Günther;
        Weber-Drohl, Ernst
Evening Herald 120

F

Fairview Park, Dublin 199–200, 201–2
Fantasia (film) 139
Farrell, Marie and Bridie 119, 155, 170, 171, 173
Fascio di Dublino Michele D'Angelo 24
fascism 1, 8, 24, 29, 64, 68, 174
Federal Bureau of Investigation (FBI) 190
Fenian Brotherhood 32, 64
Fianna Fáil 6–7, 29, 43, 68, 186, 199, 201
Fine Gael 90, 186, 199, 201
Finner Camp, County Donegal 113
First Inter-Party Government 181, 186
Flanagan, Oliver J. 140, 200
Floyd, George 201
flying boats 79, 112–13, 133
Foreign Office (British) xxi, 149
Foynes, County Limerick 79, 133
France
    civilians, mass evacuation of (*l'exode*) 63
    coastal towns, analysis of images 165–6
    German forces, fall to 62, 63
    German Stuka bombers, refugees attacked
        by 63
    Maginot line 62
    Mussolini's declaration of war on 63
    National Assembly 201
    Oradour-sur-Glane, Nazi massacre at 201
    Paris, liberation of 166
    Vichy France 63, 175
    see also de Gaulle, General Charles; French
        Resistance
Franco, General Francisco 68, 71
French Resistance 63, 163, 165
Friedman, William (cryptographer) 31
Fromme, Franz 35
Frongoch, Wales 3, 31

G

G2 xxii, 5, 12
  aerial photographs 14
  American diplomatic presence, concerns
    about 121
  Auslands Organisation, surveillance of 24
  Axis/IRA partnership, potential threat of 15
  coastal and air defence security division 14
  Dublin diplomatic circles, monitoring 45, 46
  external security section 14
  fascism, bulwark against 203
  German aliens, movements of 15
  German espionage in Ireland 41
  German internees, censorship of mail 158
  Görtz's coded messages 148
  Görtz's landing in Ireland 87
  Hayes, Richard J. seconded to 53–4
  Hempel, security profile of 49
  information leakage, control of 162–3
  information sources curtailed by government
    187–8
  internal security 14
  Italian aliens, movements of 15
  Kerney, investigation of 71, 77
  legacy of 197, 198, 203
  Local Defence Force (LDF) and 15
  MI5, co-operation with 18–20, 50–1, 87–8,
    89–91, 99–100, 115, 151–2
  MI5, post-war links with 188–9
  NATO, views on 186–7
  naval service, security section and 14
  OSS agent Marlin, co-operation with 136–7
  OSS, post-war relationship with 189–90
  personnel during the Emergency 12–13
  Pfaus, surveillance of 36
  post-war reorganisation of 185
  postal censorship 14
  pre-war surveillance operation 15
  Preetz monitored by 97, 99
  press censorship 14
  publicity department 14
  Red House, Dublin (HQ) 13, 20, 98, 99,
    197–8
  redesignation as J2 193
  reorganisation by Bryan 13–14
  role in guarding the Irish state 183–4
  sections and subsections 13–14
  security conference with MI5 and OSS 143
  Signal Corps 51, 52, 92–3, 97
  signals security 14–15
  Stuart, Francis and 43, 45
  Tomacelli, surveillance of 24
  Trinity College, G2 plants in 24
  US criticism of Irish neutrality 125–6
  veterans of the independence campaign 16

  see also Bryan, Colonel Dan; Coast Watching
    Service; Hayes, Richard J.; J2
GAA (Gaelic Athletic Association) 2, 38, 72,
  200
Gaelic League 2, 72
Gageby, Douglas 13, 125–6, 206
García, Juan Pujol (Garbo) 162
Garda Aliens Section 6
Garda Commissioner 89, 145, 187–8, 197
Garda Security Section 6
Garda Síochána, An 5, 187–8
  German Legation and 49
  Local Defence Force (LDF) and 15
  Metzke, Oskar and 56–7
  Scott Medal and 39
Garda Special Branch 6, 15, 24, 32, 94
  arms importation, information about 195
  Görtz and 87, 88–9, 92, 120
  IRA and 39, 118
  US soldier, incident in Dublin 132
  Weber-Drohl picked up by 83
Gartenfeld, Karl Eduard (pilot) 86
GC&CS see Government Code and Cypher
  School
General Election (1918) 3
General Election (1932) 6
genocide, Nazi Germany and 167, 171
George V, King 53
George VI, King 59, 65
George Washington, SS 65
German Academic Exchange Service 25–6
German Armed Forces see Wehrmacht
German Foreign Ministry 48, 59, 61, 65, 66, 121
German Foreign Office 54, 60, 78, 175, 176, 177
  Irish Bureau 65–6, 74, 75, 80
German High Command 33, 45, 75, 162
  Görtz and 86, 92, 148
  Hempel's reports and profiles 58
  IRA and 61, 65
German internees
  academic studies and 161
  asylum (post-war) offered by Irish state
    170–1
  complaints made to Hempel 158
  denazification, Allied policy of 168
  mail censored by G2 158
  war, end of 168–9
  see also Curragh Camp, County Kildare;
    Custume Barracks, Athlone
German Legation 24
  Garda Síochána, An and 49
  Heinkel crash, informed about 114
  Hempel and 44, 49–51, 54
  information leakage, threat of 52, 56, 57, 58
  Metzke and 54–6, 57

monitored by G2 51–2
monitored by MI5 51, 52
OSS agent Quigley's report on 140
secret wireless set at 50–1
staff increase, Irish authorities' refusal 106
wireless set seized 54
German Military Cemetery, Glencree, County
    Wicklow 57, 173
German Palatines 21
German secret service see Abwehr
German-Irish Trade Agreement (1935) 23
Germany
    East Germany 111
    intelligence-gathering, limitations on 33
    Ireland, cultural links with 21, 22
    mechanised warfare 12
    neutrality, attitude towards 12
    post-war provisional government 172
    post-World War I 33
    post-World War II 169–70
    surrender 167
    Treaty of Versailles and 33
    West Germany 111, 178, 183
    see also Nazi Germany
Gestapo 95
Gilmore, George 29
Glengad Head, Malin, County Donegal 106–7
Goethe Institute, Munich 26
Gonne, Iseult (later Stuart) 42, 87
Gonne, Maud 25, 42, 87, 94
Göring, Hermann 101, 110, 171, 172, 176
Görtz, Ellen (née Aschenborn) 84, 173
Görtz, Hermann 66, 73, 74, 81
    Abwehr and 84, 85, 86, 121
    alias Heinz Kruse 121
    Aliens Registration Office, letter from 172
    background 83–4
    bribes offered by 146–7
    Bryan, Dan and 88–9, 171–3
    code broken by Hayes, Richard J. 147–8, 151,
        152, 163, 170
    coded messages written by 92, 93, 146, 147,
        151, 170
    codename 'Dr Schmelzer' 83
    Custume Barracks, internment in 148, 152,
        153, 154–5
    daughter, concerns about 169
    Deansgrange Cemetery, burial in 173
    death by suicide 172
    Deery, Anthony and 92, 93, 145
    escape in Dublin 89
    escape plans, discovery of 147, 152
    espionage in England, conviction for 84
    espionage mission in Ireland 83, 85–6
    family 84

Farrell sisters and 119, 155, 170–1, 173
Garda Special Branch and 87, 88–9, 120
German Military Cemetery, reinterred in 173
Germany, reluctance to return to 170, 171–2
Hayes, Richard J., post-war meeting with 171
Hempel and 83, 89, 92, 120, 121
hunger strike 155
imprisonment 120, 121, 144, 145, 146
interrogation of 120–1, 146, 147
IRA and 85–6, 87, 88, 92–3, 118, 119–20
Ireland, attempts to escape from 118, 119
Irish authorities, questioned by 170
keyword used by, 'Cathleen Ni Houlihan' 148
Laragh Castle, County Wicklow 86, 87, 90,
    94, 118
Luftwaffe, attempts to join 84
mental health 121, 148, 155, 170, 171, 172
O'Donovan, Jim and 87, 94
on the run 90, 91, 94, 101, 117–19
parachute landing in Ballivor 86–7
perception of 154–5
RAF spying mission 84
Russian cipher used by 150
Schütz, disagreements with 155
security concerns about 126
Spartacist uprising (1919), quelling of 170
studies in the National Library 170–1
transmitter and 92–3
Government Code and Cypher School
    (GC&CS) 52, 53
    ISOS section 149, 150, 151
Government Communications Headquarters
    (UK) 19
Government of Ireland Act (1920) 34
Gray, David (US Envoy to Ireland) 126–7
    Aiken, suspicions about 129
    'American Note' and 142–3
    Axis spies in Ireland, views on 128, 142–3
    de Valera, difficulties with 127, 128–9, 130,
        142–3, 144
    Department of External Affairs and 189
    departure from Dublin 190
    Devers, Major General Jacob and 134
    G2's perception of 189
    Ireland, paranoia about 127–8, 135
    Irish Army, views on 128
    Irish neutrality, views on 127, 128, 142
    Marlin (OSS agent) and 135, 136, 138
    OSS and 135
    World War I, service in 127
Green, Dick 51
Griffith, Arthur 30, 69
Guilfoyle, Major Joseph 13, 20
Guiney, Commandant James 158

H

Halifax, Edward Wood, 1st Earl of 34
Haller, Kurt 72–3
Handel, George Frideric, *Messiah* 21
Hart, Francis Noyes, *Hide in the Dark* 97
Haughey, Charles J. 167, 195
Hay, Major Malcolm 149
Hayes, Michael 47
Hayes, Richard Francis (film censor) 139
Hayes, Richard J. 184, 185
  audio tapes of xvi, 206
  biography, *Codebreaker* (Mc Menamin) v–vi,
    xv
  Bryan, Dan and 192
  codebreaker, role as 202
  commemoration, lack of 202–3, 207
  criticism of Russell, Seán 38
  cryptography, achievements in xv
  cryptography unit, request for 185
  death 192
  G2, seconded to 53–4
  Görtz interrogated by 120–1, 146, 147
  Görtz, post-war meeting with 171
  Görtz's code broken by 147–8, 150, 151, 152,
    170
  Hempel's coded transmissions 53
  Kerney, Leopold H., interviewed by 79
  legacy 203
  *Manuscript Sources for the History of Irish
    Civilisation* xv
  MI5, meetings with Page and Liddell 151
  microdot system broken by 115, 116
  National Library of Ireland, Director of 53,
    79, 138, 139, 152
  O'Reilly (SD agent) interrogated by 142
  OSS (Office of Strategic Services) and 138
  Page, Denys, collaboration with 163
  Preetz, perception of 100
  Richard Hayes: Nazi Codebreaker
    (documentary) xv
  Schütz's documents analysed by 115
  SD (Sicherheitsdienst) code broken by 142
Hayes, Stephen
  Abwehr and 41
  background 38
  bombing campaign in England 39
  Görtz and 87, 155
  IRA Chief of Staff xvii, xx–xxi, 37, 38–9, 118
  IRA's investigation of 119
  Magazine Fort raided by IRA 40
  Nazi Germany and 39–40, 201
  Stuart, Francis and 44
Hayword, Inspector Thomas 179
Healy, Joseph (Joe) 13, 79

Hearne, John J. (Irish High Commissioner to
  Canada) 58
Hefferon, Colonel Michael 195
Hempel, Eduard 43–4
  Allies, favourable treatment of 115, 134, 135
  American press reports on 126
  Americans, favourable treatment of 134, 135
  asylum granted to 183
  Bryan's suspicions about 106
  coded transmissions 53, 54
  de Valera and 158, 183, 185
  death 183
  family 44
  German internees and 154, 158
  German Legation and 44, 49–51, 54
  Germany, return to 183
  Görtz, problems caused by 83, 89, 92, 120,
    121, 152
  Hitler, audience with 49
  informers and contacts 54–5, 57
  IRA volunteers, U-boat request 57
  Irish neutrality, respecting 57–8
  Irish politicians/civil servants, reports on 58
  Metzke, information gathered by 55–6
  Nazi Party membership 43, 44
  OSS agent Quigley's report on 140
  reports to Berlin 50–1, 53, 54, 58, 59, 60
  Ribbentrop and 59, 115
  Russell and 65
  Scottish Republican Brotherhood's request
    54
  security profile of 49
  staff increase, Irish authorities' refusal 106
  Stuart, Francis and 44, 45
  Walshe, Joseph, analysis of 58
  Weber-Drohl and 83
  wireless reports to Berlin 50–1, 53, 54
  wireless set acquired by 52
Hempel, Eva 44, 49
Henzl, Lieutenant Alfred (pilot) 114
Herkner, Friedrich 22
Heydrich, Reinhard 174–5
Himmler, Heinrich 66
Hindenburg, Paul von 23
Hirohito, Emperor of Japan 121
Hiroshima 167
Hitler, Adolf
  Abwehr and 33
  Breen, Dan, greetings sent by 140
  Britain, planned attacks on 63–4, 162
  Brownshirts and 1
  Canaris and 33–4, 124–5
  Chamberlain's policy of appeasement 39
  death by suicide 80, 167

Donegal Air Corridor, awareness of 112–13
France, fall of 62
Hempel's audience with 49
Hull, Cordell (US Secretary of State) and 130
Ireland, strategic importance of 63
Irish people's attitudes towards 58, 95
Nazi Party and 7, 20, 22–3
Night of the Long Knives 33–4
Normandy landings and 166
Paris, destruction ordered by 166
Poland, invasion of 11, 33, 39
power, rise to 22–3, 26, 29, 48, 66, 124
Russia, invasion of 153, 161–2
USA, concerns about 124–5
Veesenmayer and 66
Holocaust 167, 175
Holohan, Revd John 192
Hood, HMS 113
Horton, Admiral Sir Max 203
Hoven, Joseph (Jupp) 26, 27, 28, 29, 67, 70
Hulings, Captain Thomas (pilot) 133–4
Hull, Cordell (US Secretary of State) 123, 128,
    129, 130–1
Hungarian Arrow Cross party 178
Hungary
    Jews, persecution of 174, 175
    Nazi occupation of 81; 174, 175
    Shoes on the Danube Bank, The memorial
        178
Huntziger, General Charles 62
Hurley, Kathleen 103, 104
Hyde, Douglas 44, 47, 107, 127
Hyland, Detective Garda Richard, Scott Medal
    awarded to 39

I

Imitation Game (film) xx
Imperial Conference 5
Imperial Japanese Naval Air Service 125
internment 26, 38
    see also Curragh Camp, County Kildare;
        Custume Barracks, Athlone; Frongoch,
        Wales
Ireland
    Allies, co-operation with 12, 113, 115–16,
        163–4
    American diplomatic presence in 121
    Americans, attitude to 132
    anti-Hitler sentiment 58
    communist subversive activity in 188–9
    dominion status 45–6, 50
    Germany, cultural links with 21, 22
    invasion, threat of 18, 129, 183–4
    Marshall Aid and 186
    NATO, refusal to join 186–7

OSS agents in 135–41
post-war era, state security and 187–8
repatriation of servicemen's remains 114
security issues 126, 196–7
security status, Bryan's assessment of 10–11
strategic importance of 63, 64, 66, 102, 122,
    125
    see also Irish Free State; Irish neutrality;
        Northern Ireland; partition of Ireland
Irish Air Corps 11
Irish airspace
    Donegal Air Corridor 112–13
    flying boats and 112–13
    Hitler's awareness of flying boats using
        112–13
    Luftwaffe violations of 18, 105, 107
Irish Army
    Coast Watching Service 16–17
    cryptography unit, need for 185
    ex-IRA recruits 13
    First Division 16
    NATO and 187
    perception of 128
    personnel 11–12
    recruits, de Valera's appeal for 91–2
    Signal Corps 8, 14, 51
    underfunding of 9–10, 195
    see also National Army
Irish Army Mutiny (1924) 4–5
Irish Army School of Music 22
Irish Citizens Army 94
Irish Civil War (1922–3) 5, 13, 26, 43, 98, 206
    1916–1921 Club of veterans 191–2
    anti-Treaty side 4, 26, 31, 42, 68
    de Valera and 30
    post-war divisions in Ireland 6–7
Irish Defence Forces 4–5
    personnel 11–12
    regional commands 6
    see also G2; Irish Air Corps; Irish Army; Irish
        Naval Service; J2
Irish Free State 4, 35
    Allies, co-operation with 12
    Bryan's assessment of security status 10
    committee on national defence 12
    external threats 8–9
    German nationals employed in 22
    Irish Race Convention (1922), delegation
        46–7
    Irish Sea as a natural barrier 10, 11
    Northern Ireland and 5
    vulnerability to attack 12
Irish German Society 182
Irish Hospitals' Sweepstake 35–6
Irish Hospitals Trust 35, 36

Irish Independent 120
Irish Legation in Berlin 59, 76
Irish Legation in London 138
Irish Lights 92–3
Irish National Film Censor 139
Irish National War Memorial Gardens 198–9
Irish Naval Service 6, 14, 193
Irish neutrality
    American criticism of 125, 126, 127
    de Valera's defence of 183
    German attitude towards 12
    Gray, David, views on 127, 128, 142–3
    Hull's views on 130
    OSS agent Quigley's report on 140
    OSS's evaluation of 139
    World War II xv–xvi, 12, 14, 18, 19, 20, 52,
        66
Irish Race Convention (1922) 46–7
Irish Republican Army (IRA)
    Abwehr and 35, 36, 41, 44, 45
    Archer and 8
    Army Council 38
    bombing campaign in England 34, 35, 39
    Cairo Gang, assassination of 4
    Clissmann, Helmut and 25, 26–7, 181–2
    coded messages and 32
    Collins, Michael and 4
    de Valera's determination to suppress 40, 43
    disgruntled "22 men' in 15
    East Limerick Brigade 67–8
    ex-IRA men, Supplemental Intelligence
        Section (SIS) and 16
    Garda Special Branch and 39, 118
    General Army Convention 29, 32–3
    German High Command and 61
    Görtz and 85–6, 87, 88, 92–3, 118, 119–20
    government raids 40
    guerrilla warfare 12, 16, 27, 29, 85, 199
    intelligence section of 8
    internment of IRA prisoners 91, 114, 136
    Irish Hospitals Trust and 36
    Irish National War Memorial, attacks on
        198–9
    Kilmichael Ambush 27
    Magazine Fort raided by 40
    MI5's surveillance of 34
    Nazi Germany and xvii, 8, 15, 20, 27–9, 32,
        36, 39–40, 49
    Neutral IRA, O'Donoghue and 13
    in Northern Ireland 57
    Old IRA 12, 16, 36
    post-Civil War 29
    Russell, Seán, statue of 199–200
    Sabotage Plan (S-Plan) 29, 34, 36, 39
    Soviet Russia and 31

    splits in 29–30, 74, 85
    ultimatum issed to British Foreign Secretary
        34
Irish Republican Brotherhood (IRB) 2, 64
Irish Times 13, 167–8
Irish Volunteers 3, 7–8, 30–1
Irland Redaktion 45
ISIS terrorists 195–6
Italian Fascist Overseas Organisation 24
Italian Legation 24, 50
Italian nationals 15, 24, 100–1

J

J2 (joint intelligence services) 193
    Air Intelligence section 197
    British Army barracks, reconnaissance of
        194
    Defence Intelligence section 197
    Exercise Armageddon 195
    financing issues 197
    growth of 197
    Islamic extremists, threats from 195
    monitoring communist activity in Ireland
        194
    Naval Intelligence Cell and Fishery section
        197
    Northern Ireland border, concerns about 194
    nuclear weapons in Northern Ireland,
        concerns about 194
    peacekeeping duties 197
    Troubles and 194–5
    see also G2
Japan 121, 125, 126, 140
Japanese Foreign Office 149
Jersey, German invasion of 141
Jews
    Croatian 174, 175
    European Jews, list of 175
    Final Solution to the Jewish Question 174–5
    genocide, Nazis and 167, 171
    Holocaust and 167, 175
    Hungarian 174, 175, 178
    in Ireland 175, 200
    Kristallnacht and 48
    Nazi extermination camps 175, 185
    Polish Jews, killing of 33
Jodl, Alfred 167
Joyce, William (Lord Haw-Haw) 10, 45, 106,
    112, 113
Julianstown, County Meath 105

K

Kelly, Captain James 14, 194–5
Kelly, Joseph 34
Kelly, Pearse Paul (Paul Kelso) 119–20

Kenny, Enda 199
Kenny, John (SD agent) 141–2
Kent, Kathleen 103, 104
Kent, Mary Ellen 103
Kerney, Leopold H. (Irish Minister in Spain)
    background 69
    Bryan, Dan, interviewed by 79–80
    Burgos Prison, visit to Ryan in 69–70
    Clissmann, Elizabeth, meeting with 71–2
    diplomatic career 69
    G2's investigation of 71, 77, 78–9
    Hitler, sympathies on death of 80
    Irish neutrality 78, 79
    repatriation of Ryan's remains 76
    Ryan, Frank and 62, 69–71, 77, 79
    Veesenmayer and 77–8, 79, 81
Kiernan, Thomas 59, 60
Kilmichael Ambush 27
King, Alec 102
Kinnane, Michael, Garda Commissioner 89
Knockroe, Borris, County Carlow 106
Kriegsmarine 33, 63, 73, 75, 112
    Bismarck (battleship), sinking of 113
    see also U-boats
Kristallnacht 48
Kvaternik, Slavko 174

L
Labour Party (Irish) 6, 72, 200
Laragh Castle, County Wicklow 86, 87, 90, 94,
    118
Lauterpacht, Hersch 171
LDF *see* Local Defence Force
Lehane, Con 76
Lemass, Seán 32
Lemkin, Raphael 171
Lewis, Kenneth 84
Liddell, Cecil
    G2 and 90, 142, 150–1
    Görtz cipher, Hayes and 151
    Hayes, Richard J. and 151, 152
    Irish Desk within MI5 19, 188
    Liddell, Guy
    Archer, meetings with 19, 90, 91
    Bryan, Dan and 19, 152
    death 188
    Director of Counter-Espionage 19, 50–1, 90
    G2 and 99–100, 142
    Görtz's code, Hayes, Richard J. and 150
Lindbergh, Charles 124
Local Defence Force (LDF) 15–16
    aircraft crash landings and 113, 114, 134, 160
    Curragh Camp and 157–8, 159
    look-out posts (LOPs) manned by 17

North Strand bombing 108
Shelburne Co-op bombing 103
Supplemental Intelligence Section (SIS) 16
Lord Haw-Haw *see* Joyce, William
Lough Erne, County Fermanagh 112, 113
Lowe, Carli (archivist) xvi
Luftwaffe 33, 63, 64
    Görtz's attempts to join 84
    Ireland, bombings 50, 77, 101, 102–12, 105,
        106, 107–8
    Irish airspace, violations of 18, 105, 107
    navigational errors 107, 111
    Northern Ireland, bombings 131, 185
    radio signals, British jamming of 110, 111
    Y-Gerät system 110–11
Luykx, Albert 195
Lynch, Jack 195
Lynch, Joseph 146

M
McAleese, Mary 199
MacBride, Major John 25, 42
MacBride, Maud Gonne *see* Gonne, Maud
MacBride, Seán 26, 27, 32, 42, 44, 186
    Bryan, Dan, clashes with 190
    Clissmann, friendship with 25, 181, 182, 186
McCarthy, Michael 27
McCloy, John J. (US High Commissioner for
    Germany) 177–8
McCrohane children 103
McDonagh, Thomas 31
McDonald, Denis R. 189
McGarrity, Joseph 32, 33, 36, 64, 65
McGill Summer School 196
McGrath, Joseph 35–6
McKenna, Daniel (Dan), Army Chief of Staff 89
McKeown, Detective Sergeant 39
Mackey, Una (*later* Schütz) 170, 174
McLaughlin, Thomas 19
McNally, Thomas 158
MacNeill, Eoin 47, 151
MacNeill, General Hugo 151
McQuaid, John Charles, Archbishop of Dublin
    109
MacSwiney, Mary 47
Macville, SS 102
Madigan, Josepha 202
Maffey, Sir John 52, 112, 114, 116–17, 160,
    168–9
Magan, Brigadier Bill 188
Magazine Fort, Phoenix Park, Dublin 40
Mahr, Adolf 22, 23
Mannix, Garda 56
Manstein, General Erich von 62

Markievicz, Constance, Countess 47
Marlin, Ervin Ross (Spike) (OSS agent) 135–8, 142, 143
Marshall Aid 111, 186
Martin, Catherine 202–3
Martin, Micheál 196
Metzke, Oskar 54–7, 59
MI5
    Clissmann, Helmut interrogated by 180
    counter-intelligence 19
    Double Cross System 162
    Dublin Link 19, 20
    establishment of 19
    files released by xxi
    G2, co-operation with 18–20, 50–1, 87–8, 89–91, 99–100, 115, 151–2
    G2, post-war links 188–9
    Irish Desk within 19, 188
    security conference with G2 and OSS 143
    Stuart, Francis, transcription of broadcasts 45
    surveillance of the IRA 34–5
    surveillance of Pfaus 36
    wireless broadcasts from Ireland 98–9
MI6 xxi, 188
Military Archives 191, 203
Military College, County Kildare 191, 197
Military History Society of Ireland 191
Military Intelligence 5, 32, 45, 195
    see also G2; J2
Moloney, Helena 94
Montserrat, Nicholas, Cruel Sea, The 42
Moulin, Jean 163
Mountjoy Prison, Dublin 115, 117, 173
Mulcahy, Denis 26
Mulcahy, Elizabeth (Budge) (later Clissmann) 26
Mulcahy, Mary (née Murray) 26
Mulcahy, Richard 12, 22, 186, 191
Mulreane, Revd Joseph 169–70
Murphy, Lieutenant Colonel Michael C. 196–7
Murphy, Simon 103–4
Mussolini, Benito 1, 24, 63, 68

N
Nagasaki 167
National Archives (UK) xxi
National Army 1, 4, 8, 13, 97, 98
    see also Irish Army
National College of Arts 22
National Library of Ireland
    Görtz, Hermann and 170–1
    Hayes, Richard J. and 53, 79, 138, 139, 152
    Smith, Luke and 98
National Museum of Ireland 22, 23

National Security Committee 197
Nationalist Socialist German Workers' Party (NSDAP) see Nazi Party
NATO see North Atlantic Treaty Organization
Nazi concentration camps 175, 179
    liberation of 185
Nazi Germany
    Bryan's concerns about 8
    de Valera's protest about bombings 109–10
    extermination camps 175, 185
    genocide 167, 171
    Holocaust 167, 175
    IRA and xvii, 8, 20, 27–9, 30, 32, 36–7, 39–40, 49
    Jews, persecution of 33, 48, 174, 175, 178
    Kristallnacht 48
    perception of 20
    propaganda broadcasts 10, 45, 106, 112, 113
    Reichstag, capture by Soviet forces 167
    Russell, Seán and 64, 65, 83, 200, 201
    USA, concerns about 124
    see also Germany; Nazi Party; SS (Schutzstaffel); Wehrmacht
Nazi Party 7
    Auslands Organisation (AO) 23, 24
    Final Solution to the Jewish Question 174–5
    growth of 22–3, 29
    members in Ireland 43–4
    students studying abroad obliged to join 26
    Wannsee Conference 174–5, 200
Nazism 199, 202
Nelligan, Commandant Sean 14, 51, 92–3
Newbridge internment camp 26
Normandy landings 76, 133, 161, 163, 165–6
    double agent, disinformation and 162
    French coastal towns, images of 165–6
    Irish meteorological reports and 163–4
    planning of 162
    sectors, Utah, Omaha, Gold, Sword, Juno 166
North Atlantic Treaty Organization (NATO) 186, 195
    Ireland's refusal to join 186–7
    Soviet Union and 186, 187
North Strand, Dublin
    fatalities 108
    Luftwaffe's bombing of 50, 77, 102, 107–8
    West German government, compensation paid by 111
Northern Ireland 5
    Battle of the Bogside 194–5
    Belfast Blitz 131
    British/NATO nuclear weapons and 194
    IRA in 57
    Luftwaffe bombings 77, 131, 185

Roosevelt, Eleanor and 132–3
Troubles, the 193, 194–5
US technicians in 121, 130–1
US troops in 132, 132–3, 163
see also partition of Ireland
nuclear weapons 167, 194
Nuremberg Trials 171, 175–6

O

Oberkommando der Wehrmacht (OKW) 33, 167
see also German High Command;
Wehrmacht
O'Brien, Constable James (DMP) 94
O'Brien, Liam, *Documentary on One* series xviii–xix
O'Connell, Thomas J. 6
O'Donnell, Peadar 25, 29
O'Donoghue, Florence (Florrie) 13, 16, 118
O'Donovan, James (Jim)
Abwehr and 36
arrest 145
audio tapes of xx–xxi
background 36
codename Agent V-Held 36
ESB, return to work in 30
Görtz and 87, 94
Hayes, Stephen, views on 38, 39
internment 145
IRA and 26–7, 33, 34, 36–7
Nazi Germany and xvii, 36, 37
Russell, Seán, views on 37–8
S-Plan and 37
Stuart, Francis and 44
Weber-Drohl and 82–3
O'Donovan, Monty (*née* Barry) 36
O'Duffy, General Eoin 7, 35
Offences Against the State Act (1939) 39
Office of Strategic Services (OSS) 115–16, 135
agents in Ireland 135–41, 142, 143
British branch of 135
Counter-Intelligence Section in Europe 143
European branch of 136
G2's co-operation with 136–8, 143–4
G2's post-war relationship with 189–90, 190
Irish neutrality, evaluation of 139
security conference with MI5 and G2 143
see also Central Intelligence Agency (CIA)
O'Halpin, Eunan xxi, 88
O'Kelly, Seán T. 44
Old IRA 12, 16, 36
see also Irish Republican Army (IRA)
Ó Móráin, Mícheál 195
Oradour-sur-Glane, memorial site 201
O'Reilly, Bernard (RIC) 141

O'Reilly, John Francis (SD agent) 141–2
O'Sullivan, Billy 56–7
O'Sullivan, Garda Jeremiah 56
O'Sullivan, Captain John Patrick 14, 51, 54

P

Page, Denys 150, 151, 152, 163
partition of Ireland 34, 131, 145, 186, 187, 194
Patterson, Robert P. (US Under Secretary of War) 126, 137
Pearl Harbor 125, 126, 140
Pearse, Patrick 2, 29, 38
Peiper, Joachim 178
People's Rights Association 94
Pétain, Marshal Philippe 63
Peter the Great, Emperor of Russia 31
Pfaus, Oscar C. 35, 36
Phoblacht, An 25, 68
Poland, German occupation of 11, 33, 39, 174
Power, Commandant James
Allied aircraft crash investigation 113–14
audio tape of xvii
family 156
German internees and 148, 153–5, 156, 169–70
Görtz and 156, 169–70
Power, James (Jim) 156
Power, Sergeant John 146–7
Power, Samantha 156
Powers, Leon W. 176
Preetz, Sally (*née* Reynolds) 95
Preetz, Wilhelm
Abwehr and 94–6
arrest in Dublin 99
Donohue, Joe and 97, 99
espionage missions in Ireland 94–7, 137
G2's monitoring of 97, 98
internment 100, 154, 155
Ireland, post-war return to 170
lifestyle in Dublin 97, 99
Staffieri and 99, 100
transmitter and 96, 97, 99
pro-German sentiment, Irish people and v, 140

Q

Quigley, Martin S. (OSS agent) 139–41
Quinn, John, *Goodnight Ballivor, I'll Sleep in Trim* 82

R

Raeder, Grand Admiral Erich 64
Red House, Dublin 13, 20, 98, 99, 197–8
Redouane, Rachid 195–6
Republican Congress 29–30, 32, 68, 73
Rhineland, invasion of 9

Ribbentrop, Joachim von 65, 106
  execution 171, 177
  Hempel and 59, 115
  trial 176
  Tripartite Pact signed by 125
  Veesenmayer and 66, 73, 78, 175
Rieger, Bruno 73
Robinson, Seamus 3–4
Rommel, General Erwin 161
Roosevelt, Eleanor 127, 132–3
Roosevelt, Franklin D.
  Aiken's meeting with 129
  de Valera, perception of 130
  Irish neutrality, criticism of 125, 126, 127, 130
Roth, Jonathan xvi
Royal Air Force (RAF) 11, 62, 63
  Battle of the Atlantic, losses 102
  Castle Archdale, County Fermanagh 112
  Görtz's spying mission 84
  Vickers and 95
Royal Irish Constabulary (RIC) 3–4, 27
RTÉ
  Clissmann's interviews 182
  Documentary on One xviii–xix
  Gunplot xix
  Nobody Zone, The xix
  Richard Hayes: Nazi Codebreaker xv
Russell, Seán 26, 27, 29, 30–1
  Abwehr and 35, 65, 66, 67
  Army Council, election to 33
  bombing campaign (S-Plan) 33, 34, 61, 65
  codes procured by 148
  criticism of 38
  death and burial at sea 71
  Easter Rising (1916) and 30–1
  incarceration in America 65
  IRA and 32–3, 34, 36, 61
  Ireland, plans for return to 61
  Nazi Germany and 64, 65, 83, 200, 201
  perception of 200
  Pfaus, Oscar C. and 36
  Ryan, Frank and 71
  sabotage methods, training in Germany 55
  security risk posed by 81
  Soviet Union, visit to 31, 32, 200
  statue in Fairview Park 199–200, 201–2
  United States, tour of 32, 37–8, 64–5
  Veesenmayer's perception of 66–7
Ryan, Eilis 73, 76
Ryan, Frank (*alias* Francis (Frank) Richards)
  background 67–8
  Burgos Prison, incarceration in 69–71
  Clissmann, Helmut and 70, 71, 75
  Conradh na Gaeilge and 68

  death and burial in Dresden 76
  Glasnevin Cemetery, burial in 76
  ill health 71, 75, 76
  International Brigades and 68–9
  internment 68
  IRA and 67, 67–8, 72
  Irish neutrality, views on 75
  Kerney, Leopold H. and 62, 69–71, 77, 79, 80
  Operation Sea Eagle 73
  perception of 38
  Operation Taube (Dove) 71, 72–3
  Phoblacht, An, editorship of 25, 68
  repatriation of remains 76
  Republican Congress and 29, 68
  security risk posed by 81
  Stuart, Francis, meetings with 75, 76
  U-65, journey on board 71, 72
  Veesenmayer and 75–6, 77
Ryan, James (Jim) 118
Rykov, Alexei 31
Rynne, Michael 145

S
St Kilian's Deutsche Schule, Dublin 182
San José State University xv, xvi
Sandycove railway station 105
Schmidt, Fritz 95
Schütz, Günther (alias Hans Marschner) 115–16
  Aliens Registration Office, letter from 172
  arrest 115, 117
  death 174
  deportation to Germany 173–4
  espionage mission in Ireland 115, 117
  Görtz, disagreements with 155
  internment 117, 155
  interrogation of 115
  marriage to Irish woman 170, 174
  microdot coding system 115, 116, 117
  Mountjoy prison, escape from 117
Schütz, Una (*née* Mackey) 170, 174
Scotland, American workmen in 130, 132
Scottish Republican Brotherhood 54
SD *see* Sicherheitsdienst (SD)
Secret Intelligence Service (British) 19
Sexton, Sean, digitisation of audio tapes xix, xx
Shannon, Mary Ellen, Brigid and Kathleen 106
Shantough, Carrickmacross, County Monaghan 105
Sheedy, Revd James 56, 57
Shelburne Co-op, County Wexford 103–5
Shepardson, Whitney (OSS) 135
Sicherheitsdienst (SD) 141, 142, 149–50
Siemens-Schuckert 19–20
Sillitoe, Sir Percy 188

Simon, Walter (alias Karl Anderson) 94, 137, 155
Sinn Féin 3, 29, 43, 68, 200
Sligo Technical College 26
Slovakia 176–7
Smith, Luke, Jr 98
Smith, Luke Patrick 97–8
Smith, Mary Anne (Molly) 98
Smith, Ensign Tuck 113
Soloheadbeg ambush 3
South African Legation, Berlin 60
Soviet forces, Reichstag captured by 167
Soviet Union
    Boland, Gerald and 31, 200
    German invasion of 73–4, 76, 153
    NATO and 186, 187
    Russell, Seán and 31, 32, 200
    Spain and 68
    Warsaw Pact (1955) 186
Spain, Second Spanish Republic 68
Spanish Civil War 68–9, 162
    Battle of Jarama 68
    International Brigades 68–9, 169
Spartacist uprising (1919) 170
Special Powers Act 120
spies see espionage
SS (Schutzstaffel)
    Himmler and 66
    Oradour-sur-Glane massacre 201
    Panzer divisions 12, 62
    Polish Jews killed by 33
    Sicherheitsdienst (SD) and 141
    Veesenmayer and 66
    Staffieri (Italian national) 99, 100–1
Stanford University, Hoover Institute 205
Statute of Westminster (1931) 45–6
Stephan, Enno xxi
Stephenson, Sir Guy 19
Stephenson, John 19
Strachey family 149
Strachey, Oliver
    background 149
    codes broken by 149
    Government Code and Cypher School (GC&CS) 149
    ISOS section at Bletchley Park 149, 151
Stratton, Lieutenant Colonel Frederick Marrian
    Astronomical Physics 52
    British Army Signals Corps 52–3
    Cambridge University Rifles Volunteers 53
    G2, agreement with 53
    Légion d'honneur, knight of 53
    Order of the British Empire (OBE) 53
    Royal Corps of Signals 53
    Stuart, Francis xviii, 42–3

Abwehr, contact with 44–5
anti-Treaty stance 42
Aosdána and 45
background 42
Berlin University, post in 43
de Valera and 42, 43
Germany and 44–5, 64, 82
internment 43, 45
IRA members, meeting with 44
Irish republicanism and 42, 43
Irland Redaktion, broadcasts for 45
Joyce (Lord Haw-Haw) and 45
Laragh Castle, County Wicklow 86
Ryan, Frank, meetings with 75, 76
Swiss visa obtained by 44
transcription of broadcasts by G2 and MI5 45
We Have Kept the Faith 43
Stuart, Iseult (née Gonne) 42–3, 44, 87, 91, 94
Supplemental Intelligence Section (SIS) 16
Sweeney, Ted (light-house keeper) 163

T
Thomsen, Henning 55
Tiso, Jozef 176
Tomacelli, Eduardo, Count 24
Traynor, Oscar 89, 156
Treaty Ports 11, 106, 129
    de Valera and 10, 143
    USA's views on 126, 128
    Veesenmayer's interest in 74–5
Treaty of Versailles 33
Trials of War Criminals before the Nuremberg Military Tribunals 175–6
    Ministries Trial (Wilhelmstrasse Trial) 175, 176–7
Trinity College Dublin 59, 69, 135–6, 137
    Axis prisoners as students 161
    burnt document fragments 147–8
    G2 plants in 24
    German students/lecturers in 25
    VE Day and 167, 168
Turf Development Board 22
Turing, Alan xx
Twomey, Maurice (Moss) 26, 27, 30

U
U-boats
    attacks by 74, 102
    IRA and 57, 73
    landings in County Kerry 94, 96
    losses 102, 112, 114
    merchant ships targeted by 64
    Operation Sea Eagle 73
    Operation Taube (Dove) 71

Russell, Seán and 67, 71
surrender at Lisahally port 203–4
Treaty Ports and 10
Wilhelmshaven base 71
United Kingdom (UK), USA and 128
United Nations (UN) 197
United States of America (USA)
    Abwehr's operations in 124
    Britain, supplies/military hardware sent to 64
    communist activity in Ireland 189
    diplomatic presence in Ireland 121
    Hempel, American press reports on 126
    Irish neutrality, criticism of 125, 126
    Nazi Germany's concerns about 124
    Neutrality Acts 124
    Northern Ireland military bases 121, 130, 131–2
    nuclear weapons and 167, 194
    policy of isolationism 121–2, 123, 124
    Russell's tour of 32, 37–8, 64–5
    Shannon airport as transportation hub 187
    UK, special relationship with 128
    US-Irish relations 126–7, 128
    War Department 126
    World Fair 65
    see also Central Intelligence Agence (CIA);
        Normandy landings; Office of Strategic
        Services (OSS)
United States Congress 124, 125
United States Military Courts 175–6
United States Navy 124, 125, 126
United States Secret Service 64–5
University College Dublin (UCD) 36, 67, 68
    Axis prisoners enrolled at 161
    Bryan, Dan and xxi, 2, 191
    VE Day and 167

V
Varadkar, Leo 196, 201–2
VE Day (Victory in Europe Day) 167–8
Veesenmayer, Edmund 65–6, 71
    Abwehr and 174
    capture and trial of 175
    Croatia and 80–1, 174, 175
    Doetzer (defence counsel) 165
    German Foreign Ministry and 66
    Görtz's arrest 121
    Himmler and 66
    Hungarian Jews, deportation of 175, 176–7
    Hungary, Reich plenipotentiary in 81, 174
    Irish Bureau 65–6, 74, 75, 80
    Irish Treaty Ports and 74–5
    Jews, persecution of 174, 175
    Kerney, Leopold H. and 77–8, 79, 81
    Ministries Trial 176–7

Nazi Party, membership of 66, 174
Operation Sea Eagle 73, 80
Operation Taube (Dove) 71, 72–3
release from prison 177–8
retirement to Germany 178
Ribbentrop and 66, 73, 78, 175
Russell, Seán and 66–7, 200
Ryan, Frank and 75–6, 77
Vichy France 63, 175
Vickers Aircraft Company 95
Victorious, HMS (aircraft carrier) 114

W
Wall Street Crash 6, 22, 123
Walshe, Joseph 18, 115
    Clissmann assisted by 181–2
    co-operation with MI5 (Dublin Link) 18–19
    Dublin bombings 109–10
    German detainees, post-war treatment of 168–9
    Hearne, John J., letter to 58–9
    Hempel and 58, 106
    Irish diplomatic service and 18, 181
    Irish neutrality 58–9
    Kerney's correspondence with 69–70
    Maffey, Sir John and 116–17
    OSS agent Marlin and 138
Wannsee Conference 174–5, 200
war criminals
    pardons granted to 178
    see also Nuremberg Trials
War of Independence (1918–21) 4, 8, 12, 30–1, 140, 157, 206
    intelligence work during 13, 14, 97
    internment camps 26
    Kilmichael ambush 27
    Soloheadbeg ambush 3
    veterans 25, 28, 35, 36, 38, 116, 140, 191, 202
War News 21
War Office (British) 16, 149
Warnock, William (Irish Ambassador in Berlin) 59–60, 109–10
Warsaw Pact (1955) 186
Washington, George 123
Weber-Drohl, Ernst 82–3, 85, 155
Wehrmacht 33, 63
    Oberkommando der Wehrmacht (OKW) 33, 167
    see also German High Command;
        Kriegsmarine; Luftwaffe; U-boats
Weimar Republic 22
Weizsäcker, Ernst von 178
West Germany 111, 178, 183
White, Sir Dick, MI5 and MI6 188
Will, Hubert (OSS Counter-Intelligence) 143

Wilson, Hugh (OSS agent) 136
Wilson, Woodrow 124
Women's Prisoners' Defence League 94
World Fair, New York 65
World War I 3, 123
    Armistice 33
    Battle of the Somme 199
    Battle of Verdun 63
    British security procedures 9
    casualty rate 123, 124
    cenotaph in Toronto 207
    neutrality, German attitude towards 12
    Treaty of Versailles 33
    United States and 10, 124
World War II
    aftermath 185
    Allies, denazification policy 168
    Allies xxii, 76, 102, 161–2
    Ardennes offensive 62, 167
    Battle of the Atlantic 102, 112, 113
    Battle of the Beams 110
    Battle of Britain 64
    Battle of the Bulge 67, 142, 167
    Battle of Stalingrad 161
    Belfast Blitz 131
    Britain, planned attacks on 63
    Britain's declaration of war 39
    camps, prisoners of war sent to 63
    commemorations 198, 199, 201, 202, 207
    counter-espionage/Double Cross System 162
    D-Day 54, 162–3, 201
    Donegal Air Corridor 112
    Dunkirk, evacuation from 62–3, 104–5, 161
    Éire coastal signs 198
    France, fall to German forces 62, 63
    Ireland and xviii, xxi–xxii, 12, 113, 163–4,
        199, 202, 203
    Ireland, strategic importance of 63, 64, 66
    lives lost in 102, 167
    Maginot line 62
    Normandy landings 76, 133, 161, 162, 163,
        165–6
    nuclear weapons 167
    Operation Barbarossa (Germans) 73–4, 76
    Operation Fortitude (Allies) 162
    Operation Overlord (Allies) 54, 162, 166
    Operation Seelöwe (Sealion) (Germans)
        63–4, 71, 73
    Pearl Harbor, Japanese attack on 125, 126
    Russia, German invasion of 73–4, 76, 153
    surrender, Germany and 167
    Tripartite Pact (Germany/Italy/Japan) 121,
        125
    USA and 64, 126, 161

    see also G2; Irish neutrality; MI5; U-boats;
        Wehrmacht
Wymes, Sergeant Michael (later Garda
    Commissioner) 145